THE
CHAMPION'S
STRATEGY
FOR
WINNING
AT
SCRABBLE®
BRAND CROSSWORD GAME

THE CHAMPION'S STRATEGY FOR WINNING AT SCRABBLE®

BRAND CROSSWORD GAME

Joel Wapnick

STEIN AND DAY/Publishers/New York

First published in 1986
Copyright © 1986 by Joel Wapnick
All rights reserved, Stein and Day, Incorporated
Designed by Lou Ditizio
Printed in the United States of America
STEIN AND DAY/*Publishers*
Scarborough House
Briarcliff Manor, N.Y. 10510

Library of Congress Cataloging in Publication Data

Wapnick, Joel.
   The champion's strategy for winning at SCRABBLE® brand crossword game
   1. Scrabble (Game)   I. Title.
GV1507.S3W36 1986   794.2   84-40621
ISBN 0-8128-6247-3

For Emilie Juliette

CONTENTS

ACKNOWLEDGMENTS

I am grateful to a number of people for making this book possible, and for making it much better than it otherwise would have been.

In the former category are Susan Erda, my literary agent and lawyer, and Sol Stein, president of Stein and Day. I might still be looking for a publisher had Susan not been so enthusiastic, and had she not found in Sol someone whose enthusiasm matched hers.

In the latter category are principally my editor, Toby Stein; my fellow Game experts, Stephen Fisher and James Neuberger; and the publishers of *Letters for Expert Game Players (LEGP),* Al and Donna Weissman. Toby transformed my manuscript from amateur to professional status. She made it much more readable, clearer, and more lively than it otherwise would have been. Stephen's suggestions concerning the organization and content of chapters 1, 4, 5, and 6 were particularly valuable, as were Jim's comments concerning my analyses of the annotated games in Part IV. Al and Donna graciously allowed me to reprint word positions, commentary, and other material from *Letters for Expert Game Players.* This publication has greatly shaped my vision of SCRABBLE® brand crossword game strategy for a number of years now. The efforts of forty or so expert contributors to *LEGP* are thus at least partially reflected in this book.

I would also like to thank my colleagues who were kind enough to contribute material to me for this effort: Mike Wise, Ed Halper, Stephen Fisher, Dan Pratt, Sam Kantimathi, James Pate, Jim Neuberger, Alan Frank, Jeff Reeves, Chris Cree (who also helped with the analysis of Annotated Game #4), Robert Felt, Joe Edley, Jeremiah

Mead, and Ron Tiekert. Thanks, also, to Ann Sanfedele, who contributed the jacket photograph.

Finally, I am most grateful to my wife, Lisa Serbin, for her encouragement, support, and love during the time I was struggling with this book. Also during the time before and since.

PREFACE

Though I do not think of myself as an average sort of person, I concede to being "normal" in many respects. However, there is one way in which I am decidedly not normal: I have inanimate passions.

Most people are usually passionate toward a moving object such as another person, an animal, a basketball, or a sports car. I have also been known to be passionate in this way, but that is not what makes me unusual.

When I was six years old, I found my first inanimate passion: license plate "collecting." When my parents took me on a trip, I wrote down the license plate numbers of cars that we passed. I urged my parents to drive faster so that I could collect more numbers.

Six years later I became a coin collector. Nowadays, if a kid wants to start a collection, he has to go to a coin shop. In those days, however, you could actually go out and collect coins. On Friday nights, my friends Neal and John often went with me to the banking establishments of Lynbrook, New York. We exchanged currency for rolls of nickels, dimes, and quarters. After extracting the valuable coins, we rerolled our change and exchanged it for other rolls. The climax of the evening consisted of converting our entire allowances into rolls of pennies. We then went to one of our homes and spent the next two hours or so eating ice cream and combing through thousands of pennies. We often traded with each other, and *nothing* gave us greater pleasure than getting the better of a deal. Not that we knew; the pleasure came from convincing our trading partner what a clod he was to give up such-and-such for so-and-so.

My third passion was the stock exchange, and it took hold of me shortly after my Bar Mitzvah. My usual selection method was to examine the yearly highs and lows of stocks on the New York Exchange. If (1) the current price of a stock was slightly closer to its yearly high that to its yearly low, (2) its high was about 50 percent greater than its low, (3) the stock was not a preferred stock but (4) yielded a substantial dividend, and (5) had a nice name, I was interested. This passion ended when I became serious about music. I blew all my tradings profits on a Steinway grand piano.

For me, music is in a class of its own. It is much more than an inanimate passion. Though it plays an essential role in my life, it has not quenched my need for a truly inanimate passion. So when I was twenty-two and quite unhappily enrolled in a graduate psychology program, I became intrigued with horse racing betting systems. Fortunately, I never bet on my systems, for though they worked well on past data, they flopped at predicting future races. I did, in fact, develop one reliable system, but it was applicable to only one race out of twenty. It returned an average profit of a dime for every two dollars bet.

I took up chess seriously when I was in my mid-twenties. The high point of my chess career occurred during the 1971 World Open, held in New York City. My opponent, whose rating was 300 points higher than mine, had been outplaying me. I made a move and called "check." Forty-five seconds later, I noticed that "checkmate" was the more appropriate word.

SCRABBLE® brand crossword game has been my most enduring inanimate passion. I played my first game when I was nine years old and have been playing with appropriate seriousness since 1975. I suspect that it will remain a strong interest until I reach my second childhood (at which point I intend to greatly expand upon my collection of teddy bears and other stuffed animals). Why this game? I have reserved the first chapter of this book for answering this question. But first I'll tell you something about the history and current popularity of the Game, and then I'll give you the game plan of this book.

Alfred Butts invented what became SCRABBLE® brand crossword game in 1933. The Game was first mass marketed in 1949 and became tremendously popular in 1952. It has retained its phenomenal appeal.

Since 1971, the Selchow and Righter Company has controlled all of the production and trademark rights to the Game in North America. In 1973 the company established a subsidiary, SCRABBLE® CROSSWORD GAME PLAYERS®, INC., to promote the SCRABBLE® brand crossword game through three main activities: (1) publication of SCRABBLE® *PLAYERS® NEWS*, (2) licensing of SCRABBLE® PLAYERS® CLUBS throughout the United States and Canada, and (3) promotion of SCRABBLE® tournaments. Selchow and Righter is also responsible for the publication in 1978 of the *OFFICIAL* SCRABBLE® *PLAYERS® DICTIONARY* and for the establishment of a unified set of tournament rules.

As a consequence of the efforts of SCRABBLE® Crossword Game PLAYERS® and its members, serious Game activity in North America has increased steadily over the years. There are now over seven thousand subscribers to the SCRABBLE® *PLAYERS® NEWS*. More than nine thousand players regularly attend meetings at one hundred eighty SCRABBLE® PLAYERS® CLUBS throughout the United States and Canada. Dozens and dozens of tournaments take place each year, and a North American Championship sponsored by Selchow and Righter is held every other year.

In view of this pattern of growth, the need for instruction on how to play SCRABBLE® properly has also grown. I wrote this book to meet that need. It is intended for anyone who plays the Game, regardless of ability. I will cover all the important strategic elements, from the most basic to the most subtle and elegant. I'll tell you how to study intelligently in order to improve your game. You'll get the complete North American tournament rules and a description of the *OFFICIAL* SCRABBLE® *PLAYER'S® DICTIONARY*. There are chapters dealing in detail with tournament preparation and play. In addition, a major portion of the book is devoted to the analysis of games and exceptional moves played by experts. I guarantee that this book will increase your enjoyment of the Game by improving your play. It will also improve your winning percentage—assuming that your playing partners do not also read it.

If you are a beginner, don't be scared into thinking that this book is too advanced for you. Although I have presented many aspects of Game play that you probably have not considered before, there is nothing in this book that is beyond your comprehension. And while the examples I have used include obscure and unusual words that you probably have not come across before, I cannot see how exposure to them will do anything but increase your playing strength. In the few books dealing with how to play SCRABBLE® that have been published up to now, the authors concentrated on the rudiments of the Game. The "how-to-play" material in these books was not very challenging and could easily be summarized in a few pages. These books all taught their readers how to play—poorly. This book also covers rudimentary topics, but it goes way beyond them as well. If you are interested enough in this Game to read a book about how to play it, then you want to play it well.

This book will help you do just that.

THE
CHAMPION'S
STRATEGY
FOR
WINNING
AT
SCRABBLE®
BRAND CROSSWORD GAME

PART I

The Nature
of the Game

A number of Christmases ago, Selchow and Righter's advertising campaign for the SCRABBLE® brand crossword game consisted mainly of a television commercial that was widely shown across the country. The commercial featured an elegantly dressed, handsome young couple. He was formally attired, and she wore a dazzling evening gown. They had apparently just exited from an exclusive restaurant, or perhaps from the theater. They drove off in a late model luxury car and ended up across a table in a luxurious living room complete with a burning fireplace in the background and brandy snifters in the foreground. They were playing the crossword game. As they gazed at each other with looks that can only be described as lascivious, she effortlessly made the first and only play of the commercial: PANACHE.

This commercial was not repeated in following seasons. Selchow and Righter in fact changed advertising agencies shortly after this campaign. There were a number of reasons that the commercial was a failure: the product wasn't adequately displayed, nine-tenths of the viewing audience probably thought that PANACHE was what you got if you ate portions of a pan along with the food on it, and the "plot" was absurd. I objected to the commercial on more basic grounds: it wasn't a realistic portrayal of how SCRABBLE® is played.

The word *scrabble* means to scratch, grope, or claw about frantically. And *real* crossword game players scratch their heads a lot. They grope for the right play. Few plays are effortless, especially plays such as PANACHE. And no matter how charming a man finds a woman, he does not look at her with great longing and excitement immediately after finding himself on the losing end of an 86-0 score. Not if he's a serious player.

The chapters in Part I describe what the Game is really like. Chapter 1 is an appreciation of the Game. It describes its essence and spirit. If a game can be said to possess a soul, chapter 1 is a description of the soul of SCRABBLE® brand crossword game. The content of this chapter is far from metaphysical, however. In addition to describing the Game's attributes, chapter 1 includes some remarkable examples of inspired play.

Chapters 2 and 3 deal with the body rather than the soul: rules and words. Chapter 2 presents some obscure rules and clarifies some others. It is oriented toward club and tournament play. Chapter 3 describes the *Official* SCRABBLE® *Player's Dictionary,* the bible for club and tournament players in North America.

Perhaps one day my opponent in a tournament game will be a beautiful lady dressed in a dazzling evening gown. Perhaps she will even begin the game by smiling at me and effortlessly playing some obscure bingo such as MOPOKES or LEKYTHI. If so, I'll smile back and ask her as politely as I possibly can to please cover her head with a paper bag until the game is concluded.

1

An Appreciation

My purpose in writing this book is not just to help you improve your play. I also want to increase your appreciation of this marvelous game. Such an appreciation can be fully developed only by understanding the Game's finesses and complexities. Once this understanding is achieved, it will become apparent to you that SCRABBLE® is not simply another game. It is the youngest of the *great* games. Like chess, shoji, bridge, go, and perhaps a few others, it will continue to be played through the ages.

Let me tell you why. It is first and foremost a word game, and playing with words is a natural form of amusement for many humans. I'm sure that most of you, like myself, have long been fascinated with word play. For as long as I can remember, I have taken words apart in my head, rearranged the letters variously, spelled them in reverse, and attempted to find shorter words within longer ones. If *you* like doing these things, you will love SCRABBLE® brand crossword game.

Second, the Game requires a great deal of creativity. I consider this to be its most outstanding characteristic. The merely competent player will usually lose to the competent player who is also imaginative. The player who looks for the unexpected will often be rewarded by plays that yield satisfaction as well as a good point count. Most of us enjoy experiencing a "eureka" phenomenon. In SCRABBLE®, this can occur in a variety of ways. The player may discover an unusual or unlikely word, or may make five new words on one play, or may uncover hidden resources in the board position, or may even make a move that looks mundane but is actually strategically brilliant. Here are some examples.

Example #1

	A	B	C	D	E	F	G	H	I	J	K	L	M	N	O	
			V				T	O								1
		B	A		C	O	D						R			2
			A	N	E	W	E					R				3
			B		E	L						E				4
		E	Y	N	E	I						C				5
	E	H			F	U	N	K				T		D		6
							E		T	A	O		O	D		7
						S	I	Z	I	E	R		M	U		8
							O							R		9
						S	O	F	T	E	N	E	R		10
								I		A	X					11
								I	D							12
								L				P	L	Y		13
								I					A		I	14
								A	V	I	A	T	O	R	S	15

My rack   AEGNOS ☐

Example #1 is from one of my tournament games. The ☐ symbol shown in my rack is used throughout this book to represent the blank. In this position I could not find any playable seven- or eight-letter bingos. I was trying to figure out a way to create an opening so that I could play a bingo on my following turn. A bingo is the technical term for a play made utilizing all seven tiles on the rack. The value of such a play is equal to the point value of the play plus a 50-point bonus. It seems to me that using the name of another game as a SCRABBLE® brand crossword game term is absurd. Imagine calling a home run a "hockey." At any rate, while I was contemplating my move I suggenly spotted a *nine*-letter bingo: A☐ONGSIDE, 12B.* I was very proud of this play and was distressed to find from postgame analysis that it was the wrong move! I should have played ☐ON-GEALS, 13B, for an additional 17 points.

---

*Location of a word is derived from the letters running across the bottom of the diagram and the numbers running down its right border. The location given is that of the first letter of the word. If the number of this square is given before its letter, the word has been played horizontally. If the letter of the square is given first, the word has been played vertically.

Example #2

	A	B	C	D	E	F	G	H	I	J	K	L	M	N	O
1															
2		J	I	B	V			C	O	Q	U	I	N	A	
3		U		E	W									Y	
4		G		L	O	X							E	F	
5				T	I				V					I	
6					N				I					L	
7			H			G	A	L	E	A	T	E	D	T	
8	M	E	A	N			O	H	I	A		E	K	E	
9		U											C	R	
10		N					D	O	Z	I	E	R		E	
11		T	W	I	R	L	E	D			S	L	Y	D	
12	P	A	E	O	N			P							
13		R						A	B	A	T	O	R		
14		S			F	O	R	A	M						
15								T	U						

Rack CILOQSU

In Example #2, no tiles remained in the bag. My opponent placed an N in front of the A at 2N on his previous turn so that I could not unload my Q by playing QUA (2L). To my great relief and delight, I found COQUINA (2H, 38 points). Note that I did not pluralize COQUINA. I saved my S so that I could end the game on my following turn with SLY (11K).

Example #3

	A	B	C	D	E	F	G	H	I	J	K	L	M	N	O
1															
2				L											
3				I	T								C		
4			P	E	A								H		
5			A	D									A		
6		B	I	T	S							W	A	W	L
7		U	D	O		J	O	B					Q	I	
8	E	N	U			F	E	Z					U		G
9	R	N	G	E	N		T				K	A		A	
10	R		H			E	M				E				T
11	A		I	S	M		R	E	V	E	L			E	
12	T		Y	O	R	E						P		T	
13	I							D	I	G	I	T			
14	C	O	R	N		X							E		
15		E	O	N	I	A	N					S	O	F	A

Rack IOOUNS□

Example #3 comes from a game that I annotated for the SCRABBLE® *Players Newspaper* (see Appendix A) a number of years ago. Once again, no tiles were left in the bag. There were a number of acceptable moves in this position, including ERRATICS (A8), ION (14H), and ⒷESOT (10K), but the most virtuosic and probably the best move was NI[D]US (N9). It created a total of five new words.

	A	B	C	D	E	F	G	H	I	J	K	L	M	N	O	
	TWS			DLS				TWS				DLS			TWS	1
		DWS				TLS				TLS			T	DWS		2
			DWS C			B	DLS		DLS T			DWS A				3
	DLS		O	DWS F		U		DLS		I		DWS	J	U	DLS G	4
			R	O	DWS T	L				V	DWS U	G			I	5
	TLS		D	R	I	TLS B			TLS Y		H	A	TLS D	E		6
		DLS			E	X	DLS		DLS			A	DLS M	I		7
	TWS		F	DLS O	L	I	O	S			Z	A	DLS N	TWS Y	8
		DLS		P			DLS		DLS H			I	DLS	E	9
	TLS			E	Q	TLS U	A	T	TLS E	S			TLS R		10
		T	A	DWS D					I			DWS R		O	11
	DLS	O	DWS W				DLS A		DLS C	T	I	DWS O	N	DLS S	12
		M	DWS E	L		W	A	DLS K	E				DWS		13
	DWS P	O	D		TLS			S	E	R	V	DWS I	N	G	14
	TWS A	N	DLS			TWS				DLS			TWS		15

Example #4

Score	Tied
Rack	EENNR ☐
Opponent's rack	EEL ☐

Example #4 is the most remarkable of this group. This position was first presented in *Letters for Expert Game Players* (see Appendix A). There is no way to win the game, but there is one way to salvage a tie:

The correct play necessitates playing the blank for no more points than if it is not played! It is BRENT[S] (3F). This move prevents the opponent from going out with BETEL (2K). Opponent's ⒜LE (F13) loses, but ⒢ELEE, LE[V]EE, or ⓂELEE (H2) result in a tie.

As creative as the examples above are, they represent only one aspect of the Game. They are illustrations of brilliant tactical plays rather than of longer range strategic planning. Thanks to both *Letters for Expert Game Players* and the SCRABBLE® *Players News,* strategy has developed greatly over the past few years. We shall see in chapters 5 and 6 that the implementation of sound strategy requires at least as much creativity as do the above brilliancies.

And then there's luck. That there is a significant element of chance in what is essentially a game of skill sometimes works in my favor, of course—but, mostly, as a skilled player I find this aspect infuriating. SCRABBLE® expertise can be achieved through dictionary study and playing experience. Nevertheless, due to the chance factor, performance will always be partially beyond the control of the most accomplished player. Strong players must therefore play as well as they can to minimize the number of upsets pulled against them by weaker players. In addition, players who wish to improve at the Game must develop the self-awareness to distinguish their own weak play from the chance aspect of the game. It is very easy to blame the tiles for a losing effort. The fault more often lies in ourselves than in our tiles.

A fourth attraction of SCRABBLE® is that it is aesthetically pleasing. The board, with its intricate pattern of differently hued blues and reds, is really quite lovely. The tiles have a nice smooth feel, and all four varieties of them that I possess (consisting of various combinations of white, blue, maroon, and black letterings and backgrounds) are very attractive. The geometrical designs of the patterns on the board can, at times, be intriguing.

Finally, I like the fast pace of the Game. Unlike some other recreational activities of consenting adults, the enjoyment derived from playing SCRABBLE® brand crossword game is inversely related to the duration of the Game. There is nothing quite so frustrating as waiting fifteen minutes for an opponent to play CAT for ten points. Fortunately, strict time limitations are generally observed in sanctioned clubs and tournaments. However, these limitations do affect the quality of play. I am unaware of anyone who has ever played a perfect game under time constraints. Experienced players expect that they will make mistakes, and that the "credit" for some of their victories properly belongs to their opponents rather than to themselves. They know that the winner of a SCRABBLE® game is usually the person who makes fewer mistakes. However, they are willing to put up with the consequences of a clocked game in order to experience the excitement, tension, and anxiety that builds up during the course of a close game. I find that even though these feelings interfere with my concentration over the board, I am glad to have them, for they help make this Game as absorbing and challenging as it is.

Leonard Bernstein once wrote that no other activity gave him as much satisfaction as the act of composing—not drinking that first glass of orange juice in the morning, nor making love. Scrabble may not afford you the satisfaction that either of the above activities might. On the other hand . . .

2

Rules

Time: 9:30 P.M. on the evening of Tuesday, August 9, 1983.
Place: A meeting room in the Drake Hotel, Chicago.
Participants: The thirty-two players who qualified to take
 part in the North American SCRABBLE® Championship,
 beginning the next day; and Jim Houle, president of
 SCRABBLE® Crossword Game PLAYERS® and tourna-
 ment director of the North American Championship.
Purpose: Clarification of the rules.

I remember this meeting very well. A cocktail reception
for the players had just ended. The reception featured the
presence of Alfred Butts and the unveiling of the tournament trophy. SCRABBLE® CROSSWORD GAME PLAYERS®
had commissioned the sculptor Milton Sherrill to create the
trophy, which, according to the SCRABBLE® *PLAYERS®*
NEWS, was "a semiabstract 's' depicting the spirit of the
classic board game." It was a handsome work of art and, if
you looked closely at some of the players at its unveiling,
you could see them salivating at the prospect of winning it.
Another feature of the reception was the consumption of a
good deal of alcohol. Anticipation of the tournament had
made a number of the competitors quite tense, and it had
occurred to some of them to drink their way to relaxation. I
was salivating at the prospect of playing them the next
morning.

The rules meeting was unbelievably adversarial. Players
disagreed among themselves and with Jim Houle about the
rules. People were constantly being interrupted. Voices were
loud and confrontational.

Here were thirty-two of the most rules-knowledgeable

players in the country, most of whom had played the Game in tournaments for years, arguing ferociously over the rules. How could this be? Didn't they know the rules by now?

Of course they knew the basic rules. This crossword game is very complex, however. Not all contingencies of play are covered by the instructions included with each game. In addition, expert players have vivid imaginations. They are very good at imagining ways in which the rules might be legally but unscrupulously bent by their opponents.

The purpose of this chapter is to clarify some of the more obscure rules of the Game. I have assumed that you know the rudiments of the Game. If you do not, please read Appendix B before continuing with this chapter. Appendix B describes the physical dimensions (board, racks, and tiles), and it tells you how to begin a game, how to make legal plays, and how to calculate your score. This chapter deals with virtually everything else and is geared toward club and tournament play.

Scoring

There are some aspects of scoring that need to be clarified. Tie games are one example. Until a few years ago, ties were broken on the basis of the single highest scoring play in the game. Whoever made that play was the winner. This is no longer the case. There are no tie breakers. A tie is a tie, and in a tournament it counts as half a win and half a loss.

The scoring at the end of the game, though unambiguously stated in the rules, is sometimes misunderstood by casual players. A player is said to play out when she makes a play that uses all the tiles on her rack and there are no replacement tiles left in the bag. Such a play ends the game. The player who plays out gets a bonus: *twice* the total value of the tiles on her opponent's rack is added to her score.

It occasionally happens that because of unwieldy tiles on the rack or a constricted board position, neither player can play out. In this case, the total value of each player's tiles remaining on the racks is deducted from the respective scores. If I am stuck with a v and my opponent is stuck with a Q, for example, 4 points are deducted from my score and 10 points are deducted from my opponent's score.

There is *no* point bonus for winning a game. In the early days of tournament playing, a 50-point cushion was award-ed to the game winner. This was done to prevent collusion on the part of the players, both of whom under the rules at that time stood to benefit from high scores rather than from winning games. A player's tournament standing nowadays depends primarily on won-lost record, so a 50-point bonus for winning is unnecessary.

Checking the Tile Distribution

In a tournament, you should always check the tile distri-bution of the set you are using before beginning a game. Make sure that you have the correct number of tiles for each letter. If you simply count the tiles and determine that there are one hundred in the set, you may be very surprised when the third V shows up! It is your right to check the tile distri-bution, and the tournament director will give you sufficient time prior to the game to do so. It is also your responsibility to check the distribution: if an incorrect distribution is dis-covered after the game has begun, the players have no recourse. They are stuck with the tiles in their bag, even if they include five Qs but only two Us.

Although you may sometimes use your own set in tour-nament play, you most likely will be playing on a set pro-vided by SCRABBLE® Crossword Game PLAYERS®, which provides an invaluable service by sending game sets out to tournaments. It sometimes happens, however, that the tile distributions of these sets gets fouled up at the end of a previous tournament. Therefore, be especially careful before the first game of a tournament to check the tile distribution of the set you are playing on.

The tile distribution can also become fouled up if two games are played at the same table and a player inadver-tently picks tiles from the wrong bag. This actually happens fairly frequently with novices and intermediates and is a tournament director's nightmare. A cheater can of course deliberately foul up the distribution by pocketing some of the more desirable tiles from a set for the next game. It happens, but very rarely.

Picking the Tiles from the Bag

According to the rules, tiles should be picked one at a time, put face down on the table in front of the rack, and then placed on the rack. I have never followed this involved procedure, and very few of my colleagues have either. The generally accepted procedure is to hold the bag with one hand at arm's length and at eye level; withdraw the tiles with the other hand, taking as many or as few at a time as is comfortable for you; place the tiles directly on your rack. Don't dawdle with your hand in the bag!

It often happens that a player will accidentally pick an extra replacement tile. When this happens, he places all eight tiles on his rack, in whatever order he chooses. This is done regardless of whether the tiles just picked have already been placed on the rack. The opponent then randomly picks a tile from the rack and returns it to the bag. The opponent is entitled to see the tile letter before returning it to the bag.

Some players feel that if a player notices that he has an extra tile among his replacement tiles but has not yet put these tiles on his rack, the opponent should pick from the replacement tiles only rather than from the player's entire rack. Still others feel that if a player has picked an extra tile but has not yet looked at the tiles just picked from the bag, he should be allowed to return the extra tile to the bag immediately. This is certainly very sportsmanlike play. You should be aware, however, that if you pick an extra tile your opponent has the right to make you add it to your rack. Be very careful not to pick excess tiles when you hold the blank or else you may lose it! It once happened to me in a tournament game.

The rule for picking excess tiles from the full rack may be abused by the unethical player. A player who is stuck with a u-less Q, for example, may *intentionally* pick an eighth tile in the hope that the opponent will pick the Q from the rack. There is of course no way of knowing the player's true intentions. If I were to pick a Q from my opponent's rack in a tournament game, however, I would not hesitate to call over the tournament director. An argument may ensue concerning whether or not the Q had been on the rack before your opponent picked replacement tiles. The tournament director should probably consider such an argument irrelevant to her decision, since there would be no way of determining with certainty whether the Q had or had not been on the rack before replacement tiles were picked. She should at the very least force your opponent to keep the Q. If you, on the other hand, accidentally pick an eighth tile while holding an unplayable Q, and your opponent then picks the Q off your rack, you should take the initiative and tell your opponent to pick another tile. Incidentally, this problem cannot be resolved by picking only from the replacement tiles; your opponent may not discover his error until after he has mixed the replacement tiles in with the others on his rack. He may then "not remember" what his replacement tiles were.

Time Limitations

All tournament SCRABBLE® games require the competitors to adhere to some form of time constraint. There are two systems currently in use. The first employs sand timers. Each player is allotted three minutes per move. If the sand runs out before the player announces her score, she loses her turn. It is the player's responsibility to start her opponent's timer once she has completed her play. In tournaments involving sand timers, a maximum time limit of fifty to sixty minutes per round is established by the tournament director. Unfinished games are terminated when this time has expired, and the total value of the tiles left on each player's rack at this point is deducted from that player's score. The player who made the last move of the game must replenish her rack (if tiles remain in the bag) before adding up the points to be deducted from her score.

The use of sand timers has been roundly criticized by many expert players, for a number of reasons. It has been the cause of a number of arguments, along the lines of:

> *Player #1:* You are out of time.
>
> *Player #2:* What do you mean? I announced my score just before the sand ran out.
>
> *Player #1:* No you didn't. The sand ran out at least three seconds before you said 26, which was the wrong score anyway!
>
> *Player #2:* You are absolutely incorrect! Tournament director! I want the tournament director!

Another problem with sand timers is that the cheapos in use in tournament play are woefully inaccurate. They vary from two minutes to four minutes. A third problem is that three minutes per move is too slow. As a result, many games are not concluded before the total time alloted for the round is used up. The biggest problem, however, is that sand timers do not allow for conservation of time so that saved time may be used when needed. Some moves take only a few seconds' deliberation. Complex situations, however, may require five minutes or more to evaluate properly. A time-per-move system does not allow for proper consideration of difficult situations, and will therefore, at times, affect adversely the quality of play.

As a result of the above considerations, sand timers have given way to chess clocks in most strong tournaments. For the uninitiated, a chess clock is a little box that houses two clock faces. Two buttons protrude from the box's top casing, one directly above each of the clock faces. When the button above one of the two clocks is depressed, the clock beneath it stops. At the same time, the other button is propelled upward and the opponent's clock begins ticking. Needless to say, the player is supposed to press the button after making a play.

The time allowance has varied over the past few years from twenty to twenty-five minutes per player. At present, twenty-five minutes is the standard in most tournaments, including the North American Championship. The penalty for exceeding the time limit is ten points subtracted from the player's score for each excess minute or fraction thereof.

Correct procedure for using the chess clock is simple. The buttons above the two clock faces are put in a neutral position so that neither clock is ticking. The clocks are then set. This involves moving the minute hands of both clocks to the appropriate number of minutes before 12. The clocks are designed so that, as time runs down, the minute hand elevates a small flag near the 12 on the clock face. The time limit has been exceeded if the minute hand has moved far enough to the right to cause the flag to drop back down.

Once the player who goes first verifies that seven tiles have been picked from the bag, the opponent presses the button over his own clock face, starting the first player's clock. After the first player has made a play and announces her score, she presses the button over her clock. It is incorrect to push the button before announcing one's score. She then records her score, and only after doing so she picks replacement tiles from the bag. Players who repeatedly press their clock buttons before announcing their scores, or who pick replacement tiles before recording their scores, may be penalized if the opponent notices this happening and informs the tournament director. At present, however, the actual penalty to be assessed has not been resolved.

The sequence of forming a word, announcing the score, depressing the clock button, recording the score, and selecting replacement tiles from the bag is repeated after every succeeding move in the game. It is the player's responsibility to remember to depress the clock button after making a play.

If there is a break in the action (during a challenge, when the players detect that one or both of them have made an addition mistake during the course of the game, or when a player must leave the table for some reason), the buttons are adjusted so that neither clock is running.

An unsportsmanlike competitor could take advantage of these procedures by immediately blurting out any number after making a play. Time on his clock would thus be saved, since he could afterward correctly tally his score for the play while his opponent's clock rather than his own was running. (An incorrect score can be corrected at any point during or after the game, until the players hand in the tournament record sheets to the tournament director.) The way to deal with this situation is to call to the table the tournament director, who should then warn the player that another instance of this behavior will lead to expulsion. We shall see that there are other potentially unpleasant situations like this one. I should mention, however, that they rarely occur among experienced players. I have witnessed only two expulsions in all the tournaments I have attended, and in neither case was the expulsion due to the behavior described above. In the first case, a male player punched a female player (not his opponent!) in the jaw. In the second, a player attempted to push a pencil up his opponent's nose.

Challenges

A challenge must result in the loss of a turn for one of the players. If the word in question is ruled acceptable, the challenger loses the turn. If the word is unacceptable, the person who has been challenged removes her tiles from the board, receives no points, and forfeits her turn. In order to be ruled acceptable, the word in question need only be in the *Official* SCRABBLE® *Player's Dictionary*. The player whose word is challenged does not have to know the meaning of her challenged word.

Bluffing is part of the game. If a player plays a phony word and her opponent does not challenge it, the word stays on the board, and the player adds to her score however many points the play is worth.

If possible, someone other than the players should consult the dictionary to determine a challenged word's legality, since information found by looking up the word might

affect future play. One of my opponents once played
ARRASE[S], which I challenged. No one else was present, so I
looked it up. I saw that ARRASES was a phony, but could not
avoid noticing that ARRASED was acceptable. That was useful to know should my opponent try to play ARRASE[D] on his
next turn. But I should not have been able to use that
information in this particular game. If my opponent had
looked up ARRASES, his knowledge of ARRASED might have
posed an ethical dilemma for him on *his* next turn.

There are a number of procedural niceties associated with
challenging. One challenges by verbal declaration. This
should be done *only after the player challenged has depressed the button over his clock face,* officially ending his
turn, but *before he has replenished his rack with tiles from
the bag.* If a player challenges after the word is placed on the
board and the score is tallied, but before his opponent
depresses the clock button, his opponent has every right to
withdraw the word and make a different play if he so
wishes. There is a gray area here, for the challenger's
reminder to his opponent to press his clock button may tip
off his opponent that a challenge is imminent. The reminder
must nevertheless be made before the opponent picks new
tiles. Purposefully refraining from pressing the clock button
in order to see if an opponent will challenge is of course
unethical. The correct way to handle this behavior is to call
over the tournament director. The director will no doubt
warn the competitor that continuance of this practice will
result in expulsion from the tournament.

This situation raises the question of whether a player
should inform the opponent of the fact that the opponent
has neglected to press the clock button after making a play.
The player could simply refrain from making a move until
after the opponent noticed the oversight. This would cost
the opponent valuable time. The rules in fact plainly specify
that it is not the player's responsibility to inform the opponent of the failure to press the clock button. Nevertheless, I
would not want to win a game in this way. I always inform

my opponents if they have forgotten to press their clock buttons, except if they forget repeatedly. Then they are on their own.

Once a challenge is declared, both clocks are stopped. One of the players raises a hand to get the attention of a tournament official. The player then writes the challenged word on a special challenge slip and shows the slip to the opponent to confirm that the word on the challenge slip is the same as the word being challenged. The tournament official takes the slip to the front of the room, where the status of the word is determined. The slip is then returned to the players, marked either "acceptable" or "not acceptable." At this point, either of the players has the right to ask for a review decision. This occurs when a player feels strongly that the word judge has erred (an infrequent but not unheard of occurrence). The word is then rechecked, usually by a different tournament official. A final decision is reached, the appropriate adjustments are made by the players, and the game proceeds from that point.

The prospective challenger need not challenge immediately after her opponent makes his play. She may instead declare "Hold." Once she does this, her opponent cannot pick tiles from the bag. The prospective challenger considers whether to challenge or not on her own time, however, as her opponent has already pressed his clock button.

We shall see in chapter 6 that the decision to challenge or not to challenge often depends on a number of factors and may be very difficult to make. It is thus in the interest of maximizing best play to allow the prospective challenger as much time as she needs to come to a decision. The only problem with allowing unlimited time for challenging is that the player who made the play that may be challenged must wait during this interval without seeing his new tiles. A player who thus routinely declares "hold" after every move would be depriving her opponent of the opportunity to formulate moves during the time she is "deliberating" whether or not to challenge. At present, there is no clear-cut rule concerning the maximum amount of time a player may take to decide whether or not to challenge. Some tournaments permit fifteen seconds. Others permit one minute, still others unlimited time. My feeling is that unlimited time should be allowed, and any player abusing this rule by routinely declaring "hold" should be dealt with by the tournament director.

If the play made creates two or more new words, the challenger has the right to challenge all of the new words at the same time. The play is ruled unacceptable if any one of the words challenged is phony. In this case, however, the players are informed that the *whole play* is unacceptable; they receive no knowledge concerning which of the words challenged are good and which are phony. They know for sure only that at least one of the words must be unacceptable.

There is no penalty for challenging the last play of the game. If your opponent plays out and you are even slightly unsure of whether the play is acceptable, you should therefore challenge. Similarly, there is no real penalty for challenging more than one new word formed on a given play versus simply challenging one word. The challenge to the additional words can thus also be regarded as "free" challenges.

Exchanging and Passing

As long as there are at least seven tiles remaining in the bag, a player may exchange any or all of the tiles on his rack for new ones. He simply announces "I exchange X [a number from one to seven] tiles," places the tiles to be exchanged face down on the table, depresses his clock button, picks the replacement tiles from the bag and places them on his rack, and returns the tiles to be exchanged to the bag. He receives no points for exchanging. There is no limit to the number of times that a player is allowed to exchange tiles during a game.

Passing consists of forfeiting a turn without tile replacement. The player announces "I pass" and then presses her clock button. A player may pass at any time during the game. Sometimes a player must pass. This happens when there are fewer than seven tiles in the bag and the player is unable to make a legal play. There are times, however, when a player passes even though she need not do so. Examples of this are discussed in chapter 6.

Ending the Game by Repeated Passing and Exchanging

After six exchanges or passes in a row (three plays of either type by each player), either player may terminate the game by simply declaring the game to be over. The total value of the tiles on each of the players' racks is then subtracted from the respective scores, and a winner is determined. If neither player declares the game over, play continues. A player cannot later in the game retroactively declare the game ended at this point.

A successfully challenged word does not count as a pass. Also, there has been some consideration of changing the rule for ending the game by successive passes and exchanges so that it applies only to passes. In any event, the premature termination of a game in this fashion must be very rare. I have never seen it happen.

Phony Blanks

Occasionally it will come to pass that you (by accident, of course) or your opponent (by accident or on purpose) will play a lettered tile as if it were a blank. *Always verify that the blank played by your opponent is truly a blank.* Turn it over to make sure that there isn't a letter on the other side. Your opponent, if he is an experienced player, will not be offended by your apparent distrust of him. Checking the blank is a routine procedure and is done by all seasoned players.

If you do not check your opponent's blank and, after you have made your next play, discover that it is not a blank, there is nothing you can do about it. The tile stays on the board as a blank, your opponent keeps his points for the move on which he played the phony blank, and the offending tile continues to represent the letter that the opponent originally declared it to represent. If you do detect a phony blank immediately after it is played, however, your opponent's tiles are returned to his rack and he loses his turn. Your opponent loses his turn *even if the phony blank turns out to be the tile it was supposed to represent!*

Tournament Pairings and Determinations of Players' Final Standings

Most of the current tournaments employ a modified Swiss system for determining pairings among players. This means that pairings are made on the basis of similar won-lost records. If after five rounds you have won three games, for example, you are likely to play in the next round someone who has also won three games. The tournament winner is the player who has won the most games. Point-spread differentials (the total number of points scored by a player in the tournament minus the total number of points scored against that player) are used to break ties in the case of competitors who have identical won-lost records.

A few tournaments employ credit systems for determining their winners. Credit systems weight total points scored and point differentials between winners and losers more heavily than does the standard won-lost system. A typical such system is one that was used for the biannual Game Room Tournament (New York City): the winner of a game gets a credit for every 10 points scored to a maximum of thirty credits, plus ten credits for winning, plus one credit for every 10 points' difference between the scores of the players. The maximum number of credits that can be earned in one game is sixty, so it is not useful to win a game by more than 200 points. The loser of a game gets a credit for every 10 points scored to a maximum of thirty credits, minus a credit for every 10 points' difference between the game scores to a maximum of twenty credits lost in this fashion. The player who earns the most credits over the ten-game tournament is the winner.

Other Lands, Other Rules

There are some major rules differences in the way the SCRABBLE® brand crossword game is played in North America and how it is played elsewhere. Tournaments held in the French-speaking world (including Quebec), for example, emphasize fairness. Their game is called *"le* SCRABBLE® *Duplicate."* Players sit individually at tables and do not play against each other. Instead, a master board is set up at the front of the room. A tournament official selects seven oversized tiles and places them where they can be easily seen by everyone in the room. The players then have three minutes to come up with the highest scoring play they can find. This is the sole criterion of excellence in duplicate Game playing. Each player gets credit for the number of points earned (a player gets no points for playing a phony word), and the highest scoring play found by any of the players is added to the board. A tournament official then picks replacement tiles, and the game continues until the tiles are used up.

I must confess that I find this a sterile way of playing the Game. The chance factor is removed, but so are all of the lovely strategic considerations discussed in chapters 5 and 6. Le SCRABBLE® *Duplicate* is to North American English SCRABBLE® what a foul-shooting contest is to basketball.

In Great Britain and Australia, the Game is closer to North American style play than it is French, in that the games consist of contests between two players. There are numerous rule differences, however, the two most significant of which are: (1) the winner of a tournament is not the player who wins the most games, but the player who scores the most points over the course of the tournament; and (2) bluffing is not allowed, as there is no penalty for challenging a questionable word that turns out to be acceptable.

The emphasis on scoring points encourages wide open,

high-scoring games. The British apparently consider these
games to be inherently good. This is about as logical as
thinking that a soccer game in which the final score is 13 to
11 must have been a marvelous experience. Wide open
games may be less frustrating than some of the crablike
configurations my opponents occasionally throw at me.
Nevertheless, the goodness of a game depends solely on the
craftiness and inventiveness of the players, and these qualities are most necessary when the competitors must struggle
to win rather than to maximize their point totals.

I also object to the elimination of bluffing from SCRAB-
BLE® brand crossword game. I have heard people describe
the purposeful playing of phonies as dishonest, unaesthetic,
and a form of cheating. I could not disagree more. Bluffing
is as inherent to SCRABBLE® as it is to poker. It places the
greatest possible burden on the players to know their words.
In a game with a significant luck factor, it is one more tool
that the expert player may use in order to win a game. We
shall see in chapter 6 that the proper playing of phonies is a
skill rather than an accident. It requires both cleverness
and good timing.

This does not mean that it is always proper to try to win
by bluffing. In a tournament game I would feel no compunc-
tion about playing phonies whenever I thought that playing them would be to my advantage. In club and informal
play, however, it is unconscionable to play intentional phonies for the express purpose of beating up on an obviously
weaker player. Unless you want your colleagues to think of
you as the lowest of the low, don't do it.

Upside-Down Plays

It is fitting that we end this rather sober chapter with
some silliness. A number of years ago the SCRABBLE® *Players News* reported on a game in which one of the players
placed an upside-down word on the board. It was a vertically played word, and its letters were facing in the direction
opposite to the direction in which all of the other vertical

words on the board were facing. Believe it or not, this game was played between two experts! The word was not challenged and wasn't noticed by either player until a turn or two later in the game.

The ruling from SCRABBLE® Crossword Game PLAYERS® headquarters was that the upside-down word had to come off the board. The game would revert to the point at which this play was made, and the player who made the word would lose her turn. This ruling struck many players as incorrect. A more logical approach would have been to consider that the player had simply placed her individual letters on the board upside down. Some players do this routinely with is, os, ns, ss, and so forth. The letters look the same as when they are correctly placed, but the tile values are upside down—in the upper left-hand corner rather than right-side-up in the lower right-hand corner. An upside-down play of BLOCK for example is really KCOLB. If the opponent challenges upside-down BLOCK, he should write KCOLB on the challenge sheet!

There are some interesting implications of this interpretation. If, for example, one player plays CARES upside down, her opponent might challenge SERAC—a legal word. The challenger would lose the challenge, though she presumably would have the right to turn the upside-down tiles right-side up—if she so desired.

There is also the problem of what happens if the first word of a game is played upside down relative to the letterings on the premium squares. Due to the fact that the board is symmetrical, neither player may notice that all or almost all of the words on the board are phonies! One player could conceivably challenge BOX in the middle of such a game, claiming that the word just played is not BOX but XOB. I assume that most rational tournament directors would, in this circumstance, consider the letterings on the premium squares to be irrelevant to the game.

Shortly after the upside-down play article appeared in the

SCRABBLE® *Players News,* a tournament was held at the Game Room. Sure enough, one of the questions asked during the rules discussion prior to the start of the tournament was "What happens if your opponent plays an upside-down word?" This was followed by a question from Hymie Ripps, an expert player and a real character: "What if [while attempting to make a play] you miss the board?"

3

Words

The rules booklet included in every SCRABBLE® brand
crossword game set contains a sample game. The first ten
words formed in this game are HORN, FARM, PASTE, MOB,
DIAL, PREVENT, MODELS, QUITE, PRANK, and SIR. Expert
players sometimes play common words like these, but about
half the time they play words that are unfamiliar to the
casual player. Some of the words played by Joe Edley and
me in just one tournament game were AGLEY, BIAXAL,
VAHINE, QUATE, POGONIAS, GARRON, RECK, PEISED, FON,
MHO, and LINTEL.

The *Official* SCRABBLE® *Player's Dictionary* (henceforth
referred to as the *OSPD*) contains about 95,000 words. Most
people have a vocabulary that is only a small fraction of this
number. A good club and tournament player might know
50,000 of the words in the *OSPD*. The top players are familiar with all but perhaps a few hundred of the *OSPD* words.

I have encountered a number of people (both players and
nonplayers) who belittle the achievements of those of us
who have chosen to study the *OSPD*. Their most common
criticisms are: it is ridiculous to study the *OSPD* because the
OSPD includes too many ridiculous and nonsensical words;
students of the Game often do not know the meanings of the
words they play; and SCRABBLE® itself is only a game and
does not foster knowledge of the English language.

As we shall soon see, the *OSPD* does indeed contain some
questionable entries. Some of these entries may strike you
as ridiculous, absurd, improper, obscure, and incorrect.
Some of them certainly seem that way to me. Nevertheless,
try not to be too much of a language chauvinist. All of the

words in the *OSPD* appear in at least one of five respected American collegiate dictionaries. Lexicographers are responsible for these words, not crazed fanatics who try to shove the linguistic equivalent of the kitchen sink into the *OSPD*. I might not like a word here and there, but who am I to argue with a bunch of lexicographers?

It is true that expert players often play words that they cannot adequately define. So? Do you know how your automobile engine works? Would you be willing to forgo using it until you find out? I personally am grateful that the proper beating of my heart does not depend upon my knowing how and why it beats.

It has often been suggested that SCRABBLE® players be required to define any challenged words. There are two problems with this suggestion. First, the adequacy of a definition may be a matter of sharp dispute; and second, some players might be unable to define words whose meaning they in fact do know. Both points are illustrated by the following imaginary dialogue, occurring immediately after Player #1 challenges Player #2's word: THE.

> *Player #1:* All you have to do to win this challenge is successfully define the word THE.
>
> *Player #2:* I don't have to. You obviously know what it means already, otherwise you wouldn't have used the phrase, "define the word, THE."
>
> *Player #1:* Okay, I'll change my phraseology. Define THE.
>
> *Player #2:* The what?
>
> *Player #1:* [getting exasperated]: The word!
>
> *Player #2:* There you go again!

[A number of minutes pass, after which Player #1 successfully convinces Player #2 to make a stab at defining THE.]

> *Player #2:* It's an article.
>
> *Player #1:* [laughing derisively]: Of what? Clothing? Maybe it's from a magazine?
>
> *Player #2:* No, no. It's an article of speech. Like A, or AN.

Player #1: What's an article of speech?
Player #2: THE.

It should also be remembered that SCRABBLE® brand crossword game experts do know the definitions of many of the strange words they play. I have often seen them at tournaments conversing in what seems like a code—until I realize that the "code" is in fact the English language! Obscure, but English (North American variety) nevertheless.

Why do we experts study? It all boils down to the fact that we love the game and that we believe it is a good enough game to justify trying to become as good a player as possible. We study words to improve our play, not to learn about words. Sometimes we do study definitions, but we learn them in order to help us remember the words. SCRABBLE® may not teach us all that much about word meanings, but who cares? Does javelin throwing keep the enemy away or put food on the table? We play games and sports because we like them, not because they are useful.

Finally we come to the issue of the Game's educational value. To say that it has no educational value is like saying that bowling teaches nothing about mechanical physics, or that music teaches nothing about acoustics. To belabor the point just a little, imagine the following *very* hypothetical dialogue, between a young man and woman. It is 1:30 A.M., and he is on his way out of her apartment:

He: I really enjoyed this evening very much. It was both pleasurable and enlightening.

She: I enjoyed it also, very much. Perhaps we can get together again soon.

He: No, I don't think so.

She [puzzled and a bit crestfallen]: No? Why not? Did I do something to . . . ?

He: Oh no. It's just that I don't think that future visits with you will serve any further educational purpose. What more can you teach me about physiology, biology, and anatomy?

She: You're right. But I can teach you something about gravity. [kicks him down a flight of stairs]

One final point needs to be made regarding these issues: players who have mastered the Game have done so not just because they have learned weird words that they may not be able to define, but because they have also learned strategy and tactics. The belittlers think that players who know the dictionary must win over players who don't have such word arsenals. This is a little bit like saying that people who are extremely wealthy know how to enjoy life. You've got to know what to do with it!

The Official Dictionaries

In North American tournament and club play, there are two official dictionaries for the Game: the *Official* SCRABBLE® *Player's®* *Dictionary* and *Webster's New Collegiate Dictionary,* latest available edition (both published by Merriam-Webster). The *OSPD* is used to determine the legality of all two- to eight-letter words, plus certain words of nine letters or more. Words of nine or more letters appear in the *OSPD* only if they are closely related to shorter words. They are invariably pluralizations (e.g., COUNTESSES) or conjugations (e.g., PETITIONING) of the shorter main entries in the *OSPD. Webster's New Collegiate Dictionary* is used for determining the legality of all other nine- to fifteen-letter words.

The *OSPD* is intended as a rule book for players, not as an all-purpose dictionary. No pronunciation guides or etymologies are included. Only one definition per word is given, and the definitions are very brief. If you really want to know a word's meaning, look it up somewhere else.

The *OSPD* has one great advantage over other dictionaries, however: it is unambiguous. A challenged word is either in the dictionary or unacceptable. The *OSPD* includes all acceptable conjugations and noun plurals. It specifies which adjectives take -IER and -IEST, and which do not. It tells you when it is permissible to tack an s onto a word ending in -ING. The Funk and Wagnall *Standard College Dictionary,* which was the official tournament dictionary before the *OSPD* was published, does not always specify these things, and neither does any other dictionary. There are no gray areas in the *OSPD,* and there is therefore no need for a word judge to make subjective interpretations.

Some Characteristics of the *OSPD*

Words of foreign (non-English) origin. Foreign words are not allowable in Scrabble. However, it is sometimes difficult to distinguish between a foreign word and a word of foreign origin that has become part of the North American English language. The *OSPD* is filled with words of foreign origin, reflecting thereby the fact that both Canada and the United States are cultural melting pots. Here are some examples: ABO, JOEY, COOEE; DA, ZITI, LINGUINI, MAFIA, PAISAN; ZAFTIG, ZOFTIG, GONIF, SCHLEPP, SCHLOCK; GOR, BEGORRAH, GAE, GORSE, MUN, WAE; DE, COUTEAU, ROUSSEAU, EAU, MONSIEUR, CHEZ; HAJ, DJIN, IMAM, JIHAD, HAFIZ; YOM, EPHAH, HAZAN, KIBBUTZ; HAIKU, DOJO, NISEI, ISSEI, KAMIKAZE, SUMO; ZARZUELA, JEFE, JIPIJAPA, JOTA, GAZPACHO, LLANO, PAMPA; SAHIB, MEMSAHIB, SUTRA, SUTTEE, DHARMA, DHARNA, DHOLE, DHOTI; OUZO, BOUZOUKI, ILIAD, NOMOS, EXODOI; MOUJIK, KULAK, KOLKHOZ, PIROG; WOK, YIN, YANG; ANGST, STREUSEL, FUEHRER, NAZI, FRAULEIN; BWANA, MBIRA, MAKUTA; FJORD, SKIJORER, TELEMARK.

Some of these words may strike you as exclusively foreign rather than of foreign origin. Remember, however, that the creators of the *OSPD* did not concern themselves with this distinction. The only criterion for a word's inclusion was whether or not it made it into at least one of the collegiate dictionaries consulted.

Prefixes and suffixes. Prefixes and suffixes figure in thousands of *OSPD* words. Though this is not surprising, some of the specific entries are. Here are some rather unusual inclusions: BEBLOOD, BECHALK, BEDIAPER, BEFINGER, BEUNCLED, DENUDER, ENDAMAGE, MISMEET, MISTRYST, NONEGO, OUTCHIDE, OUTECHO, OUTFROWN, OUTGNAW, OUTHOWL, OUTPLOD, OUTSNORE, OUTSULK, OUTYELP, OVERCOY, OVERFAT, OVERFOUL, OVERHOLY, OVERMEEK, OVERPERT, OVERSUP, SEMIHOBO, SUBSHRUB, BIDEABLE, TAKEABLE, GIVEABLE, DOGDOM, MOVIEDOM, SODALESS, LORNNESS, LOSTNESS, SISSIEST, SELFWARD. Among my favorites are unusual nouns ending in -ER such as PRE-FACER, OUTLIVER, VOMITER, PRELUDER, SUBSIDER, UP-DATER, and RESELLER.

There are two special lists in the *OSPD*. One presents RE- verbs, and the other UN- adjectives and adverbs. Some choice entries from these lists are RECLASP, REEJECT, RE-PLUNGE, RESTUFF, REUTTER, UNCHEWED, UNCLOYED, UN-COMELY, UNFUSSY, UNHOLILY, UNSPRUNG, and UNWRUNG. It really pays to know these lists, as it is not at all unusual for opponents to play RE- and UN- words. If you don't know which of these plays are acceptable and which are not, you will lose a lot of games that you might otherwise win.

Exclamations and utterances. The *OSPD* contains an admirably expressive collection of exclamations, oaths, utterances, and vocalizations. Among them are ARF, AHA, OCHONE, HUH, OHO, PHT, PSST, GOR, PHPHT, RAH, SH, SHH, NERTS, NERTZ, OW, OUCH, WHEE, PHEW, PUGH, and ZOWIE. Naturally, none of these words can be pluralized. You should be aware, however, that certain words appearing to be exclamations are actually verbs. These include AAH, OH, TSK, TSKTSK, HUMPH, and PSHAW. They can be conjugated as well as pluralized. There are, additionally, at least two nouns that are more commonly thought of as exclamations: UGH and HAH. UGHS sounds very strange, but it's in the book.

"Poor" English and slang. The *OSPD* includes words such as ET, HET (the past tense of the verb HEAT), FORGAT, AFEARED, ITHER and YEAH. It also includes "shorthand" slang words such as LEGIT (a noun!), INFO, AMMO, AWOL, EXEC, NUDIE, NUKE, BIO, BOD, TRAD, UMP, FESS (meaning to confess), LOOIE and LOUIE (short for lieutenant), and DEMO. A MAXI is a type of dress or coat, and a MINI is "something distinctively smaller than others of its kind." ELHI is short for "pertaining to school grades 1 through 12" (elementary-high school).

Among the many other slang or near-slang words are FED and GAY (both nouns), LULU ("something remarkable"), JOHN, FATSO, FROSH, HOMO, ADMAN, BROMO, YACK and YUK. You may not like some of these words, but it cannot be denied that they are an integral part of our language.

Obscenities. One of the most controversial aspects of the *OSPD* is its inclusion of a large number of obscene and vulgar words. A number of players have complained vigorously about these words. There is even a club in California that forbids them to be played.

I believe that the *OSPD* should list all words used in our society (and obscenities are among the most used), whether we like them or not. Different sets of words may be offensive to different groups of people. Some can't abide the "F word" and the "S word"; others consider RAPE and NAPALMED to be even more obscene. Wanting to banish a word from the language is not the same as accomplishing it: we may deplore certain words, but as long as we cannot deny their existence they should be playable in the Game.

Ethnic and racial slurs. I personally find ethnic and racial slur words to be infinitely more despicable than obscenities. As long as we have an imperfect society, however, these words belong in the *OSPD*. Still, they make me uncomfortable. I can see myself playing an obscene word against someone's kindly grandmother, but I think that I would have a more difficult time playing DARKY against a black person.

Unusual spellings. The *OSPD* contains a considerable number of variant spellings that may strike you as incorrect. Some examples are DANDRIFF, DROWND, PASTROMI, VITAMINE, BROCOLI, and SURVIVER.

Strange comparative forms. The *OSPD* also includes bizarre comparatives such as UNIQUER, PERFECTER, ABSOLUTER, DOGGONEDER, GLADLIER, WINSOMER, UNRIPER, UNHANDIER, and UNIFORMER. The number of these words is fortunately small. If more were included, the *OSPD* would become an even "unusualer" book than it already is.

Unexpected, irregular, and inconsistent pluralizations. There are a considerable number of words in the *OSPD* that appear to be adjectives but are nouns as well. Since they are nouns, they can be pluralized. The *OSPD* thus includes words such as IMMATURES, ADAMANTS, ECSTATICS, RAWS, OLDS, NEEDFULS, UNWASHEDS and BIZARRES. (I would like to say that these words are bizarres, but that would be incorrect—a bizarre is a kind of flower.) There are many, many more of these unexpected pluralizations.

Occasionally a word that appears to be a verbal past tense is also a noun. A TORE is "a large convex molding." A CAME is a window rod, and a STANK is a pond. A LAMED is a Hebrew letter. You may draw a challenge by tacking an s onto any of these words, so it pays to know them and others like them.

You should also be aware that virtually every noun can be pluralized. Some very strange-looking words can be formed in this manner, among them DEADS, OVERMUCHES, MUCHNESSES, TWOFOLDS, TENFOLDS, TENNISES and OXYGENS. My favorite is TRECENTOS. Its definition in the singular is "the fourteenth century."

The *OSPD* is a mine field of irregular and inconsistent pluralizations. When experts play weaker players, they often play words that take irregular pluralizations on purpose, even if a slightly stronger but less deceptive play is available. This creates an opportunity for their opponents to lose a turn by incorrectly pluralizing these words or by incorrectly challenging the experts' correct pluralizations. They may also fail to challenge experts' incorrect pluralizations. The following discussion will give you an idea of how varied and confusing pluralizations can be:

Sometimes a pluralization does not alter the word (CATTLE, ZORI, NGWEE). At other times, the pluralization is irregular. A number of words are pluralized by adding E only (BACCA/BACCAE, MUSCA/MUSCAE, APHTHA/APTHAE). Others take either E or S (AMEBA/AMEBAE/AMEBAS, LAMINA/LAMINAE/LAMINAS, PATINA/PATINAE/PATINAS). Some words sound as if they should obey the same rules but don't. For example, QUAICHS and QUAICHES are acceptable plurals of QUAICH, but LAICHS (and not LAICHES) is the only plural of LAICH.

Words ending in -US are sometimes pluralized with an I only (ACINUS/ACINI; ACARUS/ACARI), sometimes with -USES only (HIATUS/HIATUSES); sometimes with either -I or -US (PAPYRUS/PAPYRI/PAPYRUSES); and sometimes with neither (the plural of CANTUS is CANTUS)! Similarly, although singular nouns ending with a Y are most often pluralized by dropping the Y and adding -IES in its place, a few allow -YS as well as -IES (SHINDY/SHINDYS/SHINDIES; HENRY/HENRYS/HENRIES). Others allow only the -YS ending (ZLOTY/ZLOTYS, BENDY/BENDYS, BLUEY/BLUEYS).

These examples only scratch the surface. Words can be pluralized by adding -IM (BAAL/BAALIM), -Y (KORUNA/KORUNY; GROSZ/GROSZY), -EN (AUTOBAHN/AUTOBAHNEN), -TA (BEMA/BEMATA), -U (HALER/HALERU), -I (DJINN/DJINNI), -R (KRONE/KRONER), -N (SCHUL/SCHULN); by replacing -S with -OI (NOMOS/NOMOI; EXODOS/EXODOI), -F with -VES (TURF/TURVES; CORF/CORVES), -X with -CES (CALX/CALCES), -IUM with -IA (CORIUM/CORIA), -S with -NTES (ATLAS/ATLANTES), -S with -DES (OTITIS/OTITIDES), et cetera, et cetera. Sometimes plurals are only remotely related to their singular forms (LIKUTA-MAKUTA). Additional confusion results from the fact that some but not all words with irregular pluralizations can also be pluralized with -s.

The *OSPD* is not consistent in its pluralizations of similar words. For example, though SHUL and SCHUL have the same definition, SHUL can be pluralized with an s or an N but SCHUL can be pluralized only with an N. OBLIGATO and OSTINATO are both listed as nouns in the *OSPD*. OBLIGATO's plurals are OBLIGATOS and OBLIGATI, but OSTINATI is a phony; the only plural of OSTINATO is OSTINATOS. Similarly, MUNGOOSE is an alternate spelling of MONGOOSE in the *OSPD*. Both words take -s plurals, but though MONGEESE is an acceptable alternative pluralization of MONGOOSE, MUNGEESE is a phony. ENOSISES and NOESISES are both allowable, but DIESISES isn't.

Finally, you should be aware that many words appearing to be pluralizable by adding -s are not. I consider knowledge of these words so important that I study them thoroughly before every tournament I play in. I also try to play them against weaker players, in the hope that I might win a challenge should they attempt to hook an -s onto them. Some examples of these words are AVA, FEY, GEY, MIM, VEG, WUD, CORF, LEVA, SYBO, VITA, YELD, ALGID, KRONA, LYARD, PELON, and VOGIE. There are hundreds more.

Other inconsistencies. The *OSPD*'s inconsistencies are infuriating at first, but they become real weapons once they are learned. Some examples are: INSOFAR is acceptable, INASMUCH is not; though INQUIRE and ENQUIRE are both in the *OSPD*, INQUIRER is acceptable and ENQUIRER is not; FEMME is allowable, HOMME is not; FIXT, MIXT, UNFIXT, UNMIXT and REMIXT are good, but REFIXT, OVERMIXT, and INTERMIXT are phonys; LOUDLIER is good, SOFTLIER is not; TIMIDEST is okay, but don't try RIGIDEST against an expert player (play RIDGIEST instead); COLOR, COLOUR, and RECOLOR are fine, but RECOLOUR is phony; and AXLIKE is acceptable but AXELIKE is not.

In summary, the two most notable characteristics of the *OSPD* are that (1) it is permissive in that it includes many words of foreign origin, unusual applications of prefixes and suffixes, exclamations (some of which are even listed as verbs or nouns), examples of "poor" English, slang, obscenities, ethnic and racial slurs, strange spellings and comparative forms, and pluralizations that might not be allowed in other North American dictionaries; and that (2) it is often internally inconsistent with respect to the ways in which similar words are dealt with. Both characteristics increase the challenge for the serious SCRABBLE® brand crossword game player. The *OSPD*'s permissiveness means that there are more words to learn, and its inconsistency means that it's easy to get confused. I wouldn't want it any other way.

PART II

How to Play
the Game

Several years ago I played on a city league slow-pitch soft-ball team in Binghamton, New York. Our team made it to the final play-offs in its first year of existence and won league championships the following two seasons. Despite this record, we always looked like losers. The other teams had uniforms, about fifteen bats each, and bulging muscles. We had no uniforms, three bats to choose from, and lots of scrawn. For the first few games we were intimidated by the opposing team's batting practice. A succession of Neander-thaloid Goliaths would step up to the plate, take hefty swings, and smite balls into the stratosphere.

We were able to win because softball, like all great games and sports, allows "mind over matter" to prevail. "Mind" in this sense means knowing how to play. We noticed, for example, that most of the ball fields we played on had no fences. Our outfielders would simply retreat when con-fronted with a "heavy hitter," resulting in many long fly outs. In contrast, we practiced hitting line drives and ground balls. This type of contact was most likely to get us on base, either through honest base hits or opponents' errors. We also practiced fundamentals such as hitting the cutoff man, backing up throws from the outfield, tag plays, and the like. We were prepared to play an intelligent game.

In SCRABBLE® brand crossword game, the player who is a "walking dictionary" is the counterpart of softball's Go-liath. It cannot be denied that word knowledge is of great importance in the Game, just as it cannot be denied that physical strength can be used to advantage in softball.

However, of even greater importance is knowing how to play the game. That is what the following three chapters are all about.

4

Scoring Points

This chapter is concerned with the ability to find high-scoring plays. It is not concerned with long-term strategic considerations. A well-developed scoring ability is necessary for sound strategic play, however. Imagine, for example, that you are ahead by 40 points late in the game and you wish to close down the board to protect your lead (a strategic consideration). This is difficult to accomplish if you are unable to assess accurately which openings on the board are the most dangerous ones.

The key to maximizing your score is to look for locations on the board that harmonize well with the tiles on the rack. The expert player does not examine every possible play. This would be a very inefficient use of that most precious commodity, time. Instead, the expert's attention is drawn to those portions of the board that are most relevant to the situation. You must be aware of both the available premium squares and the hidden possibilities implicit in the board position. I shall use Example 5 to illustrate these ideas:

	A	B	C	D	E	F	G	H	I	J	K	L	M	N	O
1	TWS			DLS				TWS				DLS			TWS
2		DWS				TLS				**H**				DWS	
3			DWS				DLS		**W**	**A**	**G**	**O**	**N**	**E**	**D**
4	DLS			DWS				DLS		**R**		DWS			**E**
5					DWS					**M**	DWS				**L**
6		TLS				TLS				**E**				TLS	**I**
7			DLS				DLS		DLS	**R**			DLS		**G**
8	TWS			**J**	**A**	**R**	**G**	**O**	**N**	**[S]**		DLS			**H**
9			**C**	**O**	**X**		**R**		DLS				DLS		**T**
10		TLS		**T**		TLS	**D**	**E**		TLS				TLS	**S**
11				**T**	DWS		**R**	**E**			DWS				
12	DLS			**E**			**A**	**N**				DWS			DLS
13	**Q**	**A**	**I**	**D**			**W**	**E**					DWS		
14		DWS				TLS	**[S]**			TLS				DWS	
15	TWS			**P**	**L**	**O**	**T**	**T**	**I**	**E**	**S**	DLS			TWS

Example #5

Simple openings. A simple opening is one that allows a play to be made from, through, or to a letter of one previously played word. Only one word is added to the game board. There are several places on this board where simple openings may be utilized for high-scoring plays. The most blatantly obvious one is column A. With the Q placed on A13, possible plays range from QUA for 36 points to words such as ROQUE, TOQUE, SILIQUE, SILIQUA, ANTIQUE, MANQUE, BARQUE, BEZIQUE, CAZIQUE, and dozens of others. Less likely but also possible are triple-triple plays that score hundreds of points. POSTIQUE and PRATIQUE are two examples.

Other potentially high-scoring simple openings are those permitting combination premium square plays. These include B10 to B14 or B15 (a triple letter-double word combination), L1 to L4, L5, L6, or L7, (a double letter-double word combination), and the double-double word opening through the M at 5J (5E to 5K). The opening at B10 downward is particularly dangerous, as the z has not yet played. Possible plays here scoring 68 points or more are ZANANA, ZENANA, ZETAS, ZIRAM, ZOEAE, ZOEAL, ZOEAS, ZONAL, ZONARY, ZONATE, ZOUAVE, and ZYMASE. The z may also be played at L1 for 40+ points (there are numerous ZOO- words in the

OSPD), though such a play allows counterplay along the top row.

Hooks and overlaps. A *hook* is a letter that can be added to the beginning or end of a word already on the board, transforming that word into a different one. The main word played is made perpendicularly to the hooked word. The most obvious hook location on this board is at J1. A player holding the remaining C could convert HARMERS to CHARMERS and likely play along row 1 so that the horizontal word made would cover one of the triple word squares at H1 or O1.

Another hook location is at L15. PLOTTY is an adjective as well as a noun, and thus a word played down column L and ending in T at L15 is a possibility. This hook is easier to overlook than the previously mentioned one. However, there are hooks that are even more "hidden," usually because the hook letter radically changes the new word's pronunciation (for example, SLANDER-ISLANDER). Many hook plays elude even expert players. In a game (not shown here) played in the 1980 North American Championship, my opponent played Ⓜ︎ARQUES, 7H. He deliberated before making this move and momentarily could not decide whether to make the blank a B or an M (both BARQUES and MARQUES are *OSPD*-acceptable words). He made the wrong choice: I was able to make a big play down column O by using my S, converting Ⓜ︎ARQUES to Ⓜ︎ARQUESS. I ultimately won the game by 16 points, and the victory was very probably due to my opponent's oversight.

An *overlap* is a multiple hook play. The main word played creates subsidiary words by hooking onto letters from a previously played word that is parallel and adjacent to the main play. These subsidiary words are usually adjacent to each other. An example might be LOAVES, 14I. This play produces three two-letter words (LI, OE, and AS). Potentially high-scoring overlap locations are from 14I or 14J to or beyond 14N; and from N1 or N2 to N6. One should also be aware of premium squares that are adjacent to vowels or to medium- and high-point letters (2N, 4L, 5K, 6N, and 14J, for example). These openings permit two-way plays that are invariably worth 20 points or more. Typical such plays on this board might be GEY, K3; WAB, 2L; or YORE, 4L. The spot at H12 for a Y should be kept in mind as well.

Openings and hooks for bingos. The hook location at 1J and L15 are of especial importance, as they are possible locations for seven-letter bingos. The other openings for seven-letter bingos are at N9-15, where the bonus play must begin with two vowels (e.g., EARNERS, AUTUMNS, etc.), and 14I-O, where the beginning three letters must be a consonant and two vowels (e.g., BAITERS), two consonants and a vowel (e.g., TRAILER), or an A, a consonant, and a vowel (e.g., ABATERS).

The aware player must keep in mind locations for eight- and nine-letter bingos as well as for seven-letter plays. Strong players in fact play about twice as many eight-letter as seven-letter bingos. There are quite a number of openings for eight-letter plays on this board. In addition to the triple-triple opening down column A, eight-letter bingos may be played through the M or E in HARMERS, and the O or N in WAGONED. It is less likely that a bingo will be played through the R at 4J, though it is certainly possible to end a bingo here or with the R at F8. Nine-letter bingos are considerably rarer, but should be kept in mind when the board situation warrants it. In the diagram for Example 5, for example, RE at 11F-G suggests possible RE- prefix plays. Such plays occur with a fair degree of regularity in tournament play.

Almost unheard of are bingos of ten or more letters. SCRABBLE® players dream of plays such as STOREFRONT (11C), but almost never get to make such pretty plays.

Inside plays. Inside plays occur when the main word forms other words by "filling them in." Inside plays are thus special forms of overlaps. Examples of this type of play on

Example 5 are ATAXIA, E6, AXIAL, E8, and TRIAXIAL, E5. The
first play creates TIDE (10D) and TARE (11D); the others also
form ELAN (12D). Plays such as these are often extremely
satisfying from an aesthetic point of view. I have in fact
sometimes made lovely inside plays that were not the best
plays simply to show my opponent how creative I could be.

Word extensions. The inside plays demonstrated above
are also examples of word extensions. Ax is transformed
into another word by adding letters after it, or after it and
before it. It would of course also be possible to add letters
before it only (e.g., RELAX, POLEAX, OVERTAX, TOADFLAX,
etc.).

The most common word extension plays are made by
tacking on -s plurals, prefixes, or suffixes to previously
played words. For example, one player begins a game by
plunking down RALLY, 8H. The other then adds -ING to it for
an easy 36 points. Other prefixes and suffixes that are
commonly used for word extensions are BE-, UN-, DE-, NON-,
OUT-, OVER-, SEMI-, -ERS, -IER, -EST, and -IEST.

It is also possible to make word extension plays that are
considerably less plebeian. I once began a tournament
game with HIVES, 8D. Late in the game, my opponent
hooked a C onto it, creating CHIVES (8C) by making a play
from 8C to 8H. I was able to win the game on my last turn by
playing A**R**CHIVES, 8A, for 45 points. In a club game, my
opponent opened with MAKE, 8G. I had AAEBSTW in my rack.
My play was the very surprising and unusual word MAKE-
BATES (8G, 48 points). Our last example comes from the by
now overworked position in Example 5. The expert tactician
will be aware that an S and an I in the rack may be used to
create SIDELIGHTS, O1. SCRABBLE® requires eternal vigi-
lance!

Scoring Records and Norms

I have been asked the following three questions many
times over:

(1) What is the greatest number of points you have ever scored on a single turn?

(2) What is the greatest number of points you have ever scored in one game?

(3) How many points do you average per game?

The answers to these questions are (1) 185 (the play was BESCOURS, A1), (2) 609, and (3) 435 against club competition, 410 in tournament play. The answers to the first two questions are not particularly distinguished in comparison with the current North American records. On the other hand, high scores are freak events and do not reflect true playing ability. Only the third question gives you some idea of my playing strength, and it does that only because I have specified to a limited extent the quality of my competition. One should not get hung up over numbers. While it is true that I have played well in most of the games in which I have scored 500 or more points, my scores in some of my most thoughtful wins have been in the 300-320 range. A 500+ score simply means that you have been lucky, that your opponent is overmatched, or both. Where's the merit in that?

A number of years ago in a tournament I played a woman who tried to intimidate me by informing me before the game that she averaged 450 points per game against her friends. She had never played in a tournament before and had never attended a SCRABBLE® club. I won the game by a score of something like 490 to 250. This simply shows that averages mean little without some kind of frame of reference.

It cannot be denied, however, that if you play regularly in a sanctioned club and your average has been rising steadily, your play has very likely been improving. SCRABBLE® clubs vary greatly in strength. Nevertheless, an average of over 300 in most clubs is considered respectable. A 350 average is well above the mean, and an average of 400 is exceptional. Regardless of averages, you will never know how good you really are until you play against true experts.

Incidentally, the North American record for the greatest

number of points garnered on one turn in sanctioned club or tournament play is 302, and it was set by Ron Manson of Toronto. The game board just before he made his play is shown in Example #6. Can you find his move?

	A	B	C	D	E	F	G	H	I	J	K	L	M	N	O
1															
2								V							
3								I							
4							C	L	O	W	N				
5								E	F						
6									F						
7		P	U	N	D	I	T	S		B	E				
8								H	I	R	E	R			
9						M	I			G					
10				B	O	U	T								
11			N	O	M										
12															
13															
14															
15															

Example #6

Ron's Rack EEQRSU□

Ron's play was the lovely triple-triple, REEQUIPS (A1).

The North American record for the greatest number of points scored by one player in a sanctioned SCRABBLE® club meeting or tournament is 719. This record was set by Chris Reslock in an Ohio tournament in 1980. Chris played five unchallenged phonies in the game.

5

Strategy

The strategic element is what elevates SCRABBLE® brand crossword game from a merely excellent game to an exquisite one. Unfortunately, strategy is also the most obscure and neglected part of the game. Casual players are usually unaware of the profundity and subtlety of thought that can underlie a great player's finest plays. Newspaper reporters and interviewers are certainly in the dark in this respect. They want to know about unusual words played, favorite words, highest scoring plays, and so forth. Never has an interviewer asked me to explain the strategy behind what I thought was my best play in a game or in a tournament.

A mastery of strategy is essential to winning consistently in the Game at the club or tournament level. We shall see that attainment of this mastery is no simple matter!

I have divided the discussion of strategy into two chapters. In this chapter, general strategic principles are presented and illustrated. Chapter 6 deals with more particular situations that players often have to deal with.

General Strategic Principles

For clarity's sake, I have not in this chapter fully discussed the ways in which strategic principles may interact with each other. It is often impossible to make a play in which all of the game principles are adhered to. Strategic ideas sometimes conflict with each other, and the proper assessment of which of these ideas should prevail is often difficult. The need to maximize point count may conflict with rack management, for example. The idea of conservation of resources will at times be diametrically opposed to the principle of playing away as many tiles as possible.

Issues such as these are considered to some degree in this chapter, and are more fully dealt with in the annotated games section of this book.

Play away as many tiles on each turn as possible. The more tiles played away, the greater the chance of picking valuable tiles such as the blank, S, X, Z, and J. This principle is especially important in the early stages of the game, when most of the good tiles are still in the bag.

It is, of course, more difficult to play a long word than to play a shorter one. It is my feeling, however, that many six- and seven-letter words are missed due to inattention rather than to poor anagramming ability. It is easy to become complacent and to stop looking for a better play after finding a satisfactory one. Imagine, for example, that you are in the situation presented in Example #7:

TWS			DLS				TWS				DLS			TWS	1
	DWS				TLS				TLS				DWS		2
		DWS				DLS		DLS				DWS			3
DLS			DWS				DLS				DWS			DLS	4
				DWS					DWS						5
	TLS				TLS				TLS				TLS		6
		DLS				DLS		DLS				DLS			7
TWS			DLS	**F**	**O**	**V**	**E**	**A**			DLS			TWS	8
		DLS				DLS		DLS				DLS			9
	TLS				TLS				TLS				TLS		10
				DWS					DWS						11
DLS			DWS				DLS				DWS			DLS	12
		DWS				DLS		DLS				DWS			13
	DWS				TLS				TLS				DWS		14
TWS			DLS				TWS				DLS			TWS	15
A	B	C	D	E	F	G	H	I	J	K	L	M	N	O	

Example #7

Score You: 0 Opponent: 30
Your rack ELMNORW

If you know that FOVEA takes an -E hook (to form the plural), it does not take much effort to find MEWL, I 7. This play scores 28 points, and the NOR left on the rack is quite decent. However, perseverance is necessary to look farther for the longer word and the better play: REFLOWN (D6, 26 points). REFLOWN is two points less than MEWL, but the chance of picking a blank or an S after playing it is 50 percent greater than after playing MEWL.

Example #8

Score   You: 0   Opponent: 74
Your rack   DDIKNRT

It is often worthwhile to sacrifice a few points in order to play away more tiles. In the early stages of a game, I consider each additional tile played to be worth a sacrifice of two to three points. In Example #8, your highest scoring play is KIND (F6, 19 points). However, KINDRED (H3, 14 points) uses three more tiles, and for that reason is a finer play than KIND though it scores five points less. More problematic is KIDDER (H4, 17 points) versus KINDRED. Is the opportunity to draw one more tile worth sacrificing three points? In this case, I would say yes. Your opponent's substantial lead makes it that much more urgent for you to increase your probability of picking good tiles.

The value of playing away as many tiles as possible varies with the progress of each individual game. If the game is half over and no blanks have yet been played, it is extremely important to play away as many tiles as possible. If, on the other hand, most of the good tiles have been played early in the game, it may not be wise to sacrifice any points at all for the opportunity to pick additional tiles.

Balance your rack. Rack management refers to play-making that maximizes the chances for making good plays on future turns. The unplayed tiles (henceforth called the rack leave) should "go together" well. There are a number of considerations that must be kept in mind in order to achieve this:

Your rack leave should not be overly laden with vowels or with consonants. Almost all of the words in the English language consist of a combination of consonants and vowels. If you have five or more vowels, or six or more consonants on your rack, the number of possible words that can be formed from the rack is likely to be much smaller than if the rack were more evenly balanced.

Despite the fact that there are more consonants than vowels in the Game's tile distribution (56 to 42, counting the two YS as consonants), too many vowels on the rack (voweli-tis) is a much more common affliction than too many consonants. There are a number of reasons for this. First, many consonants combine with each other in groups of twos and threes (e.g., BL-, BR-, CH-, CHR-, CL-, CR-, DR-, FL-, FR-, GL-, GR-, KN-, PH-, PL-, PR-, SC-, SCH-, SH-, SHR-, SK-, SL-, SM-, SN-, SP-, SPL-, SPR-, ST-, STR-, SW-, TH-, THR-, TR-, TW-, WR-; -CH, -CK, -CT, -FT, -LM, -LT, -MB, -MP, -NT, -PT, -SH, -SK, -SP, -ST, -TCH, -PHY, -GHT, etc.). As a result, it will often take only one available vowel on the board or from the rack to make a play utilizing three or more consonants from the rack. Vowels do not go together quite as well. Although it is possible to rid oneself of a number of vowels if the right consonant is available (e.g., AGIO, EIDE, UNAI, UNAU, AREAE, AUREI, URAEI, OIDIA, AINEE, COOEE, etc.), there are relatively few words serving this function as compared to the number of words that can be formed from many consonants and one vowel. Second, all vowels are worth one point. A play made to dump vowels from the rack is therefore not likely to score well. In contrast, twenty-three of the consonant tiles are worth three points or more. Disposing of consonants is thus generally more profitable as well as easier than disposing of vowels. Finally, it is easier to play away more consonants than vowels when the rack is balanced. As a result, racks that are initially balanced may become vowel-heavy over three or four successive turns.

It is good policy to play for a rack leave that alleviates or guards against vowelitis. I once began a game with EGIO-RUU on my rack. The highest scoring plays are ERUGO, ROGUE, and ROUGE, but I did not consider any of them because of the two-vowel leave. Instead, I played OURIE. I often make plays resulting in more consonants left on my rack than vowels, even though an alternate play might yield the same number of vowels as consonants. For example, with the rack of AABDENS on the first play of the game, I would play BAAED (retaining SN) over BANED (retaining AS). The leave of AS after BANED is certainly nothing to be alarmed about. The NS leave is slightly better, however; it pretty much ensures that I will not have to worry about too many vowels on my next rack. With five tiles to pick, I would not be concerned about accumulating too many consonants.

Sometimes, however, too many consonants do clog up the rack. This is normally a concern only under the following conditions: (1) the board is closed, so there are no useful vowels on it to play through; (2) the consonants do not work well with each other; and (3) there are few vowels left in the bag. Under any of these conditions, you must make a choice between exchanging tiles—if still an option—and making the best play possible, taking into consideration the point count and the rack leave. For example, imagine that your opening rack is CCFTUVW. You could play CUT for ten points, but the leave of CFVW is highly unpromising. My choice would be to exchange all seven tiles and hope for better things in the future.

Avoid leaving more than one tile of the same letter on the rack. A number of years ago, this was thought to be a very important principle. The idea behind it was that letter duplication restricted the player's options. Having six or fewer different tiles limited the number of plays that could be made.

This principle is perhaps less important than it might seem: there are just too many words in the *OSPD* in which there is at least one instance of letter duplication. It is nonetheless important to be aware of which letters go well together and which do not. Doubled DS, ES, FS, LS, MS, NS, OS, PS, SS, and TS on the rack are not likely to hurt. On the other hand, the following doubles are notoriously unproductive and should be avoided like the plague: IS, US, VS, WS, and YS. It should also be borne in mind that there is some danger in leaving duplicates of *any* one- or two-point letter on the rack, as doubles increase the likelihood of ending up with three or four tiles of these letters. Two of a kind may not be much of a liability, but three or more of a kind can be crippling.

An important factor in determining the degree to which duplicate letters may impede your play is the board position. If, for example, your leave contains two YS but there are lucrative openings available for them (as in Example 5, page 58), there is little problem. On the other hand, if you have a blank or an S and bingo-conducive tiles accompanying the YS, you most likely will have to play at least one Y away first before playing the bingo. You might even have to play both YS away on separate turns.

Another consideration affecting the importance of tile duplication upon one's play is the contents of the bag. Imagine, for example, the following scenario: only a few points separate your score from your opponent's, the board is closed with few opportunities for big scores, and there are eight tiles in the bag. Under these conditions, the winner is often the player who goes out first. You have been considering two moves. Both use four letters from your rack. Neither move creates glaring openings that your opponent is likely to take advantage of. One play scores six points more than the other, but the higher scoring play yields a leave including two Rs. The lower scoring play leaves only one R on the rack. *Only one R has been played in the game so far.* There are six Rs in a set, which means that three are unaccounted for. Your choice is whether to grab the additional six points and risk facing tripled or quadrupled Rs on your next rack after drawing from the bag, or to sacrifice the points in an attempt to make your next rack more flexible. If you end up with a glut of Rs you will have a very difficult time going out before your opponent does. On the other hand, the additional points from your higher scoring play may make the difference between defeat and victory.

Now imagine the same scenario as the one just described, with a major difference: *four Rs have previously been played.* The determination of the correct play in both cases depends, of course, upon the specifics of the board, score, and all of the tiles remaining in the bag. In most cases, however, the correct move when three Rs remain unseen will be the lower scoring play. With no Rs unaccounted for, it will likely be correct to take the additional points.

Try to achieve a good balance between low- and high-point tiles on the rack. Players sometimes part with high-point tiles (tiles worth three points or more) too quickly and without sufficient scoring compensation for them. They do this in the hope that the exclusive retention of one- and two-pointers is more likely to produce bingos than is the retention of tiles including one or more high-pointers. It is true that over 80 percent of all bingos played in tournaments have no or only one high-point letter in them. Nevertheless, playing for bingos by denuding the rack of high-point tiles is not good strategy. Although the 50-point bonus is tempting, bingo making is an unreliable venture. In addition, dispensing with high-point tiles often means that a low-scoring play on the following turn is the likely alternative to playing a bingo.

Consider this opening rack: ABHINOO. There are two main

choices here: HOBO (8E or 8G) and ABOON (8H). HOBO is inferior to ABOON in that it leaves more vowels than consonants on the rack, and one fewer tile is drawn from the bag. On the other hand, ABOON has its drawbacks: a B can be tacked onto its beginning, it scores two points less than HOBO, and the leave of HI after playing ABOON is less likely to result in a bingo on the next turn than is the AIN leave after HOBO. It is for this last reason that many players would choose HOBO My choice is ABOON, however, and the main reason for my selection is that retention of the high-point tile may help me net a good score on my next turn even if I am unable to play a bingo.

A balance between high- and low-point tiles does not mean that you should have three or four of each. This is impossible over the long run, as seventy-seven of the one hundred tiles in a game are worth less than three points. It is also undesirable, as three or more high-pointers may leave you with a "muscle bound" rack: plenty of power, but little suppleness due to a lack of the right vowels and other low-point tiles. A rack that is well balanced in terms of low- and high-point tiles will have only one or two high-point tiles on it.

In summary, a balance of high- and low-point tiles on the rack will ensure consistently good scores on successive plays. Plays that consistently empty the rack of high-point tiles will do the opposite: their following plays will either be low-scoring or will be bingos. In the long run, consistent scoring will win out over bingo hunting.

There are certain two-letter combinations (other than the deleterious duplicates discussed above) that combine to form relatively few words. At least one of the two letters should be played away as soon as possible. The combinations are: BF, BP, BV, BW, CV, CW, FH, FK, FP, FV, FW, GK, JQ, JX, JZ, KQ, KV, KZ, MW, PV, PZ, QV, QW, QX, QZ, UW, VX, VZ, WZ, and XZ. Among the vowels, A and O do not combine particularly well. Even worse are combinations such as AAO, AOO, and AAOO.

The number of points that should be sacrificed in order to

make a play divesting the rack of the above combinations, as opposed to making a higher scoring play which does not break them up, is variable, and depends on the particular combination on the rack, the board and score situations, the other tiles in the rack, and the tiles remaining in the bag.

Conserve your "good" tiles. The good tiles of course include the blanks and the ss. Other valuable tiles are the x, z, j, and q with u.

Conserving one's resources versus playing for maximum point count is an extremely complex problem. It's nice to be able to keep the good tiles, but not at the expense of sacrificing too many points. Most players are too miserly in this respect. They refuse to part with their ss when it is advantageous to do so, and they stubbornly cling to their blanks until they find a playable bingo.

What follows are some general guidelines for determining whether to spend or save. These guidelines will not automatically lead to clear, unequivocal choices for all of your moves. You can, in fact, expect an average of about four "borderline" decisions per game that you will have to make. In order to keep your hair from turning gray prematurely, I would advise you to heed Wapnick's Rule in these situations:

Wapnick's Rule: When in doubt, take the additional points.

This will help to counteract the characteristic human tendency to hoard, which can be as detrimental over the board as in real life.

Spending or saving the s. An s should be spent if the play using it yields at least six to eight points more than plays not using it. This is not an ironclad rule. For example, if you are behind near the end of the game and can win only by playing a bingo, it might be necessary to keep the s even if using it means an additional 15 or 20 points. The s is especially valuable if the three other ss in the set are all showing on the board, as you may be able to prepare high-scoring s-hook plays that your opponent can neither use nor block.

In this case, eight or more points may not be sufficient compensation for the s. Finally, you would be ill-advised to spend the s for only six to eight points if you also have a blank on your rack but no playable bingo, and there are openings on the board for playing bingos. In this case, you should raise your threshhold for spending the s to perhaps 12 to 15 points versus not playing it. The blank combines very well with an s for forming bingos, and you should not jeopardize the bingo opportunity without sufficient compensation. In most cases, however, six or more additional points are worth making a play using the s. Example #9 is typical:

Example #9

Score You: 160 Opponent: 120
Opponent's last play PIPETTE (E1, 22 points)
Your rack ADGINRS

The highest scoring play in which the s is retained is PAR-ING (1E, 27 points). SPADING (1D) uses the s and scores nine more points. Take the additional points here, especially as by picking six fresh tiles (with the other three ss unaccounted for) you would have a good chance of picking another s.

If you have two ss on the rack, you should freely spend one of them for a good deal less than the additional six or more points. Under most conditions, having two ss on the rack is not better than having one s. The s duplicate may in fact hinder your play rather than help it. This is especially true if no other ss have been played, as picking a third s would surely hurt. Even if the other ss have been played, however, retaining both ss in the hope of playing them separately for big scores on consecutive plays, or together for a bingo, is usually bad strategy.

In some instances, playing away an s for an additional two or three points will telegraph to your opponent that you are holding another s in your rack. Consider the opening rack of CEIMRSS. You would like to play CRIMES (8D), but by tacking the s onto CRIME for only two more points and the opportunity to pick one more tile, your opponent would undoubtedly correctly surmise that your remaining tile must be another s. Why else would you spend the s for so little? Having realized this, your opponent would be less likely to make a play that would give you a lucrative s hook than if you had made a play that better disguised your rack leave.

There are two ways of dealing with situations such as these. The first is to find an alternative play that does not disclose your leave. In the above situation, SCRIM (8H) fits the bill. Your opponent cannot determine that you have another s from this play, and may indeed think that you have two consonants left rather than ES. The second is to *make* the telegraphing play, in effect saying to your opponent, "I've got another s; what are you going to do about it?" The idea behind this ploy is that you will gain by inducing your opponent to play more defensively than he may have liked to. He may sacrifice points, play away fewer tiles than he otherwise would have, and may have a less satisfactory leave than would have been the case if you *did not* in effect tell him that your remaining tile was an s. The example

given above is a borderline case. I would, therefore, follow
Wapnick's Rule and play CRIMES, though I would guess that
a fair number of experts would disagree and play SCRIM
instead. Either of these moves is superior to CRIME.

We have so far seen that playing away an s for a minimum of six additional points is generally worth doing, but
that it may be advisable to get rid of an s for considerably
less if there is another s on the rack. Now we will deal with
the situation in which playing away two ss at the same time
scores more points than playing away one or no ss. There
are usually some complicating factors involved here. For
one thing, a word using two ss is likely to use many more
letters on the rack than other plays. This is usually to the
player's advantage, as discussed above. For another, racks
in which appreciably higher scores are possible using two
ss, rather than only using one, most probably also contain
many low-point tiles, most of which will be vowels. Double-s
plays thus often have the advantage of curing vowelitis.

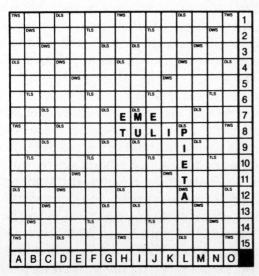

Example #10

Score   You: 39   Opponent: 14
Opponent's last play   PIETA (L8, 14 points)
Your rack   AEIOSSS

The highest scoring play in Example #10 in which only one s is used is SAE (6H, 18 points). OASES (6F) uses two of the three ss, and scores four more points. OASES is the better move; even though two ss are kept after SAE, the IOSS leave is not very promising either for separate high-scoring s plays or for creating a bingo. The IS leave after OASES, on the other hand, cleans out three of the four vowels and provides a greater opportunity for picking one of the blanks or some high-point tiles. Incidentally, if you are unfortunate enough to have three or all four ss clogging up your rack, you may be tempted to exchange some of them. Try instead to play them away, so that your opponent will not be able to pick them.

The decision to play OASES is not really very painful here, as one s is still left in the rack. However, it is sometimes necessary to choose between playing no, one, or two ss when two are on the rack. The opening rack of DEEIISS is an example. There are three playable six-letter words, all of which can be played for 18 points and all of which spend both ss: SEISED, DIESES, and DIESIS. DIESIS is the best of the three, as it gets rid of both IS. Other plays using no ss or one s score at least 8 points less and use at most four tiles (SIDE, DIES, EIDE, SEI). Is DIESIS worth the additional points and tiles?

Logic would seem to demand that if parting with one s when that s is the only one on the rack is worth seven or so additional points, then parting with two ss when there are two ss on the rack must require a greater payoff. As previously mentioned, however, there is no advantage in having two ss on the rack versus having one s. It therefore makes sense to spend two ss, when two are on the rack, for essentially the same payoff as spending one s when one is on the rack: a minimum of six to eight additional points over plays using *either* no ss or one s. That's why DIESIS in the example above is the correct play. Don't fall into the trap of assessing a move without reference to your other plays (e.g., "But I'm using two ss for only 18 points!").

Spending or saving the blank. The general rule for playing a blank is that it should be spent if it nets an additional

40 or so points versus not spending it. As was the case with the S, however, there may be extenuating circumstances. Consider, for example, the following situation. Your opponent goes first and exchanges one tile. You have CDHMPZ▯ in your rack. Your options are to exchange tiles (CDHMP, and perhaps the Z) or to play CH▯E▯Z (8F or 8G) for 34 points. CH▯E▯Z is the correct play. Though it scores only 34 points, it is good defensively. By exchanging one tile, your opponent has indicated to you that she is bingo hunting. CH▯E▯Z (unlike PH▯I▯Z allows no seven-letter bingos, and your opponent may well be unable to play an eight-letter bingo through your letters.

Incidentally, the correct placement of CH▯E▯Z is far from clear. Placements at 8E and 8H are out, as they open up access to double word squares unnecessarily. The placements at 8F and 8G are both problematic. The most likely letter to be used in CHEZ by the opponent for an eight-letter bingo is the E. By putting it on the star (8F placement), you are allowing your opponent more of an opportunity to cover the triple word squares at 1H or 15H than would be the case if CHEZ was placed at 8G. On the other hand, the 8G placement opens up the double letter squares at 7I and 9I. Your opponent is unlikely to take advantage of them, since by exchanging one tile she has indicated that she is bingo hunting and has therefore retained six low-point tiles. However, the one tile she picks might be an F, H, W or X, just the letters likely to foul up her bingo quest. The 8G placement would then backfire, since she would then be able to make a 23+ point play at 7H or 9H while retaining most of her bingo-conducive tiles.

Occasionally you will have two blanks in your rack and the opportunity to play away one or both for big scores. The same general rule holds: Play away both blanks if the play scores about 40 or more points than plays using only one blank. Situations in which it is advantageous to play one blank when two are on the rack and the two can be played together for a bingo are very rare. One borderline case is shown in Example #11:

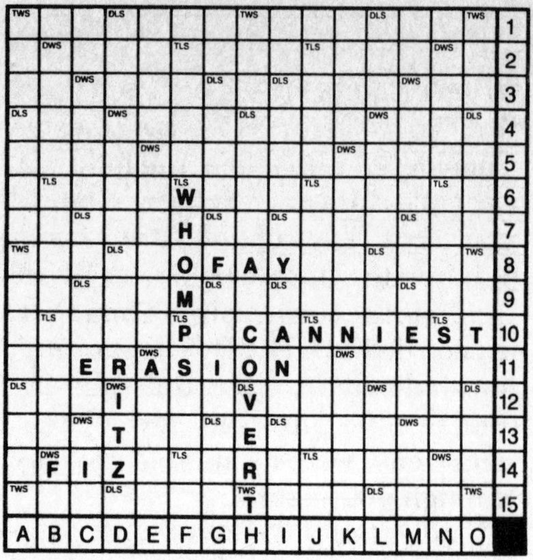

Example #11

Score You: 100 Opponent: 196
Opponent's last play CANNIEST (10H, 66 points)
Your rack BIOSX[ ][ ]

There are seven playable bingos here, the best of which is S[U]BOXI[D]E at M3 (96 points). There are also two plays which utilize only one of the two blanks: BOXI[E]ST (O4, 54 points) and TOXI[N]S (O10, 60 points). The position is actually quite complex. S[U]BOXI[D]E ties the game, but at the cost of using both blanks plus allowing the opponent opportunities to use the triple word scores at O8 or O15. TOXI[N]S is not as weak defensively, but decreases the probability of playing a bingo with the other blank next turn, as it limits possible plays through the E, R, and T of COVERT. Also, retention of the B along with the blank may hinder the creation of a bingo. BOXI[E]ST scores the least, but probably offers the best long-term prospects; the board is kept wide open for a bingo, which you are more likely than your opponent to play, but the triple word squares in column O are no longer available for your opponent.

	A	B	C	D	E	F	G	H	I	J	K	L	M	N	O
1															B
2														M	U
3					C	O	X	I	N	G				O	M
4													O	I	
5				P					J	O	Y	S		S	
6				E					W		D			T	
7			I	R	R	E	A	L		A		I		E	H
8	F	A	D		K			O	U	R	I	E		N	O
9								R		T					O
10						Z	E	D			Y	E			D
11											N				
12											G				
13															
14															
15															

Example #12

Score	You: 180	Opponent: 177
Opponent's last play		FAD (8A, 24 points)
Your rack		BEGHLRT

Conserving other resources. Depending on the board situation, any tile in the bag may be a great deal more valuable at a given moment than it normally is. If you are holding such a tile, you should save it if plays not using it score slightly less or the same as plays on which it is spent. In Example #12, the two best plays are GLOBE and BROTH (both at H1, 33 points). EH (2I) scores two more points, but creates an opening along row 1 for the opponent and leaves five consonants on the rack. The correct play is GLOBE, for it conserves the H. There are two good locations for the H: 6F and 2J. GLOBE makes it very likely that you will score a minimum of 26 points on the next turn, whereas BROTH does very little for your next turn.

The third and fourth US with the Q unplayed and not on your rack. If you and your opponent are within 50 points of each other near the end of the game, getting stuck with an unplayable Q is likely to spell disaster. A player with a 50-point lead and a Q but no U on the rack really only has at best a 30-point lead, since the opponent will gain at least 20 points upon going out. In addition, the opponent may often be able to score many points by playing one tile away at a time, since there is no pressure to go out first. Beware the U-less Q!

Example #13 is from the final game of the 1983 North American Championship, and my opponent was Joe Edley, the 1980 North American Champion. Had I lost the game I would have lost the championship and he would have retained his title.

Example #13

	Score	Tied at 218
	Joe's last play	VIMEN (4A, 40 points)
	My rack	DEKOOSU

In this position I made an incredible blunder: I played KUDO (2A, 24 points), parting with what should have been a treasured last U. Much, much better would have been OKE at 2B (not at 2D, since HOWE is a word; with no HS yet played Joe could have scored over 50 points by using the H hook at 1D in combination with the triple word score at 1A). I compounded my error later on by making a six-letter play with nine tiles in the bag and the Q not yet showing, when I could have played only three tiles away while scoring one more point than my six-letter play. Fortunately for me, Joe picked the Q and I instead picked the J, Z, and another S.

If the Q has not been played and both blanks and two or three US are on the board, keep one U on your rack unless its expenditure is required for many, many points (e.g., for playing a bingo). This is especially true if the score is close and the game is nearing its conclusion. Remember that with six or fewer tiles in the bag you will not be able to exchange the Q away.

Spending or saving bingo-conducive letter combinations. Scrabble players love to play bingos. It's an emotional thing, and it's only remotely related to the prime objective of winning the game. The satisfaction derived from clearing the rack transcends the 50 bonus points. A player will often sacrifice points on turn after turn in order to "work for a bingo" by retaining letter combinations on the rack such as AERT, ING, ERS, and IEST. The technical term for this practice is "fishing." The technical term for a weak player is a "fish," and the similarity between these two terms is no accident.

In the vast majority of cases, fishing is bad policy. The reason for this is that bingos are hard to come by. They are rarely worth the accumulated sacrifice of points over successive turns, and of course there is no guarantee that fishing will ultimately lead to a bingo. The very best players average only about one and a half bingos per game. Weaker players often achieve an average that is almost as high, but at the expense of many wasted intervening turns. I attribute much of my success to my opponents' penchant for fishing. My best results usually occur in tournaments in which the combined opposition has formed about the same number of bingos as myself. In two qualifying tournaments for the 1983 North American Championship, for example, my opponents played thirty-two bingos against me. I played the same number of bingos against them, but won twenty-two of the twenty-four games.

It makes sense to fish when the probability of playing a

bingo on the next turn is extremely high, when the cost of fishing is low relative to other plays (e.g., scoring 21 versus 22 points) or when a prospective bingo is absolutely essential for winning the game. The first condition is illustrated by Example #14:

	A	B	C	D	E	F	G	H	I	J	K	L	M	N	O	
	J	O	S	H												1
		F	O	I	N											2
				V												3
			P	E	S											4
			U		A											5
		E	R	R	I	N	G									6
		R		L												7
			P	A	C	E	D									8
				B		F	O	H								9
				L			T	A	V							10
				B	E											11
		M	E													12
	G	O	Y													13
	O	R														14
	W	A	N	T	E	D										15

Example #14

Score	You: 195	Opponent: 198
Opponent's last play		GOA (B13, 19 points)
Your rack		AEIRSTU

My choice here was between playing SATIN (F2, 25 points) or passing the U. One slight negative of SATIN is that the opponent may be able to use the triple word square at 1H by hooking an I before SATIN, changing it to ISATIN. Twenty-five points is a much larger positive. On the other hand, passing the U leaves me with the SATIRE letter combination, well-known among SCRABBLE® players. SATIRE combines with eighteen of the twenty-six different letters in the alphabet to form seven-letter words. These eighteen letters account for approximately 75 percent of the tile pool. Given that there are two different bingo openings available (row 14 and the S hook at K10; the S hook cannot be blocked unless the opponent has an s), passing the u is probably worth the point sacrifice. If the opponent makes a downward play from K10 in an attempt to block both openings, there is a good probability of forming an eight-letter bingo through one of the letters in his word. In the game, I picked an i and played AIRIEST (K5) on my next turn.

There are several other six-letter combinations that combine with many tiles to form seven-letter bingos. Among them are AEINST (the most bingo-conducive: it combines successfully with twenty-three different tiles comprising 90 percent of the tile pool), AENRST, AEERST, EINRST, and AEINRT. Combinations like these will often make fishing worthwhile if the board is open for bingos. The same is almost never true for combinations of fewer than six letters.

I would also recommend fishing as a desperation measure. In one game at the 1980 Canadian Championship, I was losing by 86 points and there were about twelve tiles in the bag. My rack was not very promising (something like BGIMOVW), and both blanks and three of the four ss had already been played. I exchanged all seven tiles, eschewing a 22-point play in the process. Even though I had no good tiles to build upon, I had to exchange in order to raise above zero my probability of winning. I was extremely fortunate. I picked the remaining s and was able to play a bingo on my next turn. My opponent unsuccessfully challenged the word (PEARTEST), and I won the game by 6 points.

Limit your opponent's scoring opportunities. It is excellent strategy to deny your opponent access to premium squares and to openings for playing bingos. You should remember, however, that by limiting your opponent you may also be obstructing your own game. You should take care to block only those openings that your opponent is likely to utilize before you do. If you have a blank in your rack but no playable bingo, for example, you most probably will not want to make a play that blocks a spot for your bingo on a subsequent turn.

As with the other principles discussed so far, limiting your opponent's possibilities often involves a trade-off. That trade-off, as usual, is your own point count. It is important that you do not sacrifice too much of your own scoring clout in order to handcuff your opponent. Consider the following opening rack: DGIPUVY. PUDGY is the play, and it should be made at 8D even though placement at 8H yields two additional points. The two points are not worth the risk of placing a vowel adjacent to the double letter squares at 7I and 9I. Your opponent might be able to score well by making an overlapping play in which a P is placed at 9I, or an M or (Heaven forbid) an X is placed at 7I. PUDGY at 8H isn't tremendously dangerous, but the 2-point sacrifice by playing the word at 8D is excellent low-cost insurance. I would not give up more than 2 points in order to avoid placing a vowel next to a double letter square, however.

It is much more dangerous to place a vowel next to a triple letter square, particularly if such a play allows a subsequent J or X placed on the triple letter square to be scored both horizontally and vertically. Such a play will score more than 50 points. In Example #15, you have the bingo AVENGED in your rack:

Example #15

Score   You: 0   Opponent: 38
     Your rack   ADEEGNV

There are no playable eight-letter bingos, so you must choose between placing the bingo at 7H or 9H. The 7H placement is correct. If AVENGED is played at 9H and if your opponent has the X and a U, she will score 52 points on her next turn by making a XU at 9J. After the 7H placement, however, the opponent's X is considerably less dangerous to you. The likelihood is that your opponent will not have an X and a U in her rack, but why take chances?

You should also strive to avoid making plays in which high-point tiles are placed next to double or triple word squares in such a manner that a vowel placed on the premium square forms a two-letter word with the high-point tile. Consider Example #16:

Example #16

Score   You: 74   Opponent: 141
Opponent's last play   BOOK (A12, 37 points)
     Your rack   DEILRX☐

Your two best moves are XERIC (C3, 28 points) and EXILED

(L2, 28 points). XERIC is the better move, for EXILED may allow your opponent to make a high-scoring vertical play down column M if he has an I or a U to be placed at M3. With seven IS and all four US not yet played, the danger is quite real. EXILED also permits the opponent to make a simple horizontal play along row 3 using both the X and the double word square next to it. XERIC has its dangers as well, particularly if the opponent is able to make a play from D1 to D4 or D5. In most cases it will prove to be less dangerous than EXILED, however, since the X in XERIC counts for only eight points if it is used by the opponent.

Nonexpert players are often inordinately fearful of opening up a triple word square for the opponent. All triple word squares are not equally valuable, however.

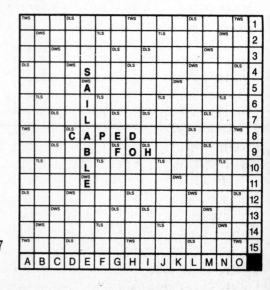

Example #17

Score   You: 90   Opponent: 55
Opponent's last play   FOH (9G, 29 points)
Your rack   EEGIHNV

You can give your opponent access to a triple word square in two ways, both of which are illustrated in Example #17. HIVE at D11 (25 points) allows your opponent to hook onto your word if he has a D or an S for placement at 15D. Your opponent doesn't need a hook tile if you play HIVE at D1 (32 points), however, as you have placed one of your tiles in a row containing the triple word squares.

You have a third option, and that is to play INVEIGH, 6E. This play is more defensive than the others (the opponent could use the triple word square at 1H by forming a six-letter word ending in E, but this is unlikely), but sacrifices 5 and 12 points relative to HIVE at D11 and D1, respectively.

My feeling is that INVEIGH and HIVE (D11) are about equally good, primarily because the point differential between them is offset by the chance to pick two more tiles after INVEIGH. When the score is taken into account, INVEIGH makes more sense: why jeopardize a lead for only 5 more points? However, HIVE (D1) is superior to both of the other plays, even though the likelihood that the opponent will make a play utilizing a triple word square is higher after this move than after the others. The reason for HIVE's superiority is that *on the average* the opponent will not be able to score 7 points more following this play than if HIVE (D11) had been played; nor will she be able to make up the 12-point difference on her turn after HIVE (D1) than had INVEIGH been played. I know this through much, much experience with situations of this sort.

The expert player does not play to avoid catastrophe; he plays the odds. In the situation above, he does not ruminate on disaster: e.g., "If I play HIVE at D1 my opponent might be able to crush me with WISHBONE, 1A." He makes the play that is most likely to result in winning the game. He knows that on a significant proportion of turns in situations like this, the opening he has created will not even be used. The opponent may not have good tiles or may have a better play elsewhere. The opponent may even feel obliged to block the opening if she cannot take advantage of it. Most of the time, however, the opening will be taken, usually for from 21 to 33 points. If the opponent has tiles good enough to score very well here, she will likely have been able to score almost equally well somewhere else on the board.

The player who adopts the strategy I am proposing must be prepared to accept an occasional drubbing. It's built into the system; taking a small risk many times over, one is bound to get burned eventually. Example #18 comes from a tournament game that I was very lucky to win:

Row	A	B	C	D	E	F	G	H	I	J	K	L	M	N	O
1	TWS			DLS				TWS				DLS			TWS
2		DWS				TLS				TLS				DWS	
3			DWS				W	O	P				DWS		
4	DLS	G	A	U	C	H	O					DWS			DLS
5					R		T	O	R	R	I	D			
6		TLS			U	TLS		i		TLS				TLS	
7			DLS		M		DLS		DLS				DLS		
8	TWS			DLS	B	I	L	K				DLS			TWS
9			DLS				DLS		DLS				DLS		
10		TLS				TLS				TLS				TLS	
11					DWS						DWS				
12	DLS			DWS				DLS				DWS			DLS
13			DWS				DLS		DLS				DWS		
14		DWS				TLS				TLS				DWS	
15	TWS			DLS				TWS				DLS			TWS

Example #18

Score	Me: 46	Opponent: 64
Opponent's last play		TORRID (5G, 20 points)
My rack		AADEFNT

My play was FATED (L1, 26 points), and it was fated to be followed by my opponent's triple-triple RAT□FIES (1H, 140 points). Nevertheless, this disaster was a rare exception to the rule.

I am not advocating that triple word squares be opened willy-nilly for additional points. On the contrary, one must particularly beware of creating triple word square openings that permit a high-point tile to be placed on the double letter score in the same row or column as the triple word square. These openings are doubly dangerous if the letter placed on the double letter square scores both vertically and horizontally. In Example #18, I would think hard before making a play such as AZIDE, 9H. If my opponent had an H, M, P, W, or Y, he would be likely to score over 40 points by making a simple four-letter word beginning at 8L.

I would also think hard about opening a triple word square on a board that is otherwise totally bereft of scoring opportunities. In this case, the discrepancy between what the opponent might have scored had the opening not been created and what the opponent would be likely to score from using the new opening may more than offset my additional points.

Sometimes your opponent's play will create an opening for you that you cannot use. In this situation, you have three options: (1) block the opening so that your opponent cannot take advantage of it; (2) ignore the opening and play elsewhere; and (3) create a second opening. The idea behind creating a second opening is that, after you have made your play and picked fresh tiles from the bag, there will be at least one opening on the board for you to take advantage of. The disadvantages of creating a second opening are that you may have to forgo a higher scoring play elsewhere on the board in order to create the opening, and that your opponent gets her choice of two openings rather than access only to the one she created by her last move. Furthermore, the two openings are rarely equal in value, and your opponent gets the first shot at the better one. The strategy sometimes even backfires; your opponent takes one of the two openings, and you cannot use the other. I generally shy away from creating a second opening unless the play is good for other reasons (e.g., it scores many points, balances the rack, etc.).

The decision whether to block an opening you cannot use, play elsewhere, or create a second opening is a complex one. It depends on how dangerous the existing opening is, how dangerous the opening you are thinking of creating would be, the game score, the number of points scored for your play, your rack leave, and the general configuration of the board. The game score is perhaps the most critical factor. If you have a lead of 60 or more points, blocking the existing opening will in most cases be correct. If the score is close or if you are behind, however, you usually cannot go terribly wrong by taking the play that nets you the most points.

To summarize, it is often good strategy to limit your opponent's scoring opportunities. Weigh the advantages of doing so versus possible self-inflicted punishment. When there is little or no cost to yourself, play defensively. You will often find yourself in the position of having to decide whether to make a safe play or a higher scoring, more dangerous one. Decisions of this sort must be based on a number of factors, including the game score, other openings available, and the tiles yet to be played. Try not to be too fearful about creating openings, however: the high-scoring aggressive play is the correct one more often than you might think.

Let the game score dictate your strategy. The importance of this maxim cannot be overemphasized. A move on the SCRABBLE® brand crossword game board that is ideal if you are 50 points behind your opponent may be disastrous if you hold a 50-point lead. Specifically:

If you are behind, try to create an open board with numerous scoring chances. The only way to catch up is to outscore your opponent. If the board is closed so that no bingos can be played and few high-scoring nonbingo opportunities are available, you will assuredly lose. If the board is replete with possibilities, however, you may get slaughtered —but you will at least have some hope of winning. The solution to Example #19 is a particularly brilliant demonstration of how to open the board so that it cannot be totally blocked by the opponent. It was found by Dr. Richard Silberg, a SCRABBLE® expert from Baltimore. The game is nearing its conclusion, and in order to have any chance of winning, you must play a bingo. The problem is that it is impossible to play a seven-letter bingo on this board, and the playable eight-letter bingos are very unlikely: they require that a G, O, or U be the fifth letter in the word, or that G is the fourth letter. Silberg's unusual solution was OTTO,

Example #19

	A	B	C	D	E	F	G	H	I	J	K	L	M	N	O
1														D	
2										P	U	N	N	Y	
3								O						A	
4			G					L						D	
5			O					I	A						
6			U					N	O						
7			T					Y							
8			I			U	N	H	I	P			P	A	X
9		B	E	F	I	T		O				E	E	N	U
10			S					W				E		S	
11			T									R		E	
12												I		R	
13						Z	A	G			B	E	D	I	M
14								L	I	A	I	S	O	N	
15			V	A	L	V	A	T	E			W	E	D	

Score   You: 283   Opponent: 348

Opponent's last play   GOUTIES🆃 (E4, 82 points)

Your rack   AGLOOTT

7C. The beauty of this move is that it sets up two hook locations: B7 for the L on the rack or the remaining M if it is picked, and G7 for the last s if it is picked. OTTO also makes it difficult for the opponent to play the Q away should he pick it. (It makes little difference if you can play the Q if you pick it, as you would lose whether you could play it away or not.)

If you are ahead, try to close down the board and limit scoring opportunities. This will help prevent you from snatching defeat from the claws of victory. My last moves from the following tournament game (Example #20) are a good illustration. My opponent was Mike Wise, an expert player from Toronto.

Example #20

	A	B	C	D	E	F	G	H	I	J	K	L	M	N	O	
1								J				C	A	P		1
2								D	O	M		H	I	E		2
3								Y		O	H	O				3
4								E		N	O	W	T			4
5								T	O	M		U				5
6							Q		E		A		I	T		6
7							U				A		G	U		7
8							T	A	L	K	I	E		I		8
9							L				O					9
10						V	E	E			D					10
11						I			V	Y	I	N	G			11
12						C					D			D		12
13						E				N	E	A		I		13
14										S	W	A	I	N		14
15														E		15

Score — Me: 203   Mike: 168
Mike's last play — VICE (F10, 9 points)

It is important to realize that at this stage of the game the bingo-making tiles were still in the bag: no blanks and only one s had been played. However, the board was sufficiently closed so that I felt confident of my ability to eke out a victory through defensive play. Take a pencil and fill in the remaining plays of the game.

My play following VICE was FEZ (13E, 25 points). This prevented bingos through rows 12, 13, and 14. Mike then made REC, 12D. I responded with RIN (11E), which prevented Mike from playing a possible bingo ending in the R at 12D.

Attention then shifted to the upper left quadrant of the board. Mike's play was BEY, 3G. I was relieved to see this move, as I was concerned that Mike might have been able to play a bingo from 3A or 4A. Nevertheless, the move made bingos possible at 4A and F1 (if he had an o for placement at 3F). I blocked both with OLLA, F3. Both HS had previously been played, so I didn't have to worry about Mike playing one at 2F, forming the word HOLLA.

After the game was over, Mike informed me that he would have played a bingo on his next turn had I not prevented him. Instead, he had to settle for ROLE, 4D. My FUBS (7C) settled the issue by preventing him from playing a bingo through the R at D4 or by hooking a [P] in front of ROLE at C4. At this point only one tile was left in the bag. I won the game by a score of 318 to 254. It was my lowest score of the tournament, but one of my better efforts.

Example #21 — board position:

```
    A  B  C  D  E  F  G  H  I  J  K  L  M  N  O
 1  .  .  .  .  .  .  .  .  .  .  .  .  .  .  .
 2  .  .  .  .  .  .  .  .  .  .  .  .  .  .  .
 3  .  .  .  .  C  .  .  .  .  .  .  P* .  .  .
 4  .  .  .  H  A  .  .  .  E  Q  U  I  P  .  .
 5  .  .  .  E  R  .  .  .  .  .  .  T  .  .  .
 6  .  K  .  W  O  .  .  .  .  .  .  E  .  .  .
 7  .  A  T  .  L  .  V  .  .  .  .  O  .  .  .
 8  E  B  O  N  I  Z  I  N  G  .  .  U  .  .  .
 9  .  G  .  .  V  .  .  .  A  S  .  S  .  .  .
10  .  .  P  A  W  E  D  .  X  .  .  .  .  .  .
11  .  .  A  B  O  .  A  J  E  E  .  E  .  .  .
12  .  .  Y  O  N  .  .  .  D  .  .  .  .  .  .
13  .  .  .  .  T  .  .  .  .  .  .  .  .  .  .
14  .  .  B* R  U  S  H  I  E  R  .  R  .  .  .
15  F  R  O  .  .  .  I  T  .  .  .  .  .  .  .
```
(* = boxed tile)

Score	You: 281	Opponent: 267
Opponent's last play		EQUIP (4I, 32 points)
Your rack		CIINOSY

Consonants from which two-letter words cannot be made (C, Q, V, Z) and from which two-letter words can be made with one vowel only (G, J, K) can be very useful for closing down the board. In Example #21, the correct strategy is to block the M and N columns (the only locations for bingos on this board) without creating any new openings. Very effective in accomplishing this is SIC (N4, 28 points). SIC is wonderful defensively, as nothing can be hooked onto its C. A play like COSY (N2, 35 points) scores more, but why give your opponent counterplay? With a 42-point lead on this board and the threat of YOD (12H, 31 points) on your next turn, the win is virtually assured.

Don't get too greedy if you are ahead late in the game. The object is to win; point spread is a secondary consideration. Sometimes an "obvious" offensive move can jeopardize one's winning chances:

Example #22

	A	B	C	D	E	F	G	H	I	J	K	L	M	N	O	
							L						D		Z	1
							H	E					E	R	E	2
				B	O	T							W	A	E	3
				Y	A	M	S							I		4
				O	N	E					P	R	A	N	K	5
				U	N									W		6
	Q				E			T	H	U	D		E	L		7
	U				D	O		J	O			V		A	I	8
	E						I	N	T	E	R	I	O	R	S	9
	E	F				V						C				10
	N	A		D	O	G	E					A				11
		C	R	O	P							R				12
	W	E														13
	I	T														14
	G															15

Score   You: 276   Opponent: 256
Opponent's last play   LETS (G1, 25 points)
Your rack   AIBFSTX

In Example #22, you *should not* play AX at either 6I or 10I. These plays score over 50 points each, but with an S and a blank unaccounted for, you must block your opponent's potential bingo openings. Use the S in your rack defensively to safeguard your victory: play FIST (13J, 25 points). This play almost certainly prevents a bingo from being played along row 12 through the R in VICAR, and it closes *all* of row 13 so that bingos originating at 13D or 13E, as well as those using the S hook at 13L, are unplayable. Your future strategy should be clear: if your opponent opens a bingo alley on his next turn, try to shut it down (hopefully without parting with the AX combination). If he plays elsewhere, make your big X play. If he blocks or uses the triple letter squares at both 6J and 10J (e.g., by making a play such as MULE, J6), play AX at H1. In a situation like this one, timing is crucial. Play defensively first, score well afterwards.

The previous two examples demonstrated how the board can be closed down to preserve a lead. Would that it were always so easy! It often happens that your opponent has more than one opening on the board where he can play a bingo or otherwise score well in order to overtake you. Example #23 is typical:

	A	B	C	D	E	F	G	H	I	J	K	L	M	N	O	
1				Q								F				1
2				U	Z						B	I				2
3				I	A			P	A	R	T	Y				3
4			U	N	A	G	I	L	E		A	S				4
5				O							C					5
6				A					W	H	E	W				6
7								J	E	E	R					7
8				H			M	O	O	T	S					8
9			P	R	O	V	I	D	E							9
10			A	T												10
11			R	E												11
12			K	L	I						V	O	T	E		12
13			A	I	N							B	O	X		13
14				E	F				M	A	T	E	D			14
15			C	O	R	O	N	A	R	Y						15

Example #23

Score	You: 368	Opponent: 344
Opponent's last play		VOTE (12L, 35 points)
Your rack		EGGLNNS

Only eight tiles remain in the bag, and a blank and an s are as yet unaccounted for. You should play defensively to maintain your lead, but how?

The only way to lose this game is to allow your opponent to bingo. The big tiles have all been played, so you needn't worry much about the nonbingo openings available such as 1L-O and row 5. You in fact might be able to take advantage of these openings on subsequent turns to maintain your lead (e.g., FENS, 1L; NOES, 5C).

The available bingo locations on this board are N4-10 (yes, WHEW is a noun and takes an S), along row 10 (beginning at 10G, 10H, or 10I), and 6A-H. The last opening is probably the least dangerous, due to its limited flexibility: an eight-letter bingo is required, and its fourth letter must be an A. Attention should therefore be focussed on the other openings first.

You are unable to use the S hooks at 10I and N6 to block *both* row 10 and column N. There is another way, however: GLOBE, M10! It scores only 8 points, but a 32-point lead with a decent rack leave and only six tiles left in the bag should make you feel pretty comfortable. Unless your opponent opens up a new bingo alley next turn, you should block the 6A opening on your next play, possibly with NOES. The idea is that if you cannot block your opponent completely, at least block him partially so that he has only one shot at hurting you. Your opponent must bingo next turn, open a new bingo alley (not so easy on this board), or lose.

In situations in which you have a lead and the board is completely wide open, you should take the offensive. Play to maintain your lead by scoring a lot of points rather than by trying to limit your opponent. Defending an open board against a good player is an almost hopeless task.

Know your opponent, and use this knowledge to adapt your playing style to maximize the probability of winning. If your opponent's word knowledge is much greater than yours, try to avoid creating an open board. An open board will contain many high-scoring opportunities, and in such a circumstance a player stronger than you is very likely to outplay you. Try instead to close the board down. This can be accomplished by playing words that don't take hook letters before or after them, by using the "difficult" consonants to close off whole sections of the board to future play (e.g., the Vs at 10F and 11I in Example #20; the C at N6 in Example #21 after SIC is played), and by making overlapping plays so that the tiles in your play do not extend out into open space.

A closed board makes the two of you "more equal." On an open board, for example, it might be possible to create eight-letter bingos through six or seven available letters. No eight-letter bingos might be playable on a tightly closed board. If your opponent knows more of these bingos than you do and/or is better at anagramming long words than you are, you will be more competitive with her if *neither* of you can put such words on the board. I occasionally lose games to players who are much weaker than I. This invariably occurs over a closed board, and causes me great frustration.

Such losses can be caused partly by luck, but are mainly attributable to an inability in these games to create scoring chances. The stronger player must strive to open the board to lessen the risk of being upset. He should create openings for hooks (without being too reckless about it), especially if the hook letter changes the existing word into one that the opponent is unlikely to know and a hook tile is retained in the leave. He should play long words, as these create multiple openings that are difficult to block. He should also try to play to the left and to the upper portions of the board, since these sectors can be more easily blocked off from play by an opponent than can the right and lower portions of the board. By opening them up early, he will make it more difficult for his opponent to strangle play.

It may of course become necessary to reevaluate the adoption of a particular playing style as a game progresses. A player who falls behind early in the game to a stronger player will be insuring defeat by continuing to try to close up the board. Conversely, a player who has achieved a substantial lead over a weaker player should not continue to open the board, but should close it down to protect that lead.

What if your opponent is of approximately the same strength as you are? It is my experience that evenly matched players can have radically different styles. Some—including me—like a wide-open, speculative, "swashbuckling" game. Others consider themselves to be at the mercy of the gods in such situations and prefer a somewhat tighter board over which they can exercise some semblance of control. If you are versatile enough to feel comfortable on either an open or closed board, you might try steering the game away from the style that your opponent most likes. If you have a strong stylistic preference, however, play in accordance with it. When your opponent's style is similar to your own, do not alter your approach, because you will only irritate both your opponent and yourself. Unless your partner has a very low tolerance for frustration, you will be no more successful than if you followed your own stylistic inclinations. Your enjoyment of the game will in all likelihood diminish, whatever your opponent's misery threshold.

Try to infer your opponent's rack leave from the plays she makes. Try also to deduce from her plays what tiles she is likely not to have in her leave. There are two main sources of uncertainty in this crossword game. The first is the selection of tiles. The second is the contents of your opponent's rack. It goes without saying that if you could reduce these uncertainties you would win more games.

The technical term for reducing uncertainty concerning the selection of tiles is cheating. I will have more to say about this topic in chapter 7. Suffice it to say now that there is no ethical way to control one's tile selection. The technical term for deducing your opponent's rack is prescience (or X-ray vision), which in most of us is oddly lacking. Nevertheless, it is possible to increase one's prescience through a careful examination of a player's preceding move or moves. Consider Example #24:

Example #24

Score   You: 0   Opponent: 14

Your rack   ADEOPUZ

There are three main possibilities here: OOZED (F8, 35 points), ZOO (F6, 32 points), and OUZO (F8, 33 points). In terms of rack leave, OUZO is clearly best. Its main drawback is the placement of an O at 11F, right next to a double word square. If the opponent has the J, he could easily score 38 points or more on his next turn by making a vertical play from E11. (The 20+ points that would result from playing an H or a W at E11 are not significant enough to deter you from playing OUZO.) The opponent probably does not have the J, however, and this deduction is based on his first play. Had the J been in his opening rack, he would have at least played JOWL instead of WOOL. The four replacement tiles after WOOL come from a bag containing eighty-six tiles. Since there is only one J in the tile distribution, the probability of his picking the J is less than 5 percent. OUZO is thus a very safe bet.

It might be argued that the S hook at 12F is also quite dangerous. A play made using it and the double word square at 12D is only likely to score in the high 20s or low 30s, however. Furthermore, the probability is that the opponent does not have an s. If he had one in his opening rack, he should have played WOOLS (8D) for the extra 10 points. Given that there are four ss in the tile distribution, he has only about an 18 percent chance of picking at least one of them with his four replacement tiles.

It is at times possible to ascertain what is, as well as what is not, on your opponent's rack. If your opponent goes first and passes one tile on his opening play, for example, you can be pretty sure that he has bingo-conducive tiles. If he makes an -s hook setup play similar to my tenth move against Mike Spencer in Annotated Game #1 (see page 181), and three ss and both blanks have already been played, you can be positive that he has the remaining s. If he makes a play such as THUD shown in Example #22 (page 94—7H; this was the play made immediately before LETS, the opponent's last play), it is very probable that he has the x. THUD sets up the x; better, if he didn't have the x, would be THUD at C5 for an additional four points. You also learn from this play that he did not have an A or an O (or he would have made the 52-point play at 10I). Knowledge of part of your opponent's rack is often just plain scary rather than useful. Sometimes, however, this information is an important consideration in determining your next play. This discussion leads directly into the presentation of the last principle presented in this chapter, namely:

Keep a record of the tiles that have been played. It is allowable to keep a running written record of the tiles as they have been played during the course of a game. This procedure is called tile tracking. A few years ago it was done by only a few players, but it is now universally practiced by most tournament players.

The rationale behind tile tracking is not hard to surmise. It enables you to know *exactly* what tiles your opponent has at the end of the game. In a close game, this information could well be the difference between winning and losing. Tracking can help you earlier in the game as well. If you know, for example, that six of twenty tiles remaining in the bag or on your opponent's rack are IS, you might (correctly) think twice before making a play that expends five of your tiles but not the I already on your rack.

Some people object to the whole idea of tile tracking. They feel that players should not have access to a written record of the tiles that have been played; instead they should develop the ability to track tiles in their heads. Tracking is illegal in most card games, so why should it be allowed in this board game?

My feeling is that tile tracking enhances play and should continue to be allowed. Moreover, it is unfair to compare the ability to keep a hundred SCRABBLE® tiles in your head with the ability to remember only about half as many cards. The fact is that in a timed game it is virtually impossible for almost any mortal to track tiles accurately without recording them. Written tracking improves the quality of play and allows for the calculation of potentially brilliant moves in the endgame that would not otherwise be possible.

Tile tracking has its disadvantages. It takes time away from the consideration of plays, and it may distract one from a careful analysis of the board position. It takes much practice to track an entire game accurately. Common mistakes made by players who track tiles are forgetting to track one or more plays, recording the same tile twice (most typically by recording the entire word played, not just the letters from the last turn contributing to it), and erroneously recording the letter that a blank represents rather than the blank.

It took me one full year of about three hundred games played with tile tracking before I felt that my tracking ability was reliable under tournament conditions. I experimented with a number of different systems before settling on the one I am about to describe.

Tiles can be tracked in two basic ways. In the first, the player writes down on a blank portion of the score sheet the one hundred tile letters or a symbolic representation of them, just after the game has begun. In the past, some players brought preprinted lists of the letters with them to the playing table in order to save the time needed to write them down during the game. This is now illegal. It is in fact illegal to bring anything written to the playing table other than an unmarked score sheet. Many players write out each letter individually and then cross them off as they are played. Others simply write the letter and the number of tiles of the letter in the distribution after it. When a certain letter is played, the number next to that letter in the player's tracking scheme is crossed off and replaced by the next lower number. The letters need not be listed alphabetically. Some players group their letters according to categories such as vowels, high-point letters, and so forth.

The alternative method of tracking consists of recording the letters as they are played. This is the method I use, and it involves numerical representation. When the first tile of a given letter is played, I write it down. As subsequent tiles of the letter appear, I write numbers next to the letter that indicate how many tiles of the letter have come out to that point in the game. I continue this process for all of the letters throughout the game. After all the tiles of a letter have been played, I circle the letter so that I can easily recognize that its tiles have been depleted. Experienced players will have memorized the tile distribution of a set, but it's not necessary to do that; it's printed on every board.

My tracking scheme is organized alphabetically, with the As written in at the top of the left margin of my score sheet and the z and blanks at the bottom. I used to track on the reverse side of the score sheet, but found this distracting. It is a nuisance constantly to turn the sheet over and back again.

When there are fewer than seven tiles in the bag, I add the tiles on my rack to my tracking list. I then go through the list and write all of the tiles that are still unaccounted for in one place, down at the bottom of the score sheet. It is sometimes necessary to shield this portion of the sheet from my opponent, since my rack can be deduced from it. Few of my opponents try to examine my score sheet, however, which is as it should be.

I find that I am more accurate if I write the letters down as they are played, rather than if I write them out at the beginning of the game and then cross them off as the game progresses. Writing the letters out is perhaps a psychologically more active process than crossing them off, though this may not be true for other players. It definitely is a more efficient process, as time need not be spent on writing the tile distribution out at the beginning of the game.

If you track tiles, you will occasionally encounter an opponent who insists that you cease and desist from this practice. Explain to him the rationales behind tile tracking and especially how tracking not only helps a player win but also enriches the game. If he doesn't buy your arguments, continue to track tiles anyway. If this infuriates him, calmly explain that you are not tracking tiles. You are instead using your free time between moves to imitate one of the million proverbial monkeys placed in front of a million typewriters, in the hope that the letters you are scribbling in the margin of your scoresheet will somehow form the basis for the next great American novel.

6

Strategy in
Special Situations

The material in the preceding chapter was devoted to a presentation of the basic strategic principles in SCRABBLE® brand crossword game. This chapter deals with more specialized and problematic topics: challenging and bluffing, setup plays, Q strategy, exchanging tiles, and endgame finesses. Board situations that are relevant to these topics recur in play with a considerable degree of regularity, and how players deal with such situations is often of critical importance in determining the game's outcome.

Challenging and Bluffing

Common sense dictates that two basic tenets be followed with respect to challenging and bluffing: (1) challenge your opponent's play when her word is a phony, and (2) never play a phony yourself. These tenets only apply to the idealized case in which both players know the *OSPD* stone cold, however, and even then strict adherence to them may not always be advisable. For most of us, a good deal more uncertainty is involved. You may not know if the word you are thinking of challenging is allowable, and you may be unsure of whether a word you are thinking of playing is allowable and/or whether your opponent will challenge it. Here are some guidelines to follow in these circumstances:

Bluff only if the payoff from bluffing is considerably greater than the payoff from not bluffing. The loss of a turn is a severe penalty: not only does your opponent get to play twice in a row, he also gets to see some or all of your tiles. Don't risk the loss of a turn unless it's well worth it.

On the other hand, challenge a word you are fairly certain is a phony, even if it does not score particularly well. Suppose, for example, that your opponent has played VOL on a double word score for 12 points. You are 98 percent certain that VOL is no good, but you let VOL stay because your opponent scores so little for it. You should definitely challenge in situations like this one. First, 12 points may not seem like much, but it is often the difference between winning and losing. Second, your opponent may be developing her rack. She may have played VOL for the express purpose of getting rid of the v. Maybe she has another v on her rack, or maybe she is building toward a bingo by disposing of her v and keeping bingo-conducive tiles. If the best she can do on this play is 12 points, then the best she is likely to do on her next turn after losing the challenge is about the same. Finally, even if VOL doesn't do anything particularly wonderful for her rack, it should be challenged just to keep your opponent from picking potentially valuable replacement tiles from the bag.

If you are unsure whether a word you are thinking of playing is acceptable, but playing that word is the only way to win, make the play. One of my opponents in the 1980 Canadian Championship refrained from playing QUINOL on his next to last play because he wasn't sure if it was good, and because it placed the Q in a dangerous position (on A4) with one U still unaccounted for. QUINOL would have been worth 60+ points, and though I had a U, I would not have been able to take advantage of the Q to score well. QUINOL probably would have won the game (and the tournament) for my opponent, and any other play could not have done that. Always give yourself a shot at winning.

On the other hand, definitely challenge a word that you are even the slightest bit unsure of, if allowing that word

to stand means certain defeat. There are few sadder sights than a losing player who discovers only after the game that her opponent's 120-point play was a phony. The more devastating your opponent's dubious play, the more likely you should be to challenge it.

Consider playing a lucrative phony if you are way behind in the game. Your opponent may not want to risk dissipating a lead by challenging your word incorrectly. He may figure that the only way to lose the game would be to make an incorrect challenge, allowing you a free turn to catch up. Example #25 comes from a game I played against Bob Black in the 1983 Canadian Championship:

Example #25

	A	B	C	D	E	F	G	H	I	J	K	L	M	N	O
1															
2															
3															
4															
5															
6	Z														
7	E				D										
8	R	A	C	O	O	N	S								
9	S	O	R		F										
10	P		E		F	I	L	L	I	P	P				
11	A		E	H							Y				
12	Y		K	A							I				
13	I			L							N				
14	N			I											
15	G			D	R	U	M								

Score	Me: 102	Bob: 230
Bob's last play	PYIN (K10, 18 points)	
My rack	BBEISTU	

As you can see from the score, I was being crushed. I had no playable bingos that were *OSPD*-acceptable, so I played a phony: TUBBIES (L4, 86 points). I knew that TUBBIES was phony when I played it, but felt confident that Bob wouldn't challenge it. For one thing, the word was reasonably plausible (FATSO is listed as a noun in the *OSPD*), but the main reason Bob was unlikely to challenge was that if he lost the challenge, I would have the opportunity to make the game score close after my following play. By refraining from challenging, Bob retained a substantial 58-point lead and the move. His chances of winning were still excellent. Given that he did not know if TUBBIES was acceptable, he was correct not to challenge me. As it turned out, I won the game. I almost certainly would have lost it had I not played TUBBIES.

	A	B	C	D	E	F	G	H	I	J	K	L	M	N	O
1								A							W
2					Q			L					E		E
3					A			T					E		E
4					I			I			A	V	O	I	D
5			A	U	D	I	T	O	R	S					E
6		G	R	I	T	S		U		O				I	D
7					D			T						N	
8			B	L	A	Z	E	R	S					J	O
9				A				E					M	U	N
10				E				P					A	R	E
11				V				L					W	E	
12		O	H	O		A	B	Y	E				S		
13		N	U			M	E	R							
14	O	X	N			A	E	N							
15	P	I	C	K	Y			F							

Example #26

Score	Me: 354	Opponent: 394
Opponent's rack		CEEIIIR

On the other hand, when losing the challenge is the only way for you to lose the game, refrain from challenging a word unless you are absolutely positive that it is no good. Similarly, if the only way you can lose the game is if your opponent successfully challenges your word, don't play a word of which you are at all unsure. Due to the effects of tiredness and tension, it often happens that players self-destruct near the end of a tournament game. Among the most tried and true methods of self-destruction are inappropriate bluffs and challenges. The situation shown in Example #26 comes from a 1984 tournament game. I had resigned myself to a loss. There were only three tiles in the bag, and I had no bingo prospects. (My rack consisted of FHLORTT.) All my opponent had to do to win was make some sort of reasonable play preventing me from using the H hook at O12 in combination with the triple word square at O15. NIECE (14J), for example, would have pretty much wrapped up the game. Instead, she tried ICER, O12. I challenged successfully, then played HOLT in the same spot for 42 points, which she unsuccessfully challenged.

If you must play phonies, play believable phonies. A believable phony is one that can be confused with a real word. It could be a false spelling, an unacceptable "variant," a made-up compound word (e.g., HOTLINE, HIGHRISE, DOGTAG), or an incorrect conjugation, pluralization, or comparative form. Don't try words that appear ridiculous. There are some ridiculous looking words in the dictionary, but they are so unique that they are easily remembered by most SCRABBLE® players. If you play a word like MOXBIB you will lose a turn for sure.

Stephen Fisher, an expert player from Montreal, is a master of the plausible phony. In one game against me, he got away with SUBANAL. This phony is probably less likely to be challenged by an expert than by a weaker player! The expert may confuse it with SUBALAR, SUBORAL, POSTANAL, and PREANAL, all of which are acceptable. The amateur player won't know these words, and might challenge SUBANAL simply because it looks weird. I got even with Stephen later in the game when I played BOOGY and he didn't challenge it. BOOGIE, BOUGIE, and BOOGYMAN are all in the *OSPD,* but not BOOGY.

Plausible phonies may also be "hybrids" of existing words. BILINEAL, for example, sounds correct probably because it is so close to BIENNIAL and BILINEAR. I have played the phony IXTER twice and gotten away with it both times. Reason: it sounds like IXTLE and OXTER. Phony hybrids are seldom challenged because they are easily confused with acceptable words.

Another category of plausible phony is the word that "should" be in the *OSPD*, but isn't. In this category are words such as CURSOR, PASCAL, BRALESS (play BARLESS instead), and SLAMMER. Omissions of words such as these will, one hopes, be rectified in the next revision of the *OSPD*.

Take the playing strength of your opponent into consideration when deciding whether to challenge or to bluff. It is one thing to challenge an implausible word played by an amateur, and another to challenge such a word when played by an expert. Experts like to probe their opponent's vocabularies by playing unusual words early in the game. If they draw unsuccessful challenges, they will continue to play unusual words until the opponent stops challenging. *Then* they might try a phony or two.

Don't try to bluff an expert unless you enjoy this game as a spectator sport. As obvious as this advice may appear, it is much more common to lose a turn by attempting to play a phony against a stronger player than it is to lose a turn by incorrectly challenging a stronger player. An expert can recognize a bogus word as easily as she can play an unusual one.

Don't challenge a phony word without examining how placement of the word on the board might affect the game. Sometimes it is to your advantage to leave your opponent's phony on the board. The word may provide an opening for your bingo where previously there had been none. It may, on the other hand, close down the board. If you have a substantial lead in this case, your opponent's unchallenged phony may guarantee your victory!

You may also want to set a trap for the opponent. If the phony word looks like a noun, for example, and you have reason to suspect that your opponent has retained an s or a blank on his rack, you may wish to refrain from challenging until and if your opponent pluralizes his phony. Or you may wish to pluralize his phony yourself—but do this only if you have a strong sense that your opponent is convinced that his play is good. It's risky to do this, especially as SCRABBLE® players are good actors. I once played HENBITE in a club game. My opponent did not challenge this ridiculous word, perhaps because he confused it with HENBIT (which is in the *OSPD*) or perhaps because of my reputation for playing obscure but acceptable words. He tried a bingo on his next turn, in the process of which he hooked an -S onto HENBITE. He was not amused when I challenged HENBITES.

You should also be aware that if an expert plays an obviously phony word, she may actually want you to challenge her. This ploy usually occurs at the beginning of the game. Let's say, for example, that your opponent goes first and has AEIORST on her rack. She will probably pass the O, retaining the famous SATIRE leave discussed in the previous chapter. The weaknesses of doing this are that it scores no points, cedes the double word score to you, and puts you on notice that your opponent is bingo hunting. But your opponent might try, alternatively, a "creative phony" such as AORTI or RATOI. Don't be fooled into thinking that she has accidentally used an incorrect plural form of AORTA or has misspelled RATIO. She probably wants you to challenge this play. From her point of view, if you don't challenge, she gets 12 points and a very nice ES leave. If you do challenge, she may be able to play an eight-letter bingo through one of the tiles in your first play. You most definitely should challenge her play, but you should also consider exchanging tiles or playing defensively on your opening move.

A rarely used but potentially helpful resource is the "fake challenge." This refers to the purposeful challenge of a word which the challenger knows is acceptable. If you hold bingo-conducive tiles and your opponent plays an unusual word but one that you know is allowable, you might consider challenging in the hope that your opponent's next play will open the board for your bingo. The challenge disguises your intentions. If you instead simply passed, your opponent would realize that you have good tiles. He could then either play defensively, exchange tiles to improve his rack, or pass if he was leading in the game. (If he was behind, you could pass again after his pass, forcing him to play in order to avoid losing by the consecutive pass rule.)

The purposeful phony and the fake challenge can both be used to advantage in the endgame as well. Imagine, for example, that there are few tiles left in the bag, the Q has not been played, the board position and remaining unseen tiles are such that whoever draws the Q will be unable to play it away, and that you are losing by 10 or so points. You would like to pass to avoid picking the Q, but if you do so your opponent would likely follow suit. Your opponent plays an obscure word that you know is acceptable, and you challenge him in the hope that he will make another play afterwards rather than pass. As a consequence of his second play, he will draw at least one more tile from the bag than he would have had you not challenged him. You have thus increased his chances of picking the Q by making an "incorrect" challenge. If the same situation exists but it is your turn to play, you might play a purposeful phony in the hope that your opponent will challenge you, make a play, and draw the Q as a result.

Don't bluff a phony bingo with seven or fewer tiles in the bag, unless your play is absolutely essential for you to have any chance of winning the game. An unsuccessful bingo bluff near the end of the game can be very damaging. In addition to losing your turn, your opponent will be able to deduce the exact contents of the tiles in the bag. She could then determine whether she should play away many or few tiles, more vowels than consonants or the reverse, and what specific tiles should be played away in order to avoid tile duplication.

Setups

A setup is a play that changes the board position so that the player making the setup will be able to use the tiles remaining on the rack to greater advantage than otherwise would have been possible. In order for a setup to be effective, the probability that the opponent will be able to use or block the opening created by it must be small. Also, the player must avoid sacrificing too much in order to make the setup: the total number of points scored for the setup and its culmination must be greater than what the player would be likely to garner over the same two turns had a setup not been prepared.

Example #27

Score	You: 222	Opponent: 185
Opponent's last play		VUG (7M, 7 points)
Rack		AHIJNSX

In Example #27, the opponent's last play indicates that he is fishing for a bingo to get back in the game: he is creating a new opening on the board for a bingo so that you cannot block both it and the openings along rows 14 and 15. In addition, he is probably dispensing with his two least bingo-conducive tiles. Why else would he make a play creating such an opening that scores only 7 points?

Since you cannot block both of his openings, you go about the business of scoring as many points as possible while taking the more dangerous opening at O8. HANGS (O4, 39 points) is the highest scoring play you can find, but much finer is JIGS (O5, 36 points). It sacrifices three points and uses one less tile than HANGS, but prepares a 50-point X play at N6 (XI/XU) next turn. This setup can be blocked, but not very easily. Also, it doesn't *look* like a setup. Your opponent may think that you are simply making the best play you can find, perhaps the only one available to you that uses the J and the triple word square. As a result, he might not feel the necessity to block the opening even if he could.

Setups aren't made solely for the purpose of scoring as many points as possible. In the discussion of endgame finesses, we shall see that setups may help you get rid of undesirable tiles or play out before the opponent does.

Q Strategy

The Q is the most reviled letter in the alphabet for the players of this game. With the exception of only five words and their plurals (FAQIR, QAID, QINDAR, QINTAR, and QOPH), it cannot be used without an accompanying U. This makes it so unwieldy that a common problem for the player with the U-less and blank-less Q is whether to exchange it or not. Here are some guidelines that will help you make this decision:

The greater the number of Us already played, the more readily you should consider exchanging the Q. This assumes that the Us played are inaccessible for your Q. The rationale for this guideline is obvious: the fewer Us in the bag, the lower the probability that you will pick one. Consider the situation critical if two or more Us are showing on the board.

The greater the number of points by which you are losing, the more readily should you consider exchanging the

Q. The U-less Q does more than prevent you from playing bingos. It lessens the probability of making a high-scoring nonbingo play, since you have only six tiles to work with rather than the full seven. If you have a lead or if the game is close, holding on to the Q may not be so critical. If you are falling behind, however, you cannot afford the Q. You must exchange it in order to have a realistic hope of catching up.

The tighter the board is, the more readily you should exchange the Q. If the board is completely closed down, it might be wise to exchange the Q even when you have a U accompanying it. It makes no sense to keep the Q if there is no place to play it.

The fewer the number of tiles from your rack that a play you are considering making dispenses with, the greater should be your readiness instead to exchange the Q. If you only get to pick a few replacement tiles, you will not have much chance of pulling a U. Try to play away at least four tiles in lieu of exchanging the Q.

The fewer the number of points a play that you are thinking of making garners, the more willing should you be to exchange the Q. I generally exchange the Q if I cannot score at least 12 points. If you are on the verge of exchanging because your other six tiles are not particularly promising for high scoring turns anyway, then holding the Q should tip the scales in favor of exchanging. Don't pass up too many points, however. It is rarely worth exchanging the Q if you can score 15 or more points and at the same time get rid of four or more tiles.

If the game is nearing its end, exchanging the Q should be a top priority. Don't risk the chance that your opponent will play away enough tiles so that fewer than seven will remain in the bag, for then you will no longer have the option of exchanging the Q.

These guidelines are meant to be broken occasionally. It

is, in fact, rare that at least one of them is not violated by either the best available play or by exchanging. If you are able to score a great number of points without using the Q, for example, you would probably be wise to ignore any of the first four guidelines. If such a play violates *all* of these guidelines, however, it had better be a blockbuster!

Sometimes there are three or four seemingly viable solutions to U-less Q situations, as is the case in Example #28:

Example #28

Score   You: 0   Opponent: 20

Rack   AEIIOPQ

The best four of several possible options are: exchange tiles (best is either exchanging all seven or exchanging AIIOQ), EPINAOI (H5, 9 points), PATIO (F6, 15 points), and POI (7G, 18 points). Exchanging gets rid of the Q, but at a cost, versus playing POI, of 18 points. EPINAOI only scores 9 points. Six tiles are played away, however, so there is a considerable probability of picking a U or other good tiles after playing it. If another vowel was on the rack instead of the Q, EPINAOI would be preferable to exchanging, since the 9 points far outweigh the value of picking one additional tile. With the Q on the rack, however, it is not clear whether the points are sufficient compensation for keeping the Q. Both PATIO and POI score decently. However, fewer tiles are played away after these moves than after exchanging or EPINAOI.

What's the best move? I'm not at all sure, and the panel of expert contributors to *Letters for Expert Game Players* (see Appendix A) wasn't sure either: seven passed away the Q, four voted for EPINAOI, eight played POI (though PIA and PIE were advocated by one panelist each). I alone chose PATIO.

Example #29 also originally appeared in *Letters for Expert Game Players*. The choice here is between two plays:

A	B	C	D	E	F	G	H	I	J	K	L	M	N	O	
	V				F										1
	G	A	R	O	T	T	E		K						2
		R			O	P	E								3
L		I			D	O	R								4
R	A	X	I	N	G		I	N							5
	Z						L								6
A	Y						U								7
W			T	O	Y	O	S								8
N	I	M	B	I											9
				P	U	R	L								10
M	A	C	H	S											11
A															12
J	U	B	E												13
O															14
R															15

Example #29

Score   You: 193   Opponent: 193
Opponent's last play   JUBE (13A, 26 points)
Rack   EINOQST

exchanging the Q only and retaining a very bingo-conducive EINOST, or the very lovely find, OILSTONE (HB, 27 points). The virtues and drawbacks of these plays are summarized below:

Oilstone

Advantages

1. It scores 27 more points than does exchanging the Q.
2. With both blanks unseen, selection of six tiles from the bag versus exchanging only one tile is a considerable advantage. Chances are good for obtaining at least one blank or the remaining U.

Disadvantages

1. There is probably a 40 to 50 percent chance that the Q will be unplayable next turn.
2. OILSTONE opens up the board for eight-letter bingos using five different letters. With both blanks yet unseen at this stage of the game, the opponent might well have one of them. As a result, he may be able to take advantage of the openings created by OILSTONE in order to play a bingo. On the other hand, this is probably only a small disadvantage, as the board is already quite receptive for bingos.
3. Drawing a blank may prove problematic. On the following turn, you may have to decide whether to sacrifice the blank for 30 to 40 points in order to get rid of the Q, or whether to exchange the Q in order to prepare a bingo using the blank.
4. Drawing six letters to a Q is extremely unlikely to lead to a bingo on the following turn.

Exchange the Q

Advantages

1. The U-less Q is no longer on the rack!
2. The leave of EINOST combines with A, C, H, I, L, N, O, S, T, U, W, or [] to form playable bingos on this board; given the distribution of the unseen tiles, the probability of playing a bingo after exchanging the Q is about 60 percent.
3. Though the exchange of one tile may clue the opponent that you are bingo hunting, there are too many openings

on this board for the opponent effectively to close it down.

Disadvantages

1. Exchanging the Q sacrifices 27 points versus OILSTONE.
2. The probability of picking a blank is only a sixth of what it would be if OILSTONE were played.

The correct choice here is again unclear. The panel voted 12 to 7 in favor of OILSTONE, though I personally favor exchanging the Q. Regardless of whether you agree with me, you should keep in mind that U-less Q situations are among the most complex that you will face over the board. Try to be flexible in your thinking. I know players who are actually happy to see their opponents play the Q for 35 or so points because then they don't have to worry about being stuck with it themselves! Try not to develop too strong a hatred for the Q, for if you do, it will cloud your judgment when you have to deal with one. It is correct neither to rid yourself of the Q at all costs, nor to play for as many points as possible without regard to how the Q may cripple your future point production. Each situation must be evaluated individually.

If you have the QU combination on your rack and you are bent upon getting rid of the Q as quickly as possible, you may overlook plays that separate your U from your Q. Sometimes, however, your best play requires you to do just this! Consider the opening rack of BELOQUZ. No QU plays are available, and the Z cannot be played without also playing the U. This means that you must resign yourself to a maximum of 12 points (LOBE or BOLE) in order to retain the QU combination. If you play OUZEL (8H), however, you score 30 points. There is some risk that your opponent may make a play that prevents you from placing the Q above the U on your next play, but she is much more likely to play to the right of the Z, since that is where most of the action is (access to the double word squares, the -S hook at 8M). ZEBU is another of your possible plays, but you would then be unlikely to play away your Q on your next turn if your opponent hooks an -S onto ZEBU.

One more comment concerning the U-less Q: don't forget about the non-U Q words, particularly QAID. With the exception of some of the two-letter words, QAID is probably the single most often played word in North American English SCRABBLE®. If you have the Q and a D in your rack, consider making plays that keep the D on the rack if they don't entail too much of a sacrifice as compared with other plays that spend the D. As and IS are so plentiful that you stand a good chance of picking at least one of them, and the other may be open for you on the board. The execution of this idea is demonstrated in Example #30:

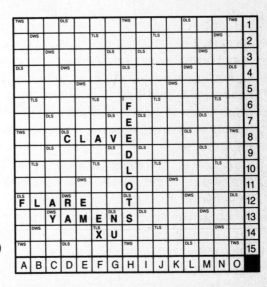

Example #30

Score	You: 104	Opponent: 139
Opponent's last play		XU (14F, 52 points)
Rack		DNOOQRT

Your highest scoring play is DOR (11C, 32 points). However, your second highest scoring play NOR (11C, 29 points) is best. It conserves the D for a sacrifice of only 3 points. With none of the nine IS in the tile distribution yet showing on the board, you stand a fairly decent chance of drawing one even though you pick only three tiles. NOR thus allows

you the distinct possibility of playing QAID at F7 on your
next play. Furthermore, your opponent is highly unlikely to
block this spot, given the other more interesting openings
on the board.

Finally, you should also keep the U-less Q words in mind
when you have the QU combination on your rack. Under-
standably enough, many players overlook these words
when they have QU.

Exchanging Tiles

The exchange is a useful option for simultaneously dispensing with undesirable tiles and increasing the probability of picking desirable tiles. The forfeiture of a scoring
opportunity is a severe penalty, however, so you should not
exchange unless it appears to be absolutely necessary. An
exchange is justified only when the points that could have
been taken instead of exchanging are more than made up
for on subsequent turns. This occurs less often than one
might think.

In my last 107 tournament games, I exchanged tiles only
thirty-nine times, or about once for every forty plays made.
In contrast, my opponents exchanged seventy-nine times. I
attribute the difference to my ability to make more effective
rack balancing plays than my opponents, my ability to use
the limited resources of a bad rack more effectively, and to
my opponents' greater readiness to fish for bingos by
exchanging. I noticed from the game scores that my opponents frequently exchanged three or four tiles, whereas I
almost always exchanged five or more, though sometimes
only one or two. An exchange of four tiles or fewer usually
indicates a fishing play, whereas an exchange of five or
more tiles indicates a horrid rack that must be returned to
the bag. I thus exchanged when my tiles were really poor
(e.g., AAIOUUV, BCFNPPW, etc.), or when I felt that I had an
excellent chance to convert a one- or two-tile fishing play
into a bingo. My opponents also exchanged in these circumstances, but were apparently more willing to fish for three or

four tiles than was I. As mentioned in the previous chapter, this type of fishing should be avoided.

On the other hand, don't shrink from exchanging when it is really necessary to do so. I occasionally watch novice and intermediate players compete, and it seems to me that some of them must consider exchanging tiles to be an almost shameful act. I have seen such players make 6-point plays that yield a rack leave of five vowels! Alfred Butts once said that in all his years of playing SCRABBLE® he never once exchanged tiles. Then, again, he never won a tournament.

Endgame Finesses

The endgame in SCRABBLE® brand crossword game is the most complicated and treacherous stage of the game. It is at this point that a game you have worked hard at winning for the better part of an hour can be kissed goodbye by one inappropriate play. I would estimate that the outcome of at least a third of all tournament games is determined by endgame play. Here are some ideas that will help you play effectively at this critical stage:

Attempt to play out rather than allow your opponent to do so. In a close game, the player who plays out usually wins. Twice the total value of the opponent's remaining tiles is added to the score of the player who plays out, and this bonus often provides the margin of victory. When the score is very close at the end of the game, it is therefore usually more important to make a play that enables you to go out on your next turn than it is to make a higher scoring play that doesn't allow you to play out. In Example #31, for example, you can score 23 points with ANTED (12A), 18 points with DADA (L3) or TAV (A1), and 17 points with DAD (7A). All of these moves lose, however, because they don't address the opponent's threats to play out: INURED or RUINED (1J) and LUNIER (3H). After your ANTED, the opponent can play out with LUNIER and win by six. And after DADA, INURED or RUINED wins by one. The correct play is AOUDAD (2H). Though AOUDAD scores only 10 points, it both

Example #31

	A	B	C	D	E	F	G	H	I	J	K	L	M	N	O
1								W						D	
2								A						I	
3	V	I	E					L						N	
4		F	L	Y				E						G	
5			E	P	E	I	R	I	C				O	E	
6		Y	O	W				H				S	H		
7								I				T			
8			J	A	R	G	O	N	S			B	A	N	
9		C	O	X		R						T			
10		Z	L		B	E						U			
11		O	T		O	E						R			
12		N	E			N						M	E		
13	Q	A	I	D		L				V	I	S	A		
14	U	T		E	K	E						G			
15	A	E		P	L	A	T	F	O	R	M	S			

Score	You: 415	Opponent: 420

Opponent's last play   VISA (13K, 30 points)

Rack   AADDOTU

Opponent's rack   EINRU

prevents your opponent from playing out and guarantees that you can play out and win the game on your next turn with either ANTE (12A) or TAV (A1). Incidentally, a phony was played in this game. Can you find it?

If you have a substantial lead, the tiles unseen are bingo-conducive, and the board is open enough to prevent you from closing off to your opponent all of the bingo alleys, avoid picking the last tile from the bag. Protect your lead. If you deplete the bag and your opponent then bingos out, he will get a nice bonus from your unplayed tiles. If you leave one or two tiles in the bag, however, you will at least get to make one more play. The points you garner from that play are in effect worth double: they are added to your score and the value of the tiles used to make your play do not contribute to your opponent's score if he should then play out on his next turn. It is sometimes worth it to pass your entire turn just to make certain that you will have a play after your opponent bingos.

In a game from the 1980 Canadian Championship, I ignored this idea and suffered a very painful loss as a consequence. My opponent was Mike Schulman, and the crucial choice point is shown in Example #32:

	A	B	C	D	E	F	G	H	I	J	K	L	M	N	O	
1								T				C	O	X	A	1
2								A		P	I	U				2
3			U	T	E	R	I	N	E			M	A			3
4								L			L	I	B			4
5								F	A	N	E					5
6								I	D		T					6
7							M	A	D	E						7
8							C	I	A	O						8
9							O									9
10			O	U	Z	O		V								10
11	B	R	A	W	N		L	E	V	E	R					11
12	E							R		N		W		G		12
13	I						J	O		T		A		U		13
14	G					P	O	D		S	A	F	E	L	Y	14
15	E					E	Y	E				T			S	15
	A	B	C	D	E	F	G	H	I	J	K	L	M	N	O	

Example #32

Score	Me: 340	Mike Schulman: 266
Mike's last play		TAIL (H1, 15 points)
My rack		GHIKNNR

I played HUNK (D2) and lost. I made this play because I thought it would prevent Mike from playing a bingo, and because I overlooked KNOWING (D8, 40 points) and HOWKING (D9, 40 points). There were two ss unaccounted for, so I figured that I would win the game by blocking both the -s hook at 5H and the T at 1H for use as part of an eight-letter play. What I failed to realize was that bingos could be played elsewhere. I emptied the bag after playing HUNK, picked the Q in the process, and Mike then bingoed out with SOIREES (N5, 73 points). His winning margin was 11 points, and it included 34 big points from my rack. Note from the following analysis that even though I could have won with HOWKING or KNOWING, my point spread differential would have been maximized by neither of these plays. Note also that adherence to sound strategic principles (in this case, avoidance of the Q and of emptying the bag when leading) could have more than made up for the tactical oversight.

At the point in the game when I played HUNK, the nine tiles unaccounted for were DEEIORSSQ. Had I been thinking properly, I would have realized that because of the location of the open U and the nature of the distribution of the unseen tiles, it would have been impossible for Mike to play a bingo including the Q. If I had therefore passed my turn instead of playing HUNK and Mike had then played a bingo, one of his two replacement tiles would be an unplayable Q. Furthermore, if the Q was already on his rack he could not have played it without using at least two other tiles (QUA is the only three-letter Q word in the *OSPD,* and all of the AS had previously been played). A Q play at D2 would leave him with at most six tiles on his rack, and he therefore would not have been able to beat me by playing a bingo on his following turn.

Actually, my loss was caused as much by using up the tiles in the bag as it was by being stuck with the Q. Passing would have guaranteed my victory, but so would have AH (13L, 20 points), since I then would have had the opportunity to score decently after his bingo. Had my replacement tile been the Q, I could have responded to SOIREES at either N5 or 5B with KNOWING (D8), winning easily.

The previous example demonstrates how voluntary passing in the endgame can be used to advantage. Most players view passing (as opposed to exchanging) as something to be done only when it must be done, namely, when there are fewer than seven tiles in the bag and a legal play cannot be found.

As you can see from Example #32, however, voluntary passing can be far from pointless even though your score does not increase and your rack does not improve. Example #33 also demonstrates the value of passing. It shows that what seems like a clear win can easily be turned into a loss if the "obvious" move is made instead of the correct one, which in this case is to pass:

A	B	C	D	E	F	G	H	I	J	K	L	M	N	O	
	N					B									1
	E	H		C	O	M	I	T	I	A	L				2
	W	O			U				N						3
		O		G	A	T	E		G						4
M	A	U	D	L	I	N			J	O	E				5
	F			A	D			N	I	T					6
	A	Y			U	P	O		V						7
T	R	E	K			A	W	E	E						8
R	H	I	T		A	X	E		S	O	P				9
O		F	I	C	E				I						10
U		V							L						11
S	B	A	Y												12
E	E	N													13
R	A	D													14
S	D														15

Example #33

Score	Me: 376	Mark Fidler: 276
Mark's last play		OIL (L9, 3 points)
My rack		AEILORT

This position is from a game I played against Mark Fidler in the 1982 Boston Open. With a 100-point lead and only three tiles left in the bag, I had this game well in hand. My first thought was to block Mark's bingo alleys, but I found it impossible to block -s hooks at both 12L and N9 in such a manner that no other openings for bingos were possible. My second thought was to play TINEAL (3J, 22 points). I then checked out the tiles that were still unaccounted for. They were AEIGNQRSTZ.

I decided to pass. My reasoning was as follows: Mark could only play a bingo if the Q was not in it. The only possible bingo involving the Q was QINTARS, and there was nowhere to place it on the board. If Mark was therefore able to play a bingo, one of his replacement tiles from the bag would then be the Q. He would be stuck with it, and I could then play out at my leisure for an easy victory. Passing guaranteed a fairly substantial victory for me.

As it turned out, Mark played SEARING, N9. I then played RELATION (14G, 60 points). I picked up 42 additional points for the tiles in Mike's rack (QTZ), and won by 126 points. Had I played TINEAL instead of passing, my rack leave after emptying the bag would have been OQRTZ. After Mark's SEARING, we would have tied at 398 apiece. Had he found ERASING (12I) instead of SEARING, he would have won by 2 points. Note also that had I made a one- or two-tile play that did not empty the bag I probably would have won. After ONE (3K, 22 points), for example, my three possible racks would have been AILRTTZ, AILQRTZ, and AILQRTT. Had I ended up with the first rack, Mark would have been stuck with the Q after his bingo. Had I ended up with either of the first two racks, ZIRAM (A1, 51 points) would have in fact won easily for me. The AILQRTT is the worst possible situation, but here I would have been able to play ADIT (14C, 7 points), preventing Mark from playing out with ADZ (14C). I again would have won easily.

Be alert to endgame setup plays: retain tiles that prevent your opponent from preparing setups, and if appropriate, try to prepare setups yourself. The endgame is particularly prone to setup plays. With many tiles already played, endgame board positions often crystallize in such a way that there are what can best be described as "nooks and crannies" on the board. These are small closed off areas within which clever little setup plays can be devised. Setups are especially effective when the opposing player has fewer than seven tiles on the rack, but cannot play out on the next turn. In this situation, your opponent's lack of tiles may make it impossible for him to block your setup.

```
   A   B   C   D   E   F   G   H   I   J   K   L   M   N   O
1  .   .   .   D   I   O   C   E   S   E   .   .   .   .   F
2  .   .   J   O   .   F   A   X   .   .   .   .   .   .   O
3  .   .   I   .   .   .   N   .   .   .   B   U   N   G   .
4  .   .   V   .   A   S   T   E   R   I   A   S   .   .   .
5  .   B   L   E   N   T   .   O   .   .   .   N   .   .   .
6  .   Y   A   .   .   .   .   K   .   .   F   .   .   .   .
7  .   E   C   U   .   L   A   M   I   A   E   .   U   .   .
8  .   .   .   .   .   .   M   E   N   .   R   E   P   E   L
9  .   .   R   .   W   H   I   T   .   .   R   .   .   .   O
10 .   .   I   L   I   A   .   .   .   .   H   E   .   .   U
11 .   .   G   .   Z   .   .   .   .   O   D   .   .   .   V
12 .   .   .   .   .   .   .   .   .   .   R   D   A   T   E
13 .   .   .   .   .   .   .   .   I   N   G   O   T   .   R
14 .   .   .   .   .   .   .   .   S   O   W   .   .   .   E
15 .   .   .   .   .   .   .   .   .   .   .   .   .   .   D
```

Example #34

Score	You: 338	Opponent: 275
Opponent's last play		WIZ (E9, 40 points)
Your rack		DQ
Opponent's rack		AIPTY

In example #34, you seem to have a safe lead despite being stuck with the Q. Appearances can be deceiving, however. That lead will dissolve into a defeat if you play ILIAD (10C, 13 points) immediately. The correct play is to pass, as the D is needed to prevent the opponent from setting up a winning play. If you play the D away, your opponent could then play ABYE (B4, 9 points), followed by PITY (A1, 48 points). You would lose by one point. If you hold on to the D, you could respond to ABYE with DA (4A), and thus preserve your win.

Incidentally, it should be mentioned here, that although passing turns out to be the best play for Examples #32, #33, and #34, don't be misled into thinking that it is an often used resource. It is valuable only when your opponent must put tiles on the board following your pass in order to have a chance of winning. It is extremely rare that passing has any value outside of the endgame. If you go first and have AEINORT in your rack, for example, you may be tempted to pass. This will signal your opponent that although you do not have a seven-letter bingo, you do have tiles that combine to form eight-letter bingos with a great many of the letters in the alphabet. Your opponent doesn't have to play one of them, however. She may instead pass herself, or exchange tiles in order to improve her own rack.

Example #35 is a demonstration of how a resourceful player may use a setup to play out:

Example #35

	A	B	C	D	E	F	G	H	I	J	K	L	M	N	O	
1	J	A	G					D	E	C	E	A	S	E	D	
2		N						U			H	E	I	R		
3		A	Z	O				I					B			
4		N		P	L	O	T	T	E	R						
5		A							O							
6						V	E	I	L	S						
7										A						
8					F	U	R	R	I	E	R					
9					L				I							
10			T	A					E					G		
11		C	O	X	A		S	E	N	S	O	R	I	A		
12	A	H	O	Y				M			W	O	M			
13	D	I	T					E			N	U		E	F	
14	I	N						E	L	K		E		D	O	
15	T							R				N			B	

Score	You: 390	Opponent: 408
Opponent's last play		ELK (14H, 17 points)
Rack		IPQUWY
Opponent's rack		GTV

The situation seems hopeless. Not only are you 18 points down, but your opponent has seemingly prevented you from unloading the Q with her last play (you could have played PIQUE, 14D, or QUEY, 13F, had she not played ELK). Then you study the board very carefully and find salvation: YAW (7I, 23 points)! The beauty of this play is not that it scores well, but that it sets up a -P hook at L7 for QUIP (L4, 42 points) as your going-out play. YAW is a remarkable play that could easily be overlooked. At an earlier point in a game, a similar oversight might not be so critical. In the endgame, however, the failure to find such a move can undo all of your earlier efforts.

Tournament Preparation and Play

It is possible that you are not interested in playing in tournaments. You may dislike the pressure of competition, or you may think that you are not good enough to compete. Don't be too quick to rule out tournament participation, however.

Tournaments are fun. The players are both easy to get along with and intelligent, and most of them try hard to make newcomers feel especially welcome. It is in the players' interest to do so, since the vitality of tournaments can be maintained only by a constant infusion of new blood. In addition, many tournaments are held in attractive resort hotels, and bargain package rates for hotels and food are standard.

A typical tournament day consists of breakfast at a civilized hour, followed by play in the morning. Then lunch, followed by more play throughout the early afternoon. Competitors are then on their own for the rest of the day. They can go sightseeing, play tennis, swim, renew old friendships or start new ones, play more SCRABBLE®, relax, or follow their fancy. Then, after enjoying a nice dinner, they can go out on the town (if there is one), play more SCRABBLE®, or do whatever else they want. A tournament adds the perfect amount of structure to a minivacation. And of course it's also an escape: no laundry to do, no kids to care for, no meals to prepare, no supermarket shopping, and no business to attend to. Sounds nice, doesn't it?

Most tournaments run three divisions: expert, intermediate, and novice. The separation of players by ability pretty much ensures that you will neither be overwhelmed or underwhelmed by your opposition. Swiss system pairings will additionally maximize the likelihood that you will play against players whose ability is approximately equal to yours.

Even if you choose not to participate in SCRABBLE® brand crossword game tournaments, however, I think that you will find much of the material in the next three chapters to be of interest. Chapter 7 presents methods for effectively improving your game through anagram practice, dictionary study, memorization, and game playing. Chapter 8 deals with your behavior at the tournament site: what proper etiquette at the playing table consists of; what you can do when you aren't playing, to stay in top playing shape; and what you should avoid doing if you wish to play your best. Finally, chapter 9 consists of a brief history of tournament play in North America, followed by listings of some of the more prominent tournaments that currently take place on a regular basis in North America.

7

Tournament Preparation

How well one does in a tournament is not solely dependent on raw talent. Raw talent helps, of course, but study and training are of at least equal importance. David Prinz won $1,500 for placing first in the 1978 North American Championship (NAC). To give you an idea of how important work was to his victory, he estimated that his prize money averaged out to about 15 cents per hour of total training time. Joe Edley won the second NAC by studying the *OSPD* three hours a day, seven days a week, for two years. I did not put in quite as much effort to win the 1983 version of this tournament, though I did work consistently and diligently for well over a year. Actually, I have been steadily trying to master the *OSPD* since it was first published in 1978.

This degree of dedication is necessary if you wish to be competitive with the best players in the game. You can become quite a decent player, however, with much less effort. If you attend Scrabble® club sessions on a regular basis for about half a year, without doing any additional studying on your own, you will learn a tremendous amount. You will know all of the two-letter words, many of the threes and fours, some of the fives, and a sprinkling of unusual seven- and eight-letter bingos. In addition, your general playing ability will improve markedly.

If you wish to be a more than decent player, however, it is necessary to spend additional time studying and training. I differentiate between these terms in that study refers to efforts intended to increase your playing vocabulary, whereas training refers to the development of playing skills such as anagramming, board resourcefulness, and strategic prowess. Intensive study and training are both necessary in order to become a fine player.

General Preparation

It is well known that many chess grandmasters keep themselves physically fit so that they can think clearly for long periods of time while playing in tournaments. The same rationale applies to tournament play in the SCRABBLE® brand crossword game. Chess masters often must concentrate for as long as five hours at a stretch. SCRABBLE® players are not required to do this, but in a tournament such as the North American Championship they may have to play six or seven games over a ten-hour period. Despite breaks for meals and short periods between games, such a schedule is grueling. The general level of play declines as the day progresses, and the number of obvious blunders and oversights increases, probably exponentially. The rate of decline in the level of play is slower, however, for the player who is physically fit then it is for the player who is out of shape.

I don't really believe that it is necessary to run ten miles a day, play one-on-one full-court basketball for an hour, and then top that off with an arduous weight training program in order to play an excellent game. What is necessary is a program of moderate and regular exercise. For me, this consists of tennis three times a week plus at least forty-five minutes a day of walking.

Exercise is, of course, only a part of physical fitness. The other components include good nutrition, plenty of rest and relaxation, low intake of alcohol, and avoidance of smoking. Smoking is not permitted at most SCRABBLE® tournaments, and many habitual smokers have a difficult time over the board without their cigarettes. My opponents who are smokers tend to get more and more antsy as the game progresses. Tension apparently heightens the need for a cigarette, and I have no doubt that the growing preoccupation with this need adversely affects play. If you are a heavy smoker and you plan to play in an upcoming tournament, you could acclimate yourself by forgoing smoking while playing practice games. Even better, give up smoking. Finally, you should avoid artificial stimulants and drugs, as they are likely to wreck both your physical health and your ability to concentrate. Space cadets don't win tournaments.

I have found that it is particularly important to feel unharried during the period leading up to an important tournament. You should arrange your life so that you don't have to fight for your study and training time. If this is not possible, try to budget a smaller amount of daily time for preparation over a longer pretournament period.

Try to avoid cramming. If you feel pressured to absorb a lot of material over a short period of time, you will forget much of what you studied. Even worse, you will be more likely to confuse new words with similar sounding non-words than if you had studied at a more relaxed pace.

A few of the top players, myself included, practice meditation regularly. Meditation with deep, controlled, slow breathing can be incredibly useful in a tournament. It has two major beneficial effects. First, it provides the mental discipline to ignore stimulation extraneous to the task at hand. When players panic, they ruminate about losing, bad luck, "if only" situations, and so forth. Meditation is an effective way of blotting out such thoughts. It enables you to focus exclusively on one thing only: the game situation. Second, meditation keeps you mentally sharp, as the deep breathing associated with it facilitates the flow of oxygen to the brain.

You don't have to go to school in order to meditate. All you have to do is make yourself comfortable in a pleasant, quiet environment. Breathe in deeply and slowly through your nose, and then exhale slowly through your mouth. Try to think of nothing else but the pace of your breathing. Meditate for a couple of minutes the first few days, and then gradually increase the time until you are meditating for about half an hour a day (one thirty-minute session or two fifteen-minute sessions). Consider yourself accomplished at meditating if you are able to focus exclusively on your breathing, and if you feel free and relaxed during the process. When you've reached this point, try meditating in a variety of places and at a variety of times during the day. Keep in mind that if you don't practice meditation before the tournament takes place, you will be unable to meditate effectively during the tournament. Meditation is a skill that must be developed over time.

The Study of Words

Before embarking upon a program of word study, one must first know which words to study. All words are not equally useful. Some can be played to advantage only very rarely, perhaps in less than one game out of a thousand. Others pop up all the time. Even if it is your ultimate goal to master the entire dictionary, you might as well start with the words that you are most likely to play rather than ones you will never see on the board. The most useful words include:

All words of five letters or less. The vast majority of plays made over the SCRABBLE® brand crossword game board form words that are five letters or less in length. Knowledge of these words is vital for doing well in tournament play. Fortunately, there are not that many of them. The total number of two- to five-letter words in the *OSPD* is less than 12,000 (85 two-letter words, 908 threes, 3,686 fours, and 7,080 fives). Many of them are familiar words, and many others are -s plurals that need not be studied separately from their singular forms. If you are a beginning player, there are probably only about 5,000 two- to five-letter words in the *OSPD* that you need to study.

Bingos containing no or only one high-point tile. About two-fifths of the seven- and eight-letter words listed in the *OSPD* have no more than one high-point tile in them. Because of the tile distribution in the Game, however, these words account for about four times as many played bingos as do all of the other seven- and eight-letter words in the dictionary. It is conceivable that a word like IDEATION could be played twice in the same session (it was once played against me twice in the same game), but it is unlikely that you will ever hear of anyone anywhere playing COBWEBBY.

Words of five or more letters containing four or more vowels. Words with many vowels in them are often difficult to find over the board. They are unlikely to have regular prefixes and suffixes, and they often do not sound as they are spelled. They are very common in SCRABBLE® play, however, and this is due to the two factors mentioned in chapter 5: the large number of vowels in the tile pool, and the relative ease with which consonants as opposed to vowels can be played away.

Hook words. As demonstrated in chapter 4, words that can be changed into other words by hooking a letter before or after them are especially useful to know.

Words that appear to take - plurals, but do not. There are several hundred of these "trick words" that are five letters or less in length. It is essential to know them both to set traps for the opponent and to avoid playing phony pluralizations yourself.

Lists. Now that you know which words to study, you are probably wondering where to find them. Most Game experts have spent endless hours constructing word lists. My own lists total 335 typed pages, but that is nothing compared to the lists put together by Charles Goldstein, a very strong expert from California. His lists are longer than the dictionary, and they don't include definitions!

List making is very tedious. Before you say to yourself, "Who needs this?," however, let me point out that access to existing lists is much easier nowadays than it once was. If you join SCRABBLE® Crossword Game Players (see Appendix A), you can request the following alphabetized lists, or back issues of the SCRABBLE® *Players News* that contain them:

(1) All two-, three, and four-letter words in the *OSPD*.

(2) Hook word lists for changing two-letter words into three-letter words, threes into fours, and fours into fives.

(3) All combinations of seven tiles that combine to form two or more bingos.

(4) Numerous six-to-make-seven bingo lists (e.g., SATIRE, TISANE, SANTER, OUTERS, etc.).

(5) Some five-to-make-seven bingo lists (AERST, AEIST, EORST, ERSTU) and five-to-make-eight bingo lists (AERST, ERSTU).

(6) The 125 seven-letter bingos most likely to be picked from a full bag of tiles.

(7) All six-, seven-, and eight-letter words ending in -INGS.

(8) All seven- and eight-letter bingos containing five vowels or more.

Also of some use is Ethel Cannon Sherard's book, *The Double List Word Book* (Gwethine Publishing Company, 201 N. Wells St., Chicago). This book is based upon the *OSPD*, and it includes two lists for each letter of the alphabet: all words beginning with the letter, and all words ending with the letter. Both lists are arranged alphabetically and are further categorized by word length. This book also contains lists of words beginning with OO, ending with EE, and beginning, ending, or containing the J, Q, X, and Z.

How to study. After you have decided upon the words that you would most like to learn, you must apply some sort of systematic method for getting these words firmly established in your head. Here are two approaches that I and other experts have found helpful:

Word recognition.

The idea behind this approach is that unfamiliar words can be absorbed through repeated presentations. When I was preparing for the 1983 North American Championship, part of my study consisted of spending about an hour a day reading lists of all bingos that I decided not to memorize. I read only a small portion of these lists each day, but after three months I had covered all of them seven or eight times over. I knew the many thousands of words on them very solidly, and this knowledge was the difference between defeat and victory in at least two of my tournament games.

You can learn words through recognition by simply reading the *OSPD* over and over again. If you choose to do this, however, I would suggest that on your first time through you use a highlighting pen to underline the words you don't know. Your study time will be spent more efficiently on subsequent passes through the dictionary, as you will not be attending to words you already know.

Another valuable method for increasing your word recognition is to prepare cassette tapes you can listen to at home or in your car. Make sure that you pronounce each word clearly, and that you then spell it out. You may also wish to include the word's definition, what part of speech it is, and if its forms are irregular in any manner.

Memorization.

Memorization differs from recognition in that it requires a series of words from a list to be recalled *in sequence,* without access to the list. Its great advantage over recognition is that memorized words are learned with much greater security than are recognized words. They are rarely forgotten. Another advantage is that memorized words are recalled without having to rely upon anagrammatic skill. This is important, as few players have perfect anagrammatic ability, especially with eight-letter words. Third, memorization helps you recognize phonies readily. If your opponent plays a word that should be at a certain place in your list but isn't, you can challenge the word and be 100 percent positive that the word will have to be removed. If your opponent plays a word in a form different from any on your lists, you can challenge the word with impunity. For example, one of the lists I have memorized contains all of the eight-letter three-vowel words with two high-point tiles in them. If an opponent tries RETHAW, I would challenge immediately, since I know that RETHAWED is not on my list. Finally, memorization is usually faster as well as more reliable than anagramming. This is true both for finding a word and for determining that the tiles on the rack cannot be used to form a bingo.

The major disadvantage of memorization is that it is time consuming. Although it takes an experienced memorizer no longer than five minutes to memorize twenty or so new words, these words must be mentally rehearsed regularly in order to keep recall from deteriorating. The more new words you memorize, the more memorized words you will have to maintain through rehearsal in the future.

It has been apparent to me for some time that I am not capable of memorizing the entire dictionary. The practical consequence of this fact is that I have had to be selective. Except for about 450 unpluralizable three-, four-, and five-letter words, I do not memorize words other than bingos. There are two reasons for this: shorter words can easily be remembered through word recognition alone, and shorter words can be much more easily anagrammed than can bingos. Most of my memorized words are eight-letter bingos rather than sevens. I thus reserve my memorization skills for the words that I am most unlikely to find over the board had I not memorized them. These include eight-letter bingos containing three or more vowels, and all seven-letter bingos containing four or more vowels. I do not memorize -s pluralizations of seven-letter bingos unless the pluralization seems strange to me (e.g., MINIMALS). I lose some precision by omitting pluralizations (I once incorrectly played CUNE-ATES, for example), but this is more than offset by the benefit of not having to memorize many thousands of additional words.

Most players use a straight alphabetical system for storing their memorized words. They arrange the tiles alphabetically on their rack from left to right, and then try to recall that portion of their list that most closely corresponds to this alphabetization. A portion of the list comprising all seven-letter bingos arranged in this manner would include the following sequence of words: ABILITY, MISBIAS, ABIOSIS, JABIRUS, KABUKIS. Their alphabetizations are ABIILTY, ABIIMSS, ABIIOSS, ABIJRSU, and ABIKKSU. If you had memorized this list and had ABIIRST on your rack, you would immediately know that you did not have a playable seven-letter bingo, since this combination "falls in the crack" between ABIOSIS and JABIRUS. My own organizational system is somewhat more involved. My grand list contains sublists arranged by how many high-point tiles the words in them contain, and these sublists are further broken down according to the number of vowels contained by the words in them. These still lengthy sub-sublists are then alphabetized by vowel combinations, and further alphabetized within each vowel combination on the basis of their consonants. To give you an idea of what I am talking about, my one-high-point-letter, four-vowel sublist begins with the following sequence: ATALAYA, CARAGANA, ANASARCA, ALAMEDA, APANAGE, ALTHAEA, AZALEAS ... It ends some 2,900 words later with . . . OUTSHOUT, TUMOROUS, TUBULOUS, UNCTUOUS, and TUMULOUS. Because of the nature of my lists, I do not arrange my tiles strictly alphabetically on my rack. I instead alphabetize the vowels and consonants separately. The vowels are placed to the left, the consonants to the right.

Regardless of how you organize your lists, you will need some sort of a mental filing system to make them manageable. Such a system will enable you to recall easily specific portions of a large list when you need them. I divide my lists into 200-word groups, and I subdivide each group into ten 20-word units. I learn only one new unit a day, though I may rehearse several hundred previously learned words on the same day. It is vitally important also to memorize the sequence of words consisting of the first word in each unit (words #1, #21, #41 ... 181 of your list), and also the sequence of words consisting of the first word in each group (words #1, #201, #401, and so forth). These guideword lists will greatly shorten the time it takes you to recall the specific portion of a long list that you most need at any given time.

How to memorize. Memorization of so many special words is difficult at first, but becomes much easier with practice. There are numerous mnemonic tools at your disposal to help you in your quest. Suppose, for example, that you wish to memorize the following sequence of words: WOBEGONE, BESOOTHE, OVERBORE, RECOOKED, LOCOWEED, COOPERED, DOVECOTE, RECHOOSE, PODOMERE, and FOVEOLET. These words are from my two-high-point-letter, four-vowel list. The key to remembering them is to find some sort of structure in them. You may notice, for example, that the first three words end in E, the second three in D, and the third three in E again. You might also categorize them by consonants: the first three contain B, the next five C. Another technique is to use tile values to help you memorize: the number 43111 represents the tile values of the initial letters in the first five words, for example.

Some players like to make up fantastic stories to help them link words together. An example of such a story, as applied to the sequence given above is:

> A WOBEGONE beggar was not BESOOTHEd when three of his colleagues OVERBORE him, and then robbed him of his only remaining possession, RECOOKED LOCOWEED. In order to recoup his loss, he entered a job retraining program sponsored by the government, where he learned to be a cooper (COOPERED). He didn't make much money, however, and the only lodging he could afford was a rather unpleasant outdoor flat located right under a DOVECOTE (yecch!). He decided to RECHOOSE his profession to better himself, and became a veterinarian specializing in insect care. His first patient was an arthropod with a broken PODOMERE which accentuated an unsightly FOVEOLET just below it.

Read through this story once or twice, and I think that you will have little problem memorizing the sequence of words embedded within it. Incidentally, I have found that the more pictorial and fantastical the story, the easier it is to remember the words. A side benefit is that you will learn the definitions of all sorts of strange words.

If you decide to memorize words for the Game, be forewarned that it will take a considerable amount of over-the-board practice before you will be able to apply your memorizations to actual play. It is one thing to recall words in the peace and quiet of your own home, and quite another to recall them in the middle of a tense tournament game. When I first attempted to use my memorized lists in tournaments, I was unable to recall them at critical moments. Like tile tracking, it was only after considerable tournament experience that I could apply this skill easily and reliably.

Training Procedures

Anagramming skill. The ability to form words from a seemingly random collection of tiles is of course central to good SCRABBLE® play. Knowing that a word is in the *OSPD* won't help you much if you can't find it over the board. Fortunately, anagramming is a skill that can be easily improved. When I first started playing the Game, I used to test my anagrammatic ability by working on the Jumbles that appear in many daily newspapers. I was initially inept, but now I can routinely find all six six-letter words in the weekend Jumbles puzzle within a total elapsed time of about ten seconds. Here are some ways for improving your anagramming ability:

Look for words with prefixes and suffixes. This is second nature to almost all players. Although the search for these words often proves fruitful, it does entail some risk. Anagramming by prefix and suffix is too easy! It does not tax the player's mind. All too often I have seen players fail to develop true creative anagramming skill because they focus exclusively on prefixes and suffixes. Look for these words, but don't begin and end your search for the best play with them.

Make up "anagram words" consisting of combinations of short words and prefixes or suffixes to help you remember real words that are difficult to anagram. You might, for example, find it useful to remember the word MRIDANGA as DRAMA + ING, KILLDEE as DEL + LIKE, or NUGATORY as OUT + ANGRY. Many players make up lists containing mnemonic rearrangements like these.

Use vocalization as a prompt. If you have what appears to be a bingo-conducive rack but you cannot find a bingo in it, make up nonsense words from your tiles and say them softly to yourself. If there is in fact a bingo in your rack that you are not unfamiliar with, vocalization of this sort often results in the bingo suddenly popping into your head. Don't ask me why this works. All I know is that it does.

Practice makes better. The more you test yourself with anagrams, the better and faster you will get at solving them. Joe Edley, the 1980 North American Champion, has mastered the *OSPD* almost exclusively by solving anagrams. He uses flash cards, each of which contains ten anagram problems. On one side of each card, ten words are listed. The letters comprising each word are presented in alphabetical order on the other side. Joe has gone through all of the bingos in the *OSPD* several times by solving their anagrams with his flash cards. His training has thus enabled him not only to recognize words in the *OSPD*, but to anagram them flawlessly as well.

Board resourcefulness. Board resourcefulness refers to the ability to find plays over the board. It is unquestionably the most important (as well as the most creative) skill that a player can develop. We shall see in the annotated games section of this book that even among experts, mistakes occur on at least one out of every three plays. Such mistakes sometimes result from inadequate vocabulary, poor anagramming skill, or inappropriate strategy. Most frequently, however, they occur because of insufficient consideration of the board position. Due to time pressure, carelessness, poor visual-spatial ability, or lack of concentration, the player simply overlooks the best play.

Board resourcefulness comes from the study of board positions. One effective approach is to record the letters of your racks on the score sheet while playing a game, so that it is possible to go back over the game later to see what you missed. *Careful* postgame analysis almost always reveals many mistakes, and sustained study of this type will most assuredly sharpen your play over the board. Be warned, however, that this type of study is time consuming and cannot be rushed. It may take three hours or more of analysis to examine adequately your moves from just one game.

A technique that I sometimes use while playing a game is to take notes on openings created by my opponent or by me. In Example 5 (page 58), for instance, I might write "keep SI for SIDELIGHT" in a corner of my score sheet so as to prevent myself from forgetting about this possibility later in the game.

One final tip: board resourcefulness can only be developed fully if you look at the board! Look for opportunities on the board such as those discussed in chapter 4: openings, hooks, overlaps, inside plays, and word extensions. Too many players spend too much time with their noses buried in their racks. Study the board, and let it guide you to the best play.

Strategic prowess. Most experts acquired their strategic prowess by playing numerous games against, and by consulting with, players who were initially much stronger than they. There is no substitute for this experience. If you want to develop a good strategic sense, you must see good strategy in action. A study of chapters 5 and 6, and of the game annotations in this book, will help a great deal, but the impact of the principles and ideas presented in these portions of the book only becomes real when they are used against you. When you play an expert, you will feel frustrated when she closes down the exact portion of the board where you were planning to play a bingo. You will feel helpless as she creates an unblockable hook for herself. You will wonder why she always seems to balance her rack while you are stuck with five vowels. In short, you will feel totally outclassed. Once you have experienced these feelings, the importance of good strategy will become obvious to you. You might have known previously that fishing should usually be avoided, but now you will have the will power to resist doing it. You might also start looking more consciously for plays that dispense with many of your tiles, instead of settling for a quick 20 or 25 points while playing away only two tiles. You will start to make plays that make your opponents feel as uncomfortable as you once felt.

Even if you already have a well-developed strategic sense, you should test yourself against good players as part of your pretournament preparation. Not only will your strategic skills be sharpened, but you will be more likely to learn a few additional words by playing strong players than by playing weaker ones. Most important, you will be forced to struggle. You will have to exert yourself on every move in order to win. If you can get yourself to adopt such a fiercely competitive attitude, you will come close to doing the best that you can in the tournament. If, instead, after making a weak move, you say to yourself, "In a tournament I wouldn't have done that," you may in fact end up *doing just that* in a tournament!

Some players avoid playing strong opponents before a tournament, apparently believing that consistent losing will destroy their self-confidence. This is a form of whistling in the dark. If you are not good enough to win, you might as well know it. If you don't know that you are not good enough, not only will you not try as hard as you should to improve, but you are likely to be very disappointed by your tournament performance. Losing can be good for you, but it feels a whole lot less painful *before* than *during* a tournament.

8

At the Tournament Site

This chapter deals with how you should handle yourself at the tournament site in order to play as well as you possibly can. The major premise underlying the last chapter was that pretourney study and training contributes greatly to successful tournament results. However, all of your preparation will go for naught if you do not look out for yourself properly at the tournament site. This involves more than maintaining your physical and mental well-being. It also requires that you know how to deal with certain situations that may arise during play so that your opponents do not take advantage of you, and so that you do not offend other players by exhibiting poor etiquette.

Taking Care of Yourself

Many players enjoy having a good time while attending a tournament. They view tournaments primarily as mini-vacations. There is nothing wrong with this attitude. Tournaments should be enjoyable, even for serious players. Nevertheless, you cannot go hog-wild at a tournament and expect to do well. If you eat and drink to excess (*very* common phenomena at tournaments held at resort hotels), if you don't get enough sleep, if you play fifteen extra games a day—do not expect to play well in the official competition. In order to do your best, you must maintain your pretournament general preparation program: regular exercise, sensible eating, plenty of rest and relaxation, and abstinence from sustances that cloud your judgment and concentration.

There are a few other things you can do that will help you conserve your energy. First, spend as little time as possible in the tournament area between games. There is usually about a fifteen-minute interlude between the end of a round and the beginning of the following round. Use this time to go back to your room by yourself and relax. If you stay around the playing room, you will inevitably get caught up in an animated conversation about how you and everyone else fared in the previous round. You can expend a great deal of energy in bemoaning your fate or in describing how brilliantly you played, and you will need this energy later on.

Be especially careful not to pig out at meals preceding tournament play. Lunch can be especially dangerous, as after three or four hard games in the morning you may be very hungry. If you eat too much before playing, however, your body's need to digest the food you have eaten will make you somnolent.

If you have a little extra time during the lunch break, go back to your room and take a shower. It will refresh you and help you play well in the afternoon. Remember to bring extra changes of clothing so that you can be as comfortable as possible throughout the tourney.

Finally, don't study on the days of the tournament. I find such study to be more harmful than helpful. It reduces your confidence by exposing you to many words that you may not be able to absorb in a short period of time; and if you do in fact know them, then the study is of little value. Studying during a tournament always makes me feel somewhat frantic, and I don't believe it has ever helped me. However, I cannot make a blanket condemnation of cramming, since I know a few experts who claim they find this type of study beneficial.

Table Manners

The nature of SCRABBLE® brand crossword game is such that it is easy to upset or distract your opponent. If you are an inexperienced tournament player, you may not even realize that your opponent is taking unfair advantage of you by engaging in such behavior. You may also unknowingly irritate your opponent. For these reasons, it is important to know something about proper SCRABBLE® etiquette.

Good etiquette. Good etiquette consists basically of playing quietly, presenting a pleasant demeanor, and making no attempt whatsoever to distract the opponent. It does not preclude a few allowable deceptions, however. You are not breaching good etiquette if you actively but quietly shuffle the tiles on your rack to give your opponent the false impression that your tiles are very promising. Your opponent might as a result make a defensive play rather than the higher scoring play she was intending. It is also allowable to stare intently at part of the board so that your opponent might think, again erroneously, that you plan to play there on your next move. You should feel free to time your plays in potential challenge situations. If you intend to play a word that you know is acceptable but you think might be challenged, you might hesitate before making the play so as to induce your opponent to think you are unsure about the word's acceptability. If you play a phony, on the other hand, you might play it immediately and with confidence so that your opponent will get the impression that you are certain the word in question is acceptable.

Bad etiquette. Bad etiquette consists mainly of talking during the game other than for the purposes of announcing the number of points scored for a play, rectifying scoring discrepancies between you and your opponent, informing him of a decision to exchange tiles or to pass, and challenging. Your opponent may be struggling to recall words from a memorized word list, working out a sensible strategy, or trying to anagram an eight-letter bingo. If you say something as innocuous as "My, what a nice day. Too bad we are cooped up in here," you will break his concentration. He will be perfectly justified in telling you to keep your mouth shut.

Other types of comments seem more intentionally designed to rile the opposing player. Among the most common are those intended to mislead the opponent about the tiles in a player's rack: "I just can't seem to pick any decent tiles today." "What junk!" or "Oh wow, finally something good." When opponents make comments like these to me, I ask them to be quiet. Sometimes this works, and sometimes it doesn't. Maybe I should say something like "Oh, really? Let me see what you've got." Regardless of how you choose to handle such comments, *never* believe your opponent, and never believe that the exact opposite of what your opponent said is true either! Make your play on what you know, not what your opponent tells you.

Other kinds of obnoxious remarks are intended to deceive you into erroneously challenging or refraining from challenging. I wish I had a dollar for every instance in which an opponent placed a word on the board and then said "I'm not really sure whether this is good." The unspoken message behind such a remark is something like "If you decide to challenge and you lose the challenge, you really aren't so dumb, since even I don't know if the word is good. So go ahead and challenge." Experience has shown me that almost without fail, plays prefaced by expressions of hesitancy are acceptable.

Another way of saying "I'm not sure if this word is good" is to place a word on the board and ask the opponent if it is acceptable. The player may be genuinely unsure if her word is allowable. And it would, therefore, be very helpful for her to know if you intend to challenge the word if she in fact plays it. Still, if you answer her question, you are a real dodo. Don't even say that you don't know if the word is good, since any indication of uncertainty on your part may be taken as a signal that you will not challenge. I usually say something like "I won't answer that now," which not only makes the point but also implies that I really do know the answer. I must admit, however, that I am on occasion sorely tempted to say "Yes, of course it's okay" when I know that it isn't, and then correctly challenge the word after my opponent presses her clock button.

Even more objectionable are comments made by your opponent implying that you do not know how to play the game, or that you did something especially dumb. In one of my games in the 1980 North American Championship, I played TABORIN[E], B1. Even though I quite clearly stated that the blank was an E, my opponent looked at me as if I were crazy. With wide eyes and great surprise in his voice, he said, "Did you say the blank was an E?" I immediately realized my blunder: I could have played TABORIN[G] instead, which would have been much better defensively since my opponent would then not be able to use the triple word square at 8A. As it turned out, my opponent played WIZ (A8) on his next turn for 57 points. I don't object to his play, but I do to his comment.

Every once in a while you will come up against a player who is determined to show you how brilliant she is. She will make a play and then say something like "See how nicely this play blocks both of the available bingo openings?" Players who make comments like these often appear to be helping you rather than interrupting your concentration. They adopt the persona of the experienced veteran who has graciously consented to share a few of her strategical tidbits with you, a newcomer. I don't object to advice given after the game has been completed, but you should realize that a player who gives advice to you during the game is simply trying to win by distracting you.

It is also bad form to pronounce the words you play. There is absolutely no reason why your opponent should be unnecessarily subjected to your voice. In addition, a mispronounced word could affect your opponent's play. I have in fact observed players *intentionally* mispronouncing words in order to deceive their opponents. They might play REUS-ING or RESTING, and say "ROOSING" or "RE-STING." If you resort to this in order to win, your colleagues will consider you a lowlife.

Players sometimes try to distract opponents by pretending to talk to themselves. Their conversation sounds something like "Hmm. Thirty points here, only 28 there, but much safer ... no, I can't do that because he might have an x ..." Such a monologue sounds innocuous, but if you are attending to it you cannot be concentrating fully on your own situation. You might also be deceived. Your opponent might say to himself that he can't make a play because it opens an x spot when in fact the x is on his own rack.

Players can also rile opponents by bemoaning their bad luck or the opponent's good luck, by complimenting an opponent for a pedestrian play, or by expressing surprise at the opponent's lack of scoring or apparent poor play: "Maybe you're just having an off day." Well-known players additionally have to put up with the occasional opponent who says, before the game starts: "What a privilege to play you! I know I'm going to lose, but this is such an honor anyway." Translation: "The pressure is on you because I'm expected to lose and you aren't. If you lose to me, you don't deserve to be considered an expert." The goal, of course, is to get the expert thinking about losing rather than about making the best play.

Then there is the opponent who babbles on mindlessly throughout the game. Some people cope with nervousness in this manner, and they often aren't intentionally trying to distract their opponents. Nevertheless, continual babble can enrage an opponent. I once lost a tournament game to a fine player who, at that time, did not have the ability to remain silent. I played her a second time in the last game of the tournament, and asked her please not to talk unnecessarily during the game. She complied with my request. The thing I remember most about that game is not that I won by 314 points, but that I was still so angry from my previous encounter with her that I played a phony bingo when I was ahead by 174 points!

There are a few nonverbal ways of exhibiting bad etiquette as well. Some players develop coughing fits that mysteriously vanish when it is their turn to play but return when it is their opponent's turn. Others squirm in their seats a great deal. A few that I have played against are experts in making faces of despair, joy, horror, and so forth. Others stare at you more than they look at their own racks. Still others shuffle their tiles as loudly as possible. I have played against an opponent who, after picking his tiles, keeps the bag on his side of the table, as far away from me as possible. Also annoying is the habit some players have of moving the board from its position in the middle of the table closer to them, or so far from them that their opponents have no room on the table for their racks. Finally, a few players seem to obtain great delight from twirling the board of a deluxe set around immediately after their opponents have made a play, causing the board to bump into their opponent's rack, spilling the tiles onto the floor. If you wish to be on good terms with your competitors, you should avoid all such behavior.

In a somewhat different category are women who compete in décolleté outfits. This does indeed happen. I have not yet heard any woman admit to doing this for the express purpose of harming her male opponent's play, but I think it fair to say that many of my male colleagues find the evidence overwhelming. It is unfair to categorize the wearing of such attire as an instance of bad etiquette, however. Philosophers have long realized that the idea of mind-body duality is illusive. Men can always counterattack by exposing their hairy chests or by playing suggestive words— neither of which is likely to be nearly as effective.

Cheating. There are numerous ways to cheat at SCRAB-BLE®, including feeling the tile surfaces inside the bag to increase the chances of picking a blank, looking into the bag, using word lists during play, picking excess tiles and storing some of them in your pockets for future play, purposely adding your score incorrectly to your advantage, and so forth. It is difficult to deal with cheating, since it is almost impossible to catch a cheater red-handed. No one wants to accuse someone falsely of cheating. On the other hand, players don't like being taken advantage of, either.

If you suspect your opponent of cheating, you are in a real bind. You can attempt to blot the thought from your mind and focus on playing well (very difficult in this circumstance), or you can watch your opponent like a hawk to prevent him from cheating in your game—in which case your own play is likely to suffer. It's a very difficult situation, and I don't really know which choice you should make. Fortunately, cheating at this game is a rare phenomenon. When it does occur, however, *everybody* knows about it, even if the cheater isn't caught. Word gets around fast. If you are an experienced player and you have cheated in the past and apparently gotten away with it, don't think that the other players are ignorant of your behavior. We know.

Board Orientation

According to the rules, you are entitled to turn the board to any position you prefer when it is your turn to play. Some players, however, find it unsettling if the board is turned during play. They may choose to play upside down so that turning the board is not necessary, or they may ask you to play sideways. Unless you have a lot of experience playing sideways, don't accede to this request, and don't feel guilty about your refusal. Your opponent may think you are being spiteful, but all you are doing is refusing to accept a handicap.

Sometimes an opponent who is used to playing sideways will want to sit to your right or your left, rather than opposite you, so that the board will appear sideways to him and right side up to you. This appears to require you to concede little, as both players seem to get what they want, but I find it even more distracting then playing sideways. The opponent is much closer to you than usual; as a result, you are likely to feel that your space is encroached upon. If you move away, which you will do almost instinctively, you will be looking at the board from an angle yourself, or bending your body sideways to maintain the visual right-side-up orientation, or tilting the board toward yourself and away from your opponent. Furthermore, if your opponent sits to your right and you are right-handed, or if your opponent sits to your left and you are left-handed, you will find that using your score sheet is awkward due to a lack of table space (if you tilt the board toward you) or due to the unaccustomed relation of your body to your score sheet. Not a big deal? For some players possibly not, but for others definitely yes.

If you are not used to playing directly opposite your opponent, with the board either right side up or upside down, I would suggest that you get used to it by playing many pretourney practice games. I would also suggest that you get into the habit of playing right side up rather than upside down. There are a number of experts who do in fact play upside down, and they claim that they are at least as adept with this orientation as they would be if they played right side up. My experience is that they have a slightly higher likelihood of playing two-letter words backwards (e.g., MO instead of OM; IX instead of XI) than do players who play right side up.

Time Pressure

Your success in tournament play will be affected considerably by how you handle time pressure. It is vitally important that you use your time as effectively as possible. If you play too quickly, you probably will make more mistakes than if you play a bit more deliberately. If you play too slowly, the consequences are likely to be even worse: you may overstep the time limit and be penalized as a result, or the necessity for you to play quickly in the endgame to keep from going over the limit may cause you to blunder. Try to pace yourself so that you have about five minutes on your clock when there are fewer than seven tiles in the bag. You can learn to do this by playing numerous pretournament practice games with the clock.

Most players squander time early in the game. The most common way of doing this is to spend five or six minutes looking for bingos that "should" be there. I would advise you not to invest such a large chunk of time for this purpose. If you cannot find a bingo within three minutes, it is extremely unlikely that you will find one within six.

Don't take a rest when it is your opponent's turn to play. You can save valuable minutes by making contingency plans during this time. Think about what you might do if your opponent plays in one sector of the board versus what you might do should she play elsewhere. If your opponent is using up a lot of time by playing slowly, you should be prepared to play even more quickly. By forcing her to think more or less exclusively on her own time, your quick play will contribute to her time trouble.

On the other hand, don't be intimidated by an opponent who plays at lightning speed. It is very easy to get caught up in the rhythm of quick play and to play faster than you should. Opponents who play quickly are experts at it. If you allow such an opponent to dictate the pace of the game, he is likely to play closer to his potential than you will to yours. The fast player may not play as well as he would if he took more time, but he usually plays rapidly better than his opponents play rapidly. I deal with what seems like excessively fast play by my opponent by letting at least a minute of time go by on my clock before moving, even if I know what I am going to do. Why rush? Maybe your opponent is dying to use the washroom. I vividly remember a game I played several years ago in which my opponent achieved a lead of 150 points after only five minutes of play. I then took some deep breaths to calm myself down, and deliberately slowed my play drastically. My opponent seemed to lose interest in the game, and I won it by a few points.

Poise

One of the dominant tournament SCRABBLE® players of the mid-1970s was Mike Senkiewicz. I played him only once, in my very first tournament. I lost the game, but what impressed me more than his play was his poise. He was remarkably still throughout the game. His eyes were focused entirely upon his rack or the board, and he seemed hardly to notice me. Both his board etiquette and his ability to concentrate were exemplary.

In contrast to this behavior, I think of my own performance at the 1980 Canadian Championship. This was a high-stakes tournament, as the top four finishers from a field of thirty-two players would qualify for an all-expense paid trip to the North American Championship to be held in Santa Monica the following month. I won the first seven games of the ten-game tournament, and then fell apart. I lost the next two games, and I would have failed to qualify had I lost my last game by more than 45 points.

My opponent in the final game was the late Reg Lever. Reg had been one of the finest players in Great Britain before he emigrated to Canada, but he was legally blind at the time of this tournament. There was a special high-intensity lamp next to the playing table to help him. Was I calm and collected, as Mike Senkiewicz had been against me? Not on your life. I was thinking about how awful it would be if I lost the game—to a blind person—and failed to qualify for the NAC. I relaxed a bit after achieving a 140-point lead, but Reg stormed back with two bingos and a 42-point play. When all of the tiles had been taken from the bag, he had a 5-point lead, the remaining blank, and it was his turn. I may not have looked like a mess, but that's what I was inside. I was perspiring a great deal, and I was unable to concentrate at all. I should have been thinking about the game situation. Instead, I was contemplating giving up tournament play forever. I felt helpless, as if my loss were preordained. I had played miserably over the preceding five or six turns and was about to get my just reward for doing so.

Fortunately for me, Reg chose this moment to play a phony, GILA. My mood brightened almost instantaneously. The challenge killed his winning chances, and my nightmare was over.

Although I have experienced similar moments of panic in tournament play since my game against Reg, I have gradually learned how to control myself better. The key to accomplishing this is to recognize and then combat the first symptoms of the problem. These symptoms include the standard physical indicants of anxiety (such as sweaty or clammy hands, difficulty in fine motor coordination, dryness of the throat, or shortness of breath) as well as the disruption of concentration. In this Game, panic-stricken players usually play either overcautiously or impulsively. Overcautious play reflects "SCRABBLE® paranoia," the unfounded belief that the opponent must have great tiles. Impulsivity, on the other hand, occurs because the afflicted player feels very uncomfortable and wants to end the game quickly. Overcaution is bad, but impulsive play can be especially damaging to your winning prospects.

A	B	C	D	E	F	G	H	I	J	K	L	M	N	O	
TWS			DLS				TWS				DLS			TWS	1
	DWS		W		TLS				TLS				DWS		2
		DWS	H			DLS		DLS				DWS			3
DLS			A				DLS				DWS			DLS	4
	W	R	I	N	G					DWS					5
	T	TLS		G	TLS				TLS				TLS		6
O		A		E		DLS		DLS				DLS			7
R	I	V	I	E	R	E					DLS			TWS	8
O		A				DLS		DLS				DLS			9
I		U	P		TLS				TLS				TLS		10
D		N	O				DWS								11
A		T	I				DLS				DWS			DLS	12
L	DWS					TLS		TLS				DWS			13
	DWS				TLS				TLS				DWS		14
TWS			DLS		TWS						DLS			TWS	15

Example #36

Opponent's rack   EOQRSTU

You should, of course, always try to play deliberately rather than impulsively. If you find a so-so play quickly, look for a better one. If you locate a good one, use a little more time to see if you can find a very good one. Example #36 comes from a club game that I played against a normally very fine player. She had in fact beaten me in each of the previous three games we had played. This particular game was the last of the session. We were both tired, and one of the reasons tiredness is so detrimental to good play is that, like anxiety, it fosters impulsive play: one just doesn't want to be bothered to look for the best play. My opponent played TORQUES (I2, 79 points) immediately after I had made my previous play, which was T⬛ROIDAL. Hers was a knee-jerk reaction play: she had planned it beforehand, and she didn't even look to see if my play had altered the board in a way that might have affected her choice. About ten seconds afterwards, she groaned horribly. She had noticed that TORQUES could have instead been played at A1 for 131 points! Too bad for her that she didn't take that extra ten seconds before making her play.

The impulsive blunder is very common among players. Another example is my TABORIN⬛, mentioned on page 150. I was so thrilled to find a bingo that I didn't even take the time to see if I had a better one. To me, the most comical form of blunder occurs when a player spends two or three minutes trying to decide between two possible plays, and then spots another play that he hadn't considered before. He makes this third play immediately, and soon afterwards usually rues his action.

There are a number of things you can do to develop good over-the-board poise. First, try to relax by using deep, slow breathing. Second, be sensitive to changes in your composure. If you know that you are falling apart, you may be more capable of limiting the damage than if you are unaware of this fact. You might then be able to make a conscious effort to restrain yourself from, for example, playing too hastily. Third, try not to allow a loss to affect your future play. It is very common for players to lose in streaks. This happens because once poise is lost it is hard to regain later in the same day. If you have blundered horribly, you may find it difficult to blot out that blunder after the game is over. Or you may think that if you have played poorly earlier in the day, there is nothing to prevent you from playing poorly throughout the tournament. Such thoughts are bound to interfere with good concentration.

To a considerable extent, good poise can only be developed from experience in tournament play. I mention this to cushion you from being disappointed if you don't do as well in your first few tournaments as you feel you should. The more time you invest in pretournament study and training, the greater will be the emotional burden you place on yourself to play well. You may think that you deserve to place well. For a few fortunate people this is in fact what happens, but most of us have to stumble through our first few competitions before we really know what is happening to us. Don't resent it if players who you know to be weaker than you are place higher than you do. This will happen less frequently as you develop more and more poise as a consequence of greater tournament experience.

9

Tournaments
Past and Present

North American tournament SCRABBLE® dates from 1973, the year that SCRABBLE® Crossword Game Players, Inc. was founded. The first officially sanctioned tournament by this subsidiary of Selchow and Righter was the Brooklyn Championship, held in the spring of that year. Five other tournaments took place in 1973, most of them in the northeastern part of the United States.

Tournament SCRABBLE® has grown enormously over the years. In 1984, sixty-six open tournaments were held throughout the United States and Canada. An additional two hundred or so club tournaments also took place. Whereas tournaments in earlier years were held almost exclusively in the northeastern United States, the Midwest (particularly Minnesota, Michigan, Ohio, and Indiana) is now the current hotbed of tournament activity. It accounted for 30 percent of all 1984 open tournaments. The Southwest was the second most active region (20 percent of all tournaments), followed closely by the New York–New Jersey metropolitan area.

Until 1978, the most important tournament of the year was the annual New York City Championship. This tournament, which was in reality the Brooklyn Championship renamed, attracted strong players from all over the Northeast. It was a gargantuan elimination tournament and involved up to nine qualifying weeks of play followed by quarterfinals, semifinals, and two weeks of round-robin finals among the twelve surviving players. In the mid-

160

1970s, it was not uncommon for this tournament to attract over a thousand contestants each year.

The North American SCRABBLE® Championships

By 1977, the growth of SCRABBLE® clubs and tournaments was sufficient to identify the best players throughout the United States and Canada. Selchow and Righter accordingly began making plans for the first North American Championship. Unlike the following North American Championships, this one had no qualifying rounds. Players were invited to participate on the basis of their previous tournament and club performances.

The North American Invitational SCRABBLE® Championship was held in New York City's Summit Hotel on May 19-21, 1978. Sixty-four players participated. Of these, no fewer than twenty-five were from New York City or its suburbs. Despite the fact that the tournament was won by David Prinz, a San Franciscan, the tournament was dominated by the New York players. They took ten of the top thirteen places, eleven if you take into consideration that Prinz was in fact a transplanted New York City tournament player. The native Californians also did quite well. The players from the Midwest were far and away the weakest. After she lost her first nine games, one of them decided to go sightseeing.

This tournament used a credit system rather than a won-lost record to determine player rankings. Three credits were awarded for a win, one was given for each 50 points scored, and one was given for each 50 points a player's score exceeded that of his opponent. For example, the winner of a 352-248 game earned twelve credits; three for winning, seven for total points scored, and two for outscoring his opponent by more than 100 but less than 150 points.

The credit system created a number of injustices. It overemphasized the big win, and in a field that was grossly uneven this meant that strong players who had the good fortune to play some of the weaker opponents benefitted more than did other strong players.

The credit system made it possible for a player to jump way up in the standings as a consequence of just one good result. My final standing was a case in point. I was forty-fifth after the next to last game, but I won my last game 503-195. The nineteen credits rocketed me up to twenty-fourth place.

The winner of this tournament should have been Daniel Pratt, then of Laurel, Maryland. He compiled a 13-3 won-lost record, far better than any of the other competitors. Prinz was only 10-6 by comparison, but some of his wins were by huge margins. One of his victories was by about 350 points. His opponent afterward lamented, "He played OUTSNORE, which I challenged. What kind of a word is that?"

The most emotional moment of the tournament came after the next to last game. Shazzi Felstein had just beaten Mike Senkiewicz, but it was she who had tears in her eyes. Reason? Mike was her boyfriend, and her victory crippled his chances of taking first place. He eventually finished third.

The second North American Championship was preceded by six elimination regional tournaments, one held in Toronto and five in the United States (San Francisco, New York City, Chicago, Baltimore, and Miami). These tournaments determined who would qualify for one of the thirty-two coveted places in the NAC. I won my regional in Toronto, but as I described in chapter 8, it was a harrowing experience.

The second NAC took place November 14-16, 1980, and was held at the Miramar-Sheraton Hotel in Santa Monica, California. As had been the case with the first NAC, a modified Swiss system was used to establish pairings among the competitors. However, there was one major difference: final placements were determined not by a credit system, but by won-lost record. The tournament consisted of seventeen games.

Once again, the strongest players were from California (specifically San Francisco and its environs) and New York

City. Jim Neuberger, then a lawyer from New York City, had dominated the tournament through its first fifteen games, winning thirteen times and usually by crushing margins. He needed only to win one of his last two games to claim first prize, which was increased from $1,500 in the 1978 NAC to $5,000. He came up short by the barest of margins: one draw, one loss. Jim's only competition at this point was Joe Edley, then a night watchman from San Francisco. Joe's record was 6-3 at one point in the tournament, but he won his remaining eight games. His last game was against Jim, and it was pretty much decided when Jim refrained from challenging Joe's phony, SALTANTS. SAL-TANT is in the *OSPD*, but it is an adjective. An unusual aspect of this tournament was that although Joe finished 14-3 to Jim's 13.5-3.5, Jim's cumulative point spread differential was almost 600 points greater than was Joe's. Under the rules of the 1978 NAC, Jim would have won this tournament easily.

As for me, I finished tenth. I actually would have finished much lower in the standings had it not been for a sparkling last game, which I won 589-332. Other competitors, friends, and family congratulated me, but inside I felt that I had not played as well as I should have. I had trained as thoroughly as any of the top finishers for the better part of a year. However, I did one very dumb thing. I spent the entire day before the tournament at Disneyland. Though I had a good time there, I would have been much smarter to stay at the hotel and rest. I returned to Montreal disappointed, but at least I learned something from the experience. Next time I would not treat such an important tournament as if it were a holiday.

The third NAC was held in August of 1983, at Chicago's Drake Hotel. Like the Santa Monica NAC, it was preceded by elimination tournaments. Mine was in Montreal the preceding February, and I won it in convincing style with a 13-1 record.

The Chicago NAC, like the one in Santa Monica, consisted of seventeen games and used won-lost record as the primary determinant of competitor placement. A new wrinkle was added, however. After ten games, the field was divided into quarters. The top eight players then played a round-robin against each other to determine the top eight places (though their performances in the first ten games still counted toward their ultimate placement), the second eight vied for ninth through sixteenth places, and so forth. The advantage of this system was that it eliminated the worst element of Swiss system pairings, which on occasion can result in a player doing well by playing poorly at the beginning of a tourney and then winning a succession of games against mediocre opposition. Its disadvantage was that it eliminated anyone who finished ninth or lower after ten games from the top eight places. Another disadvantage was that it put enormous pressure on about fifteen players in their ninth and tenth games.

My personal moment of crisis came in round 7, the first game of the second day. I had won four games the day before. Had I lost this one, I would have been back somewhere in the middle of the pack. Winning it would give me an excellent shot at making the top group of eight players.

Example #37

	A	B	C	D	E	F	G	H	I	J	K	L	M	N	O
1															
2		D						G							
3		R						N					E		
4		U		G				A	R		Q				
5		S		I				T		O		U		P	
6		E	R	E						O		I		E	
7			E	T			Y	A	K				S	A	
8	F	R	O	Z	E	A	V	O	W				E	V	
9			B		L	O	X	W	E	A	L	T	H	Y	
10			T		A	M	E	N				A			
11		P	A		M		L	O	C	I					
12		A	I		O			S		F	O	L	I	C	
13	R	I		N	N			H						U	
14	U		N					E						B	
15	E	T						D				J	E	E	R

Score	Me: 381	Charles: 379

My last play   DRUSE (B2, 21 points)

Charles' rack   GIIINT☐

My rack   DDS

My opponent was Charles Southwell, and the game was an exceedingly tight one. Two turns before the position shown in Example #37, I had blundered with CUBE (N12), allowing his JEER (15L, 57 points). Though I felt panic coming on, I was able to calm down and play DRUSE, by far the best play available with a rack of DDERSSU. I wasn't sure what Charles's tiles were, but I was fairly certain that he had the blank and an -ING bingo at 2C. It turned out that I was correct: he would have played IGNITING had my DRUSE not blocked him.

In the position shown above, Charles played GI[E]N (A1, 22 points), and it cost him the game. This play is a classic illustration of what can happen if one plays for points rather than to go out. I followed with DUD (13M, 16 points), he played IT (I13, 11 points), and I ended the game with REOBTAINS (C6, 14 points). When the dust cleared I had a 413-412 win. Had Charles played EDITING (2A), DIETING (2B), TIEING (14F) or NIGHT (13E), he would have won by playing out on his next turn.

After this win I calmed down and played a solid, deliberative game all day long. My play in the position shown in Example #38, from Round #8, was illustrative of this. My opponent was Ron Tiekert, unquestionably one of the Game's two or three greatest players.

	A	B	C	D	E	F	G	H	I	J	K	L	M	N	O
1				V			D					T	H	E	Y
2		J	O	I	N	T	E						U		
3			A	X			C				A	M	P		
4			R	E		E	E				G	U		C	
5				N	O		N				I		C		
6					V		T	F			O		E	L	
7				W	E	I	R	D	S					O	
8			C	R	I	E	R							U	
9			B			S	G							R	
10				I	F										
11				G	O										
12		I	K	O	N		N								
13		A	W	A	R	D									
14															
15															

Example #38

Score	Me: 217	Ron Tiekert: 269
My rack	AQSTTUY	

I was about to play QUASI (A8, 42 points). I lifted the tiles from my rack to do so, but then I intuitively felt that I had not examined my options sufficiently. I put the tiles back down, relaxed, took some deep breaths, and found SQUATTY (14F, 84 points). My poise turned out to be the difference between victory and defeat, for Ron afterward told me that had I not played SQUATTY he would have played SIZABLE in the same spot.

Though I won all six games I played on the second day of the NAC, going into the final day of competition I had only a slight lead over my two main rivals, Dan Pratt and Joe Edley. I lost my first game that day, falling back into second place, but then won my next two. Going into round 16, I was in the same position Jim Neuberger had been in in 1980: I needed a victory in one of my two remaining games for the championship. I was 12-3, Pratt was 11-4, and Edley was 10.5-4.5. My point spread differential was over 200 points greater than was Pratt's, however, so I was likely to take first place if the two of us ended up with the same won-lost record. As fate would have it, my final two opponents were Pratt and Edley, respectively.

I lost my game to Dan by 14 points. It wasn't as close as it sounds, however. At one point near the end of the game, Dan had a 117-point lead. I then played a 58-point play (YELKS) and a bingo (UNSWORN) on my following turn to avoid being routed. Joe had won his game, so any one of the three of us still had a chance to win going into the last game. A lot of money was riding on the final outcome, as prize money for the first three places was $5,000, $3,000, and $2,000, respectively.

I had formed a habit of returning to my room between games to rest up and regain my composure. On my way up after the loss to Dan, one of the reporters told me that when I had played YELKS I had missed a 110-point bingo: SKYLINE. (The game had been monitored by closed circuit TV to another room in the hotel.) This news didn't exactly raise my spirits. Still, I tried to blot it out of my mind so that I would play the last game decently.

I got off to a good start in my game against Joe. I bingoed on my second and third turns (SENORITA and STANDOUT) to take a 107-point lead, but drew seven vowels after STANDOUT and had to pass my tiles. Joe meanwhile played brilliantly, and managed to tie me at 218 points apiece. The game seesawed back and forth, and was decided only when Joe drew the Q. He was able to play it away, but for only 16 points. The final score was 369-342, and when it was over I felt as if God had been very good to me. I also felt a little sorry for Dan Pratt, who came in second for the second time in his three NAC attempts (he was fourth in 1980).

Selchow and Righter now plans to hold future NACs in the summers of odd-numbered years. Current plans are to enlarge the playing field to perhaps three hundred, and to lengthen the tournament so that it will consist of twenty-two games played over a four-day period.

Some Other Prominent Scrabble® Tournaments

What follows is an annotated listing of some of the more

prominent SCRABBLE® brand crossword game tournaments currently flourishing in North America. Many of these tournaments are located in vacation areas of the country, and if you are thinking of participating in a tournament as part of your vacation, this listing may be of particular value to you. Tournament specifics (dates, entry fees, whom to contact, etc.) vary from year to year for each tourney, and can be obtained by writing to SCRABBLE® Crossword Game Players. Most of the tournaments described below offer intermediate and/or novice divisions, and their open competitions all attract very strong fields.

Atlantic City. The tournament is one of the few offered in January, and it draws many of the strongest players from both the New York metropolitan area and the central Atlantic states. Placements are determined by credit system rather than by won-lost record. Tournament organizers schedule rounds so that the competitors will have some free time to take advantage of Atlantic City's attractions, and vice versa. The tournament has open, intermediate, and novice divisions, though intermediates are grouped with experts and are eligible for the top expert prizes. In 1984, eleven of the players who had competed in the 1983 NAC took part in this tourney.

New York City Championship. This granddaddy of all SCRABBLE® tournaments, though not as important as it once was, still attracts many of the strongest players from the New York metropolitan area. It is held over two consecutive weekends in early spring. The first weekend is devoted to preliminary and semifinal rounds, and a round-robin is held on the second weekend for the surviving finalists. In 1984, about one hundred competitors entered this tournament. Fourteen made it to the finals. This tournament does not have separate intermediate and novice divisions. You either play well or you are out.

Boston Championship. The Boston Championship takes place in mid-April at the Newton-Marriott Hotel. Due to very reasonable package rates for rooming and food, it has been extremely successful, drawing well over one hundred competitors in recent years. It has expert, intermediate, and novice divisions (experts and intermediates are grouped together, as in the Atlantic City tourney), and in 1984 featured a special superexpert round-robin tournament among the twelve top-rated players attending the tournament. This tourney employs a credit system for determining competitor placements. A very comfortable, pleasant tournament.

Montreal Open. The Montreal Open is held over the Memorial Day weekend so that Americans can participate more easily than otherwise might be the case. It has expert, intermediate, and novice divisions, and draws players from New England, the mid-Atlantic states, and Ontario, as well as from Montreal and its environs.

Caribbean vacation tournaments. These tournaments have been held annually since 1978 and are usually scheduled for late spring or early summer. Locations vary from year to year and have included Jamaica, Bermuda, the Bahamas (Nassau), Aruba, Antigua, and Acapulco. The entire vacation lasts about a week, and the tournament is usually scheduled over four successive days with plenty of time off for sunbathing, sightseeing, and so forth. The tournament features about fifteen rounds of play rather than the more typical ten, and does not have separate intermediate and novice divisions.

Cape Cod Fun Weekend. The Fun Weekend consists of three separate tournaments, each of which is five or six games long, held at a resort hotel on the Cape. Players can enter one, two, or all three tournaments if they wish, but only one tourney is a "normal" one. The others are a "pairs" tourney, in which players compete in teams of two rather than individually, and a "variations" tournament. The 1983 variations tournament featured "toroidal SCRABBLE®," in which it was legal to form a word that went "around the board." An example of such a play is ZONATE, 15M—O plus 15A—C. The Fun Weekend is held in early or mid October.

Grand Canyon Tournament. This tournament takes place in early November, and its main attraction is, of course, the magnificent scenery. Players come from all over North America to compete, and there are two divisions of play offered: open and recreational. This ten-game tournament allows plenty of time for sightseeing, and room rates are very reasonable.

In addition to the above offerings, the following tournaments are all held on a regular basis. They are well organized, efficiently run, moderate in cost, and attract good fields:

Location	*Time(s) of Year Held*
Abilene, Texas	June
Albuquerque, New Mexico	October, during the Albuquerque Balloon Festival; also April or May
Baltimore, Maryland	March
Birmingham, Alabama	Variable (has been held recently in January and October)
Catskill Mountains, New York	September
Chicago, Illinois	Unpredictable; two or three times a year
Cincinnati, Ohio	Unpredictable; two or three times a year
Cleves, Ohio	August
Dallas, Texas	April or July
Detroit, Michigan	June and November
Gettysburg, Pennsylvania	March
Glendale, Arizona	November

Gonzales, California	November
Houston, Texas	August
Huntsville, Alabama	June or August
Lafayette, Louisiana	February and early autumn
Lansing, Michigan	December
Lubbock, Texas	October
Marion, Indiana	October
Mesa, Arizona	January
Miami, Florida	May
Minneapolis, Minnesota	July
Oklahoma City, Oklahoma	Variable (has been held recently in June and October)
Port Huron, Michigan	May or June
Prichard, Alabama	September
Rochester, New York	April
Saginaw, Michigan	September
San Francisco, California	Late winter-early spring
Toronto, Ontario	Autumn
Washington, D.C.	April or May
Wichita, Kansas	May
Xenia, Ohio	February

Dates given are approximate and are subject to change. Consult SCRABBLE® Crossword Game Players, Inc. for current information on these tournaments.

PART IV

Annotated Games

The games included in this section were all played by expert SCRABBLE® brand crossword game players. Some of these games were beautifully played, others less well. All the games were played under strict time limitations; and, as a result, mistakes in complicated positions or in the endgame were quite common. Still, there were some remarkably good plays, as you shall see.

In order to benefit as much as possible from these games, I suggest that you get out your SCRABBLE® set and play along. If you wish, you can instead use a blank board diagram and a pencil. (Score sheets with blank board diagrams on them can be obtained from SCRABBLE® Crossword Game Players.) For each move, cover up both the portion of the page showing the player's move and the commentary below it. Now allow yourself two minutes to find a play. After this time has elapsed, write down your play. Then study the situation for a few more minutes. In many instances you will discover plays that are better than your original ones. This exercise will give you a feeling for how difficult it is to make the best play under time pressure. Try also to track tiles and to use the information gained from your tile tracking to help you choose your plays.

Only after you are satisfied that you have gotten as much out of the situation as you are going to (assuming you are that patient) should you uncover the player's move and my commentary below it. Then add the play to your board, and proceed to the next move. This approach will force you to *participate.* You may learn many new words and improve your strategy from studying my commentary, but it is actively searching for the best move that will most improve your game.

Unlike the examples presented in Part II of this book, many of the positions in these games have no clear-cut solutions. In such positions I have tried to show how competing moves that are about equally good attempt to fulfill the same priorities, or how they may differ in terms of their strengths and weaknesses.

The Best Play Percentage

I have calculated at the end of each game a *best play percentage* for the competitors. A player's best play percentage can be determined from the following formula:

$$\text{best play percentage} = \frac{\text{number of best plays made}}{\text{total number of plays made}}$$

A *best play* is one in which the move made is as good or better than any of the other possible alternatives. I have categorized other plays as either *good plays* or out-and-out *mistakes*. A good play is one that is definitely, but only slightly, inferior to the turn's best play. Good plays are scored as half a best play. Plays that are neither best nor good are mistakes, and of course do not contribute at all to increasing the numerator in the above formula.

Plays consist of both moves and challenge situations. With regard to challenges, a challenger's successful challenge is categorized as a best play for the challenger and a mistake for the other player—unless allowing the phony to stand is even more to the challenger's advantage than is challenging. Similarly, in most cases a challenger's unsuccessful challenge or failure to challenge a phony is considered a mistake. Also, phonies are eligible to be considered best plays, but only if they are not challenged and if there are no equally good or better nonphony plays.

There are some limitations to this rating system. First, the system is only as good as the annotator. It is possible

that at times I may not have fully appreciated all the good
qualities of a player's move. On the other hand, I may have
inflated a player's best play percentage by overlooking
other better moves. I may even have been biased at times—
I was a player in a number of these games, and perhaps I
was not as hard on myself as I should have been. Second,
individual games vary greatly in difficulty from one to
another. In some games, a player may have few options and
as a result make a lot of best plays that are relatively easy to
find. In others, a player may miss a number of very difficult
finds in complex situations. Third, the system does not fully
take into account how bad a mistake really is. It is one thing
to make a run-of-the-mill mistake, and it is another to make
a totally catastrophic blunder. Fourth, some plays are more
crucial than others. My system doesn't fully reflect the true
playing strength of players who are great when they need to
be but who play more sloppily at less important junctures of
the game.

Despite these inadequacies, the best play percentage
gives you at least some idea of how close to perfection each
of the competitors came. You will also see that this crossword game is only marginally a game of luck, as in all but
the last of these eight games the player with the higher best
play percentage was the winner.

Game # 1: Michael Spencer versus Joel Wapnick

1983 North American Championship, Chicago: Round 3

This game had an interesting psychological aspect to it.
Since 1980, I had been generally considered to be the best
player in Canada. This reputation was based on winning
every Canadian tournament I played in. My competition
included all the strongest players from Ontario and Quebec,

but not from the rest of Canada. I had done well in strong tournaments in the United States, whereas players from western Canada had barely begun to enter such tournaments.

Mike Spencer is from Vancouver. He qualified for the NAC by coming in second to Joe Edley in the San Francisco Tier IV tournament. This result surprised many of us in the east, as we had barely heard of him previously. His club had been in existence for only about a year, and he was very much the "new kid on the block." In Chicago, he was out to prove that he was the best Canadian player. He badly wanted to play me—and beat me. Of course, none of this was verbalized; I sensed it from his demeanor toward me at the reception the night before the beginning of the tournament, and from the grim, unsmiling, and determined look on his face just before our game began. I must add that I came to like him considerably more after I got to know him a little than I did at the outset of this game. In addition, his Game table manners were exemplary. At the beginning of this game, however, I was not kindly disposed to him at all. I was very intent on preventing him from beating me. Some people may regard this as a helpful "motivating factor." In SCRABBLE® however, anything that distracts you from concentrating on the game hurts. There were a number of poor plays in this game, and part of the reason was probably that we both wanted to win so badly.

Move		*Rack*	*Play*	*Points*	*Total*
1.	**Spencer**	AAEPTVZ	ZAP, H7	28	28

ZETA is 2 points less, uses one tile more. It is weaker than ZAP, however, as it leaves 2 high-point tiles on the rack that do not go together particularly well. This is not normally a major consideration, but with other factors about equal it makes ZAP a better bet.

	Wapnick	ADELNRU	UPLANDER, 9G	64	64

My other bingo possibilities were PENDULAR (9H), UNDER-LAP (9A), and LURDANE (G8). I rejected the other eight-letter bingos because they both permitted potential triple-triple responses as well as made it easy for Mike to use the opened triple word scores. Although LURDANE scores 3 points more than UPLANDER, it allows a high-scoring response from H12 to H15. However, it does not allow the big x play at J10 that is available after UPLANDER. The two plays are approximately equally good, and my choice of UPLANDER was based on stylistic preferences more than anything else. I like wide-open games, and UPLANDER opened up the board somewhat more than LURDANE would have. There was also a slight chance that UPLANDER might have been challenged. LURDANE never would have been, for though it is an unusual word it is known by expert players as the alternative to LAUNDER.

2.   **Spencer**   AEEINTV   VENETIAN, K2   72   100
Fine play, serving notice that I was playing no pushover. Also very frustrating, as I was preparing to play UNGREEDY at K8.

   VENETIAN at K7 would have opened a second -s hook along a triple word square alley. The idea behind such a placement is that I would have to leave at least one -s hook open after my next play. As I mentioned earlier, I am somewhat leery about creating these "two-for-one" situations, since the opponent gets first crack at the more lucrative opening.

   Wapnick   DEEGRUY   GURNEY, 4H   24   88
Characteristic of my play in Chicago was my ability to find the second best play on those turns where I missed the best play. Better than GURNEY is GYRENE, 4G. The rack leave of DE after GURNEY is better than DU following GYRENE, but this slight difference is more than offset by GYRENE's additional 4 points and the absence of the B or M hook at 3M, which exists following GURNEY. In addition, two US have already been played, lowering the probability of picking another U after GYRENE to a very acceptable risk level. As it turned out, however, I picked one!

   Plays such as GREEDY or GREYED (3I) are inferior because

the EU leave may subject one to a surfeit of vowels on the rack.

3. **Spencer** ABINTV☐ VIB[R]ANT, A10   67   167
A nice play, though not the best. Mike's move indicated to me that his word knowledge was not perfect. VIBRANT is a noun as well as an adjective, and the best play is VIBRANT[S], N6. This move scores an additional 5 points and is far superior defensively.

Example #39

Wapnick DDEGSLU   SLUDGED, O9   98   186
I was in dire straits here, and I did something that I do not recommend: I played a word that I knew was phony against an expert player. Had I lost this challenge, the likelihood is that I would not have simply lost the game. I would have been buried.

Nevertheless, I felt confident that I would not be challenged. SLUDGED sounds plausible. In addition, Mike accepted my first two plays, which were not the most common of words, with no hesitation whatsoever. Finally, having realized that Mike did not know VIBRANTS, I assumed that his dictionary knowledge would not be sufficient to know with certainty that SLUDGED was no good.

SLUDGED was one of only three phonies that I played in the seventeen-game tournament.

4.   **Spencer**   EGOOOQW   WOVE, A8   30   197
Good play, as it scored well and took the dangerous triple word square at A8. Three US were already played, but perhaps the Q could be placed at I3 next turn.

Wapnick   BCMOORT   COOMBE, 14J   36   222
I felt that I was on a roll now, and that I was really clever to find COOMBE. It was the second best move, however. The best is the 106-point crusher MOBOCRAT, E4.

5.   **Spencer**   GIOOQRR   pass 7 tiles   0   197
Scoring no points on a turn is always a serious setback. With the Q spot at I3 still open, I would probably play GORY (M1, 16 points) or VIGOR (2K, 18 points) instead.

Wapnick   HJKRTU □   JAUK, E9   30   252
Exhibiting both careless and one-dimensional thinking. The move was careless in that it dispensed with the last U though the Q had not been played. It was one-dimensional in that I focussed solely on ridding myself of the J and K so as to improve my bingo chances next turn. Much better would be HAJ (J8). It does not block potential bingo alleys through the R and A of VIBRANT, prevents Mike from possibly making a big X play, and scores 4 more points than JAUK.

6.   **Spencer**   ACIIOSY   ICKY, 12C   26   223
It's a toss-up between this play and COSY (13C), COYS, or CAYS (both at 13B). COSY and COYS score 8 more points, use one more tile, but burn the S and leave a very uncomfortable AII on the rack. With only one S played and a blank still unaccounted for, I would have taken the 8 extra points.

Wapnick   EHHRST □   THY, M2   18   270
Dreadful play. One of my weaknesses is an inability to find bingos containing only two vowels in them, such as

THRESHED or THRASHED at 12H. In addition, THY blocked the s hook at N4 and opened a dangerous column which my opponent overlooked on his next move. The best nonbingo play is probably HAH (J8).

7. **Spencer** AAFIOST AFTOSA, 11G 21 244
Much better is FOIST (N1) for 36 points. In view of this possibility, OAF (13A, 22 points) is an unjustifiable rack balancing and fishing play.

    Wapnick DEEHRS□ HEDGE, H1 30 300
Also good are FLESH and FREED (H11). My preference for HEDGE is based upon the fact that it opens the board more for an eight-letter bingo than do the H11 plays. A minor consideration is that the double-letter squares at 13G and 13I do not become available to Mike.

    Also worth consideration are HERD (12L, 26 points) and HEED (15L, 29 points). These plays leave the board relatively closed, and with a 50 plus point lead some players might prefer to limit their opponent's bingo opportunities rather than increase their own. Note, however, that the board is not completely shut off to bingos after these plays: column B and row 5 remain open.

Example #40

8.   **Spencer**   EEIIIIP   TIPI, 6K   8   252

An extremely uninspired play. PIED (15L, 25 points) would be much better, and the same is true of EVITE (2J, 20 points). Both plays result in horrid rack leaves, however. If you're in the lead or about even, PIED is probably best. Mike was 56 points behind. In this situation, passing has to be considered a reasonable alternative to PIED (though I still would have taken the 25 points).

 Wapnick   NNRRST☐   BRIT, C10   12   312

Perhaps slightly better is BRIN (C10), which undoubles the NS on the rack and provides E and G hooks instead of the T hook after BRIT.

9.   **Spencer**   EEIIRRT   RIM, M12   10   262

Dismal. At least play RIME and undouble the E. The best plays are FIRER and FRIER (H11), with a preference for FIRER since it minimizes the importance of the double-letter squares at 13G and 13I.

 Wapnick   IONNRS☐   R☐ISONNE, 2A   68   380

Finally! A better play than at 5A: with the X not yet played, the 5A play dangerously opens up the triple letter score at F6.

10.   **Spencer**   AEEIORT   ETA, 1A   18   280

The triple word score at A1 is less dangerous than it looks. Higher scoring, and more useful for curing his vowelitis, is FERIA (H11).

```
     A   B   C   D   E   F   G   H   I   J   K   L   M   N   O
 1   E   T   A   .   .   .   .   H   .   .   .   .   .   .   .
 2   R   A   I   S   O   N   N   E   .   V   T   .   .   .   .
 3   .   .   .   .   .   .   .   D   .   E   E   .   .   .   .
 4   .   .   .   .   .   .   .   G   U   R   N   E   Y   .   .
 5   .   .   .   .   .   .   .   E   .   S   .   .   .   .   .
 6   .   .   .   .   .   .   .   .   .   T   I   P   I   .   .
 7   .   .   .   .   .   Z   .   .   .   I   .   .   .   .   .
 8   W   .   .   .   .   A   .   A   .   .   .   .   .   .   .
 9   O   .   .   J   .   .   U   P   L   A   N   D   E   R   S
10   V   I   B   R   A   N   T   .   .   .   .   .   .   .   .
11   E   R   U   .   A   F   T   O   S   A   .   .   .   .   U
12   .   .   I   C   K   Y   .   .   .   .   .   R   .   .   D
13   .   .   T   .   .   .   .   .   I   .   .   .   .   .   G
14   .   .   .   .   .   .   .   .   .   C   O   O   M   B   E
15   .   .   .   .   .   .   .   .   .   .   .   .   .   .   D
```

Example #41

Wapnick   EFGLMOS   FLOG, H11   9   389

With seven tiles in the bag, I felt that this was my best shot
at avoiding the Q while retaining excellent scoring chances.
GOLEMS (O1, 37 points) would have just about assured me of
picking the Q if Mike did not already have it. I did not see
FOES (N1, 34 points), GLOM (3B, 29 points), or GEM (3A, 28
points) all of which would have been very acceptable plays.
Even if I had seen them, however, I still would have played
FLOG. Given that I was in no danger of losing, the sacrifice
of as much as 25 points was worth the retention of a tremendous threat. Besides, the sacrifice was actually less
than 25 points, given that I was guaranteed a minimum of
27 points on my next turn. This would not have been the
case had I played FOES, GLOM, or GEM.

Another advantage of FLOG was that it took the H11-15
play away from Mike.

11.   **Spencer**   AEEINOR   OARED, 12K   18   298

ROARED (12J) and AERO (2A) can be dismissed because they
empty the bag, increasing Q jeopardy. On the other hand,
they increase the probability of picking the x if I do not
already have it. (However, in this case, picking the Q is more
detrimental than picking the x is beneficial.) EVITE (2J) is

about as good as OARED, and certainly cannot be considered particularly dangerous in light of the setup created by my last move.

Mike might also have tried to block me by playing YIN or YON (F12). The loss of 10 points versus OARED might appear to be a bargain for him, but this is difficult to assess since there is no guarantee that (1) I would have a blockbuster play along row 15 or that (2) I would not have a big play available elsewhere.

Wapnick	AEFLMQS	FLAMS, 15D	69	458

Making my previous play look like a stroke of genius.

12.	**Spencer**	EIINRWX	REX, B12	0	298
		RICKY *challenged*		

A result of desperation and exhaustion. I do not think Mike would have tried this phony at the beginning of the game.

Wapnick	EOQ	VET, 2K	6	464

Setting myself up for VETO next turn.

13.	**Spencer**	EIINRWX	WE, 15L	24	322

The order of Mike's plays is of little consequence, as I cannot significantly affect the board. WE is one of the best plays here; as we shall see, EX (15K) would not make optimal use of the x.

Another possibility is to play ERE (5F), but I could then block the x spot with OE, F4. In any event, the continuation recommended below scores more points.

Wapnick	OQ	VETO, 2K	14	478

14.	**Spencer**	IINRX	SIX, D2	20	342

A waste of points. Best is SI (D2, 2 points), followed by XI (4D, 38 points), WOVEN (A8, 12 points), and ROARED (12J, 9 points).

Wapnick	Q	*pass*	0	478

15.	**Spencer**	INR	IN, E4	13	355
	Wapnick	Q	*pass*	0	478

16. **Spencer**   R   OR, 13H   3
                          plus Q x 2 = 20   378

BEST PLAYS
  Spencer: Turns 1, 2, 4, 5, 6, 11, and 13.
  Wapnick: Turns 1, 3, 7, 9, 10, 11, 12, and 13.

GOOD PLAYS
  Spencer: Turn 3.
  Wapnick: Turns 2 and 8.

BEST PLAY PERCENTAGES
  Spencer: 7.5 ÷ 17 (7.5 out of 16 moves, 1 missed challenge), 44 percent.
  Wapnick: 10 ÷ 14 (9 out of 13 moves [turns #14 and #15 not counted as best plays or mistakes], plus 1 correct challenge), 71 percent.

Game # 2: Stephen Fisher versus Joel Wapnick

1983 North American Championship, Chicago: Round 14

This was a crucial game for me. On the day before, I had won six games without a loss. As a result, I finished the day in undisputed first place with a 10-2 record. However, I lost my first game the following morning (the last day of the tournament) and slipped back to second place. I played that game poorly and afterwards was feeling nervous and shaky.

Stephen Fisher is a special opponent for, like me, he is from Montreal. We have played hundreds of games against each other over the last several years. He is a very strong player (his remarkable tournament record was further enhanced by a fourth place finish in Chicago), and in a number of tournaments we have played in together, he finished higher than I. However, in all six tournament games we have played against each other, I have been the victor. Almost every game was important and in many cases determined which of us would finish first. In fact, had he won both of our games in Chicago rather than lost them, he probably would have won the tournament. Before this game I did not feel confident. I felt that the law of averages was about to catch up with me.

Move		Rack	Play	Points	Total
1.	**Fisher**	EEGIRRU	GUIRE, 8D	0	0
			challenged		

Normally, when an expert player plays a phony word against another expert, he wants the word to be challenged. Such a situation may arise if the first player has no seven-letter bingo but his tiles combine with many other tiles to form an eight-letter word. I took a while to challenge this word, not because I thought it might be good, but because I was trying to determine why Stephen played it. His tiles combine only with an F to form REFIGURE, but of course I did not know that at the time.

	Wapnick	AAENPSU	PAEAN, 8D	20	20

APNEA (8H) is a little safer, as it does not place a vowel adjacent to the double letter squares. However, the additional four points for PAEAN more than offsets the danger, especially as Stephen's last move gave me a good indication that he would not be able to take advantage of the double letter scores at 7G and 9G.

2.	**Fisher**	EEGIRRU	PURGER, D8	18	18

Other things being equal, it is generally best to try to avoid leaving more vowels than consonants on your rack. So PUGREE (D8) is a better play than PURGER. My preference is REARGUE (E6), however, as it uses one more tile than either of the other words.

	Wapnick	EGLQSTU	QUEST, 14A	38	58

A fascinating position! In addition to the play made, the

following Q-plays are worth considering: QUEST at F6 and
9C (36 and 32 points, respectively), SEQUEL at F4 (35 points),
and SQUEG at I8 and F5 (33 and 35 points, respectively).
TUQUE (9A) does not spend the S, but is inferior to the other
plays as it dangerously allows access to triple word squares
and scores only 26 points.

I wish I could say that I saw all these possibilities during
the game and as a result of careful deliberation selected
QUEST. Actually, my eyes were riveted to the -s hook at 14D. I
nevertheless still believe that my play was at least as good
as any of the others. It scores more points than the alternatives, plays away as many or more tiles, and is not particularly dangerous. The best defensive play is SQUEG (I8), however, as it takes away the more dangerous of the -s hook
locations and makes the board relatively inhospitable for
bingos. SQUEG does give up a not inconsiderable 5 points,
however, and for this reason I believe that QUEST is slightly
better.

3.　**Fisher**　DEEILOR　　REOILED, 9F　67　85
A very nice find, typical of strong expert play.
　　Wapnick　GLMORTY　　ORGY, 8K　31　89
A must. This play uses a dangerous opening and outscores
all other potential plays (ORGY, 15E; MOLLY, J6) by a consid-
erable margin.

4.　**Fisher**　ACHNTU☐　CHAUNT[R]Y, O1　0　85
　　　　　　　　　　　challenged
A typically artful phony from Stephen. I knew that CHANT,
CHAUNT, CHANTER, CHAUNTER, and CHANTRY were all in the
OSPD, but was unsure about CHAUNTRY. I had great trepi-
dation about challenging, especially as I could see that
Stephen had other unblockable bingo possibilities. I figured
that I would lose for certain if I let Stephen get his 95 points
for this play, however, so I took my chances.
　　Wapnick　AALMTTY　　AMYL, 15E　29　118
Another easy choice for me, as there are no good competing
moves.

Example #42

5.   **Fisher**   ACHNTU☐, ⓈTAUNCHER, F1   71   156

I am sure that he would have played the much safer CHAUN-
TERⓈ (F2, 71 points) had he known it. Also to be considered
is ⓊNCAUGHT (N3, 67 points). This play prevents bingos
down columns M, N, and O. Also, an eight-letter bingo
through its available tiles is less likely than an eight-letter
bingo through the tiles of CHAUNTERⓈ. CHAUNTERⓈ is cen-
trally located on the board so that its available tiles can
serve as the first, second, third, fourth, fifth, or sixth letter of
an eight-letter play. The tiles in ⓊNCAUGHT, however, must
be either the seventh or eighth letters of such a bingo.
ⓊNCAUGHT is therefore better defensively, but its 4-point
sacrifice versus CHAUNTERⓈ makes the two plays toss-ups.

   Wapnick   AEFSSTT   FASTEST, 1D   39   157

I couldn't play the bingo FASTEST, so I played FASTEST
instead. Nothing else is close to this play: good score, occu-
pies a dangerous opening, great rack leave.

6.   **Fisher**   AEEGLOW   AGLOW, 2J   26   182

The J has not yet shown and since before AGLOW there is no
really good place for it, AGLOW is a little bit dangerous: it
allows a potential J play from 1M to 1O. Here I would have
sacrificed 4 points and played GEEGAW (11D), as this play

also balances the rack better. The two plays are about
equally good, however.

Other plays such as GLOWER (M3, 22 points), AREOLE
(13C, 21 points), and WEEL (C12, 23 points) are second-rate,
as they neither score nor balance the rack as well as AGLOW.

    Wapnick ACINSVX   TAX, G1   37   194
VINCA (7I, 24 points) retains the x as well as the s, but the
sacrifice of 13 points versus TAX is too severe a penalty.

7.   **Fisher**   BDEEEOT   BREED, 13C   31   213
Better is BETAXED (3C, 38 points). This word would be better
known if it were a past tense rather than an adjective.
Someone may be BETAXED, but cannot BETAX someone else.

    Wapnick CDINSOV   OVOID, M2   18   212
I overlooked the -v hook at 3J. VOID (3J, 33 points) is a far
superior and more beautiful play.

```
     A   B   C   D   E   F   G   H   I   J   K   L   M   N   O
 1                   F   A   S   T   E   S   T                       1
 2                       T   A       A   G   L   O   W               2
 3                       A   X                           V           3
 4                       U                               O           4
 5                       N                               I           5
 6                       C                               D           6
 7                       H                                           7
 8               P   A   E   A   N               O   R   G   Y       8
 9               U   R   E   O   I   L   E   D                       9
10               R                                                  10
11               G                                                  11
12               E                                                  12
13           B   R   E   E   D                                      13
14   Q   U   E   S   T                                              14
15               A   M   Y   L                                      15
     A   B   C   D   E   F   G   H   I   J   K   L   M   N   O
```

Example #43

8.   **Fisher**   EIILOTV   VIGIL, 11B   18   231
Only God knows the best play in this position. Here are
some alternatives to Stephen's play:

Play	Score	Rack Leave	Comments
VIOLENT, 5A	20	I	Plays away six tiles, which is very desirable given that one blank and two ss are unseen; nevertheless, a somewhat dangerous play due to the openings created down column A. Also, with five is still in the bag or on opponent's rack, picking six tiles to an I almost guarantees multiple is on the next rack.
VIOLIN, 5A	18	ET	The same dangers as VIOLENT, but an ideal rack leave is well worth the 2-point sacrifice.
EVIL, H3	21	IOT	The best scoring play, though not by much over many other options. A safe play, as it minimizes the probability of opponent playing a bingo anywhere along rows 4, 5, and 6 (e.g., through the N and C in STAUNCHER or through the O, I, and D in OVOID). Only plays away four tiles, though, and keeps an I.
FIVE, D1	20	ILOT	Not as good as EVIL: scores less, doesn't block as well, plays

			away only three tiles, and still retains an ı.
ETUI, 4D	19	IOLV	Leave is not too bad on this board, though big plays next turn are unlikely due to the low tile turnover.
IVIED, 6I	17	LOT	Succeeds in getting rid of both ıs and the v, but sacrifices a few points versus other plays to accomplish this.
VIOLET, J6	19	IL	Creates an -s hook, but in a relatively safe location. Otherwise, very good defensively, as it partially blocks rows 5, 6, 11, and 12.
VILLI, J6	18	EOT	Scores the same and yields the same leave as Stephen's VIGIL, but does not block plays from 12F.
OGIVE, 11C	18	ILT	Just as safe as VIGIL, and better protects against vowelitis. VOGIE (11B) is very slightly worse, as it allows counterplay along column B.
IOLITE, 12G	17	V	Sacrifice of points is more than made up for by maximum tile turnover, and no ıs left on the rack. Blocks bingos along rows 11 and 12, and through the L in column J. Its

only real drawback is
retention of the v.

Wapnick   ACIINPS   PECAN, K8   29   241
I had been fixating on playing PISCINA (12F), and after
Stephen blocked my opening I did not even bother to look for
other bingo possibilities. One is CAPSICIN (6A, 66 points), a
word I knew at the time.

9.   **Fisher**   EHMNOOT   MHO, L4   32   263
Creates the phony MO, which neither of us noticed until it
was pointed out after the game was over! I was so busy
looking for a bingo at the time that I hardly looked up from
my rack. Better than Stephen's play is MONTH (L11, 36
points).
   Both of us were in considerable time trouble by this stage
of the game, and some of our next moves reflected this.

Wapnick   EIIKNS☐   INKINE⒮S, 12G   77   318
I saw no reason not to take the extra points instead of
playing SKINNIE⒭ at either 12H or 5C (74 and 72 points,
respectively). SKINNIE⒭ at 5C defends against future bingos, but given the number of high-point letters in the
remaining tile pool, it seemed unlikely that another bingo
would be played. I was more concerned with preventing a
high-scoring J or Z play.

10   **Fisher**   DEFJNOT   OF, 1N   20   283
TED (N4, 28 points) not only scores more and gives Stephen
a greater chance of picking the z and the remaining s, it also
eradicates the unsightly phony from the board.

Wapnick   BINORRW   BISON, N10   26   344
The purpose of this move was to deprive Stephen of the
opportunity to play the J or Z at N10 in combination with the
double word score at N14. I made a mistake tracking tiles,
however. I mistakenly categorized the ⒮ in INKINE⒮S as an
s rather than as a blank. I thought that play along row I5
was closed off, and was I surprised when I drew what I momentarily thought was a fifth s after making this play!

The N10-14 spot must be closed off, and for that reason I would recommend wos (N10, 14 points). This move retains tiles for BRUIN (4D) or BROWN (5B) next turn.

11. **Fisher**   DEEIJNT   JINN, 5C   22   305
He saved the last D for a hook play at 5B. He could have gotten right back in the game had he seen INJECTED (6B, 69 points), however.

Wapnick   EIRRSUW   WISE, 15L   41   385
With one tile in the bag, Stephen had seven of the following eight tiles: A, D, E, E, O, T, T, Z. Had those tiles been bingo-conducive, I would have played REWAX (3C, 30 points) to block the remaining bingo alley.

12. **Fisher**   ADEEOTZ   ADZ, B4   46   351
Leaving an -E hook for his next play. Better for reducing his losing point-spread differential would have been TEE (N4, 22 points). If I responded with JUT (C5, 13), Stephen could then play out with DIAZO (J11, 38 points). If I instead played TAR (11J, 7 points), he could then play ADZ at B4, and I would play with FUR. In both scenarios he loses by fewer than thirty points. In the game, he lost by 38.

Wapnick   RRTU   THIR, 5K   14   399
Since I could not block his set-up, I played for the maximum number of points possible on this and the next turn combined.

13. **Fisher**   EEOT   TEE, 7A   18   369
Wapnick   RU   FUR, D1   6
One point better was RUE, O13.

plus O x 2 = 2   407

BEST PLAYS
Fisher: Turns 3, 6, and 13. In fairness to Stephen, many of the best plays he overlooked were very difficult finds.
Wapnick: Turns 1, 2, 3, 4, 5, 6, 9, 11, and 12.

GOOD PLAYS
Fisher: Turns 2, 8, and 12.
Wapnick: Turn 13.

BEST PLAY PERCENTAGES
Fisher: 4.5 ÷ 13 (4.5 out of 13 moves, no challenges made), 35 percent.
Wapnick: 11.5 ÷ 15 (9.5 out of 12 moves, 2 correct challenges, 1 missed opportunity to challenge a phony), 77 percent.

Game # 3: Michael Wise versus Michael Schulman

1980 North American Championship, Santa Monica, California

The two competitors in this game were both from Toronto. They were very familiar with each other's strengths and weaknesses at the time this game was played, and as we shall see, Mike Wise made use of this knowledge to help win this game.

Although the game was not particularly well played by either player, it certainly was exciting. Schulman took a sizable lead into the endgame on the strength of his three early bingos. Wise then played particularly well, and Schulman, probably because he was under extreme time pressure, became completely unglued. The game's culmination was both spectacular and sorrowful.

Mike Wise finished twelfth in the tournament, and Mike Schulman finished twenty-first.

Move		Rack	Play	Points	Total
1.	**Wise**	AUHJTYZ	HAZY, 8G	38	38

THUJA (8D, 32 points) is reasonable, but HAZY is definitely

better. In addition to the extra six points, it does not provide an -s hook for the opponent.

    Schulman ABEGINS   BEY, J6   14   14
His bingo SABEING is not playable. But Schulman's play is inferior to a number of alternatives, including BHANG (G7, 15), which does not leave the O- hook at 5J; BINGE (9C, 18 points); BEGAN (9D, 17 points); BAIZE (I5, 18 points); and what I believe is the best available play, BAYING (J6, 20 points). BAYING maximizes the point count, plays away five tiles, and results in a great rack leave. Schulman apparently preferred to fish for a bingo. The main intention of his move was to retain the ING combination and the s on his rack. Bad strategy, even though in this instance it paid off for him two moves later.

2.   **Wise**   FJOPTUW   JOW, 5I   35   73
Making good use of the O- hook. There is no plausible competing play.

    Schulman ADGGINS   ZAG, I8   14   28
He erred by sacrificing a hefty 18 points in order to retain INGS. Much, much better would be GADIS, DINGS, or DANGS (L1, 32 points). Of the three, my preference is GADIS. It is the only move that gets rid of both vowels and places the G rather than the D on row 1. The G is less dangerous because the D might allow Wise to place an E before it and lucratively play away a number of tiles while forming a word in the past tense.

    Inferior to GADIS, DINGS, and DANGS are the four-letter plays such as GIGS, GAGS, DAGS, and DIGS (L2, 26 points). These plays are good defensively in that they do not open row 1 for the opponent and they do not permit a potentially high-scoring Q play from 2J to 2N or 2O, but these aspects do not compensate for the loss of 6 points and the opportunity to pick one more tile.

3.   **Wise**   EFIPRTU   FRUG, F10   16   89
Wise noticed that Schulman was fishing, so he tried to block the -s hook while developing his own rack. Because of the

hook at L5, it is impossible to totally eliminate Schulman's opportunities. Wise's play did prevent Schulman from playing a bingo ending in -s, however, and bingos ending in -s are much more common than bingos which contain an s anywhere else in the word.

Other plays that are about equally good are FIGURE (10G, 12 points), PURGE (10F, 16 points), UPGIRT (10G, 11 points), and PEWIT (K3, 16 points). I would have played FIGURE for the additional tile turnover minus the -s hook that UPGIRT would have created at 11G. THIEF (G7, 16 points) unnecessarily opens up the triple letter score at F10.

Schulman ADGINNS   SANDING, 11I   82   110
After sacrificing a total of 24 points over the last two turns (if he had played BAYING and GADIS), he got lucky and drew a playable bingo. His placement is better than placement at L5, as the 7 additional points are more than sufficient compensation for giving his opponent a shot at the O8 and O15 triple word squares.

4.   **Wise**   EEINOPT   PINGO, O8   27   116
PENGO (O8) beats PINGO in that it undoubles the ES. Better still, however, are PEEING (O6, 27 points) and EPIGON (O8, 30 points). EPIGON is a little more dangerous, as it creates -S and -E hooks at 14O, and allows potential plays of EPIGONES and EPIGONUS (O8, 33 points). EPIGON provides the better leave, however (ET instead of OT).

Schulman CDEEOOO   DECODE, L7   22   132
The leave of OO is certainly not ideal. Better is COOEE (9C, 23 points), and best is COOEED (7C, 22 points).

	A	B	C	D	E	F	G	H	I	J	K	L	M	N	O
1															
2															
3															
4															
5							J	O	W						
6								B							
7								E		D					
8							H	A	Z	Y		E		P	
9								A		C				I	
10						F	R	U	G	O				N	
11								S	A	N	D	I	N	G	
12										E				O	
13															
14															
15															

Example #44

5. **Wise** AEEOTTW AWE, 4K 17 133

He saved the second E for a hook play at N4. With so many Es still unplayed, however, Schulman may well have been able to use the spot first. In any event, Wise's move opened potentially high-scoring counterplay along column 3. Although AWEE (9D, 20 points) is too dangerous because it opens 8A–D in conjunction with permitting a high-point consonant to be placed at 8D, TWAE (11D, 21) is certainly reasonable, as is my favorite, WHERETO (G7, 19 points). With only one S and no blanks showing among the thirty tiles on the board, tile turnover should now be an overriding concern in the selection of potential moves. WHERETO is also good defensively, as it makes it very unlikely that Schulman will be able to play a bingo by using the -D, -R, or -S hook at 13L.

Schulman DIOORST DOOR, 3K 26 158

Mike was fortunate to draw DIRST to his two OS, and he missed a great opportunity. He had DISROOT (3H, 84 points) or TOROIDS (13G, 82), and overlooked them both. My choice is TOROIDS, since with the J and the Z already played the H12–15 opening is not all that dangerous. TOROIDS also kills a high-scoring location for the Q (13I to or beyond the double word score).

6. **Wise**   DEEIOTT   TREED, N2   27   160

Solid move, as it scored a lot of points and took the sting out of the -s hook at O3 by preventing any play using the double letter square at O4. I nevertheless prefer OREIDE (N2, 29 points), despite the leave of TT. The leave of IOT after TREED is perhaps even worse, and OREIDE has the additional advantage of playing away one more tile. Inferior because of the two-vowel leaves are TENTED and TINTED (N9, 26 points). TOITED (13G) is also not as good as OREIDE: it's nice to play away an additional tile, but not at the expense of eight points and the creation of a nice triple word square opening for the opponent.

Schulman BEIPSTV Exchange BIPV   0   158

A very bad fishing play. Quite reasonable alternatives are VIS (O1, 26 points), VEST, VISE (both at 13J, 25 points), and VIBES (13H, 22 points).

7. **Wise**   IIMOTUV   Exchange   0   160
                        IIMOTUV

Not as good as THORIUM (G7, 18 points)! It is rare that exchanging is justifiable when as many as 18 points are available for the taking. Even MINT (N9, 18 points) beats exchanging, though it is not as good as THORIUM because it turns over two fewer tiles.

Schulman AAESTTU   ANT, N10   11   169

Played purely for rack leave. ANTAE (N10, 20 points) is much better, is not dangerous, and conserves the s. Its leave is superior to ANT, as it entails a much lower risk of vowelitis.

8. **Wise**   BEIILOU   LIE, 9E   16   176

It is imperative to play away more tiles in order to have a chance at picking the good ones. LOUIE (9C, 19 points) opens up the triple word square at 8A, but unlike AWEE (discussed in the commentary to Wise's fifth move), it is well worth making. No other play cleans out the rack nearly as well. Besides, LOUIE is safer than AWEE as it requires an E only to be placed at 8C if the 8A–D opening is to be used. If Schulman in fact had an E, he could probably make a play from 8A to 8E after Mike's play anyway.

Schulman AEOSTUU Exchange OUU   0   169

Mike S. sacrificed a total of almost 60 points over the last three turns in order to fish for a bingo. Best here is TOUSE, at 11C, 13I (both scoring 23 points), or 8A (20 points). I would play it at 13I, since this placement takes the most dangerous opening on the board and minimizes the possibility of Wise playing a bingo.

9.   **Wise**   BILOPUX   XI, O1   29   205

The play to make is UPBOIL (D8, 28 points)! It not only saves the x, but triples the probability of picking a blank.

Schulman AEGNSST   XIS, O1   16   185

One more fishing play. Better are STAGE (8A, 26 points), retaining one S, and SEAS (13L, 32 points). I would play STAGE; six additional points for spending a second S is normally a borderline call, but in this case the opportunity to pick one more tile favors STAGE. There are now 49 tiles on the board with nary a blank in sight.

10.   **Wise**   BILOPSU   BLOB, 6G   17   222

My commentary on Mike's last play gives this one away. He had UPBOILS at either D8 (80 points) or 13F (76 points). The 13F placement is much better defensively, as it kills lucrative play along row 13 and makes it highly unlikely that Schulman will be able to bingo on this board.

Schulman AEGNRST   GARNETS, 13F   71   256

He got his bingo, but sacrificed 84 points over his last four turns to do it.

11.   **Wise**   ACIPSUY   CRAY, H12   36   258

He knew this was phony when he played it, and he also knew from his experience in games against Schulman in Toronto that Schulman's knowledge of unusual four-letter words was questionable. Wise wanted to retain the P for the hook at 9D; he was absolutely positive that Schulman would not challenge.

Schulman AOLNRT□ ORNAT[E]LY, 15A   83   339
Perhaps this was the reason Schulman did not challenge.
He would not have had a playable bingo without the Y at
15H. ORNAT[E]LY was Schulman's only playable bingo, and
it was a very nice find.

12. **Wise**   AILPSUU   PULI, D9   18   276
PULSAR (B10, 28 points) is perhaps a little better. True, it
spends the last S and retains an unattractive IU leave, but it
opens up the board a little and gives Mike one more chance
at picking the second blank. And it does score 10 points
more.

Schulman EEMQTUV   EME, C11   16   355
An incredible blunder, explainable only by the fact that he
was already in severe time trouble at this point in the game.
Not only did he make it more difficult for himself to get rid of
the Q, but he also opened up a bingo line through column B
that Wise might have been able to take advantage of. He
obviously should have played QUEER (B11, 28).

13. **Wise**   AIIIISU   Exchange IIII   0   276
A good selection of tiles to retain. The only vowels unaccounted for from Wise's perspective at this point in the game
were EO. He was undoubtedly aware of this, and kept the
two vowels in the expectation that he would at most pick one
more from the bag. The U was of course retained as insurance against picking the Q. Everyone knows that when you
exchange a U you pick a Q, and vice versa.

Schulman EKQRTUV   ELK, 11C   14   369
Killing the S hook at B11, but also killing a play ending in
-QUE. With no available locations for his Q, he would have
been better off exchanging KQV. If Wise were to pick any of
these difficult tiles, they would interfere with his ability to
form a bingo, even with the remaining S and blank. If he
were to play a bingo and then pick the Q, Schulman would be
able to win easily.

14. **Wise** AFHNSU☐ AAH, 14I 29 305
He missed HAN**D**SFUL (E2, 76 points). It is curious that this play would lose for certain to Schulman's subsequent QUAKER (3C), but Wise should have lost after any play he made anyway.

   Schulman EEQRTUV Exchange ERV 0 369
With exactly seven tiles in the bag, this was his last chance to rid himself of the albatross Q. I would have exchanged EQV and forgone plays such as VERB (G3, 13 points), REVEL (E5, 16 points), and TEE (14D, 14 points). VROW (L1, 14 points) is an interesting alternative, however, as it prevents Wise from creating the unblockable setup that he did in fact create on his next play.

TWS		DLS			TWS				DLS			TWS X			1
	DWS		TLS			TLS				DWS T		I			2
		DWS		DLS		DLS	D	O	O	DWS R		S			3
DLS			DWS			DLS	A	DWS W	E	E		DLS			4
			DWS		J	O	DWS W			E					5
TLS			TLS	B	L	O	B	TLS		D					6
	DLS			DLS		DLS E	D		DLS						7
TWS		DLS		H	A	Z	Y	E	DLS		TWS P				8
	DLS	P	L	I	DLS E	A	DLS	C		DLS	I				9
TLS		U	TLS F	R	U	G	TLS	O		TLS A	N				10
	E	L	DWS K			S	A	N	DWS D	I	N	G			11
DLS	M	I			DLS C			DWS E		T	O	DLS			12
	DWS E		DLS G	A	R	N	E	T	S	DWS					13
DWS			TLS	A	A	TLS H				DWS					14
TWS O	R	N	DLS A	T	E	L TWS Y			DLS			TWS			15
A	B	C	D	E	F	G	H	I	J	K	L	M	N	O	

Example #45

15. **Wise** FINSTU☐ TOW, L2 6 311
Terrific play! Only he can play along row 1.
   Schulman EIIQTUV EVIL, E6 7 376
An attempt to open the board for his Q.

16. **Wise** FINRSU☐ Pass 0 311
There were three tiles in the bag at this point, and the unseen tiles from Wise's perspective were EIIMOQRTUV. As it

turned out, he would have won even if he had not passed. He was concerned about picking the Q, however, so he tried this ploy instead of playing the bingo. The idea of passing in this circumstance is dangerous only if the opponent can score well or set himself up without emptying the bag.

Schulman IIOQRTU   QUIRE, 6A   16   392

Depleting the bag was the very worst thing Schulman could have done. He should have realized that Mike's pass meant that he had a bingo, and that even if the bingo word consisted of six one-point tiles and the blank, it would win the game after QUIRE.

When one player passes in a situation such as the one shown above, the correct response is usually to pass also. This was not the case in the present circumstance, however. Had Schulman passed, Wise would have forged ahead without creating any counterplay for the Q.

One possibility for Schulman was RIB (G4, 5 points), which sets up QUIRT (4D, 30 points) next play. Had Wise then been able to block this setup with a bingo along rows 3 or 4, he undoubtedly would have created new openings for Schulman's Q.

17.   FINRSU☐ FURNIS☒,   1G 88   399

Nice play. Justice prevailed, as the player who made the higher percentage of best plays won.

                    plus EIMOTV x 2 = 22   421

BEST PLAYS
  Wise: Turns #1, 2, 3, 11, 13, 15, 16, and 17.
  Schulman: Turns #3, 10, 11, and 15.

GOOD PLAYS
  Wise: Turns 6, 9, and 12.
  Schulman: None.

BEST PLAY PERCENTAGES:
  Wise: 9.5 ÷ 17 (8 out of 17 moves, no challenge situations), 56 percent.

Schulman: 5 ÷ 17 (4 out of 16 moves, 1 potential
challenge of a phony correctly turned down, as the phony
allowed him to play a bingo), 29 percent.

Game # 4: Ron Tiekert versus Joel Wapnick

1983 North American Championship, Chicago: Round 11

In this game, Ron and I combined to produce one of the
best-played games of the tournament. The margin of difference between the two of us was very slight: only one false
challenge.

Ron Tiekert has won all the major East Coast tournaments at least once and has finished within the top seven in
all three of his North American Championship appearances. He is one of two or three players whom I consider to
be at least as good as I.

Move		Rack	Play	Points	Total
1.	**Tiekert**	BBGNQVV	Exchange	0	0
			BBGNQVV		

Inexperienced players might keep GN in the hope of picking
an I for the ING combination. As you might have surmised
from my earlier comments, I believe this to be a very weak
idea.

	Wapnick	IILOPRZ	ZORIL, 8D	48	48

Nothing to think about here.

2.	**Tiekert**	AAGONSX	AX, 7F	36	36

Gox (7E, 41 points) uses one more tile and scores five more
points, but fails to undouble the As. I would have played it,
though I am not prepared to say that it is unequivocally
better than AX.

Wapnick EILMPTV   TEMPO, E4   30   78

There is no good reason for playing VETO (E5, 24 points),
LIMP (6C, 25 points) or VIM (6D, 25 points) instead, as TEMPO
both played away at least as many tiles as these plays and
scored more points. POLITE (E7, 28 points) is a possibility,
but the M and the V left on the rack don't combine with each
other particularly well.

3.   **Tiekert** ADGINOS   GANOIDS, I2   77   113

The alternative was LOADINGS (H8, 83 points). GANOIDS is
of course defensively better, as it takes the -s hook and keeps
the board relatively closed. On the other hand, 6 points is 6
points. The two plays are about equally good, though my
choice would be for LOADINGS. This choice is consistent with
my stylistic preference for open games, in which I feel that it
is very difficult for opponents to beat me.

Wapnick EFIILLV   FIVE, D1   32   110

It's no time to be fearful of Ron's response. I had to score well
to keep up with him, and nothing else comes close to FIVE.

4.   **Tiekert** ANRSTTW   FAWNS, 1D   33   146

Another good but obvious play. From this point on until the
opening was blocked, I was on the lookout for OUTFAWNS
(1A, 42 points). WANT (J3, 22 points) keeps the S, but has two
big drawbacks: the 11-point sacrifice versus FAWNS, and it
allows me to make use of row 1.

Wapnick ILLNYY☐   LIMY, 6C   31   141

Believe it or not, there is a bingo, albeit unplayable, in this
mess: LYIN[G]LY. I'm grateful to Ron for not playing LOAD-
INGS on his third turn, for if he had I undoubtedly would
have had to add [P]LYINGLY (14C) to my list of missed bingos.

YARN (F6, 30 points) is an alternative to LIMY, but its main
drawback is that it doesn't dispense with one of the two Ls
on the rack. I was not at all afraid of the B- OR S- hooks at B6
after LIMY. If Ron were to use this opening, I would probably
have counterplay along column A. Besides, a nonbingo play
using this hook location would be unlikely to score much
more than 30 points.

5. **Tiekert** CLOQRTT LICTOR, 6H 14 160
A very nice play. This play maximized his turnover which,
with the Q in his rack, was very important. TORT (J3) is two
points more but is inferior because it plays away one less tile
than does LICTOR. It is too early to exchange the Q, as with
no US showing on the board the probability is high that he
will pick one or that I will play one that is accessible for his
Q.

    Wapnick LNRTTY□ RATTLY, 3H 18 159
The first real mistake of the game. I missed ROTT⬚NLY (L5,
72).

6. **Tiekert** AFIMNQT FILM, L1 26 186
This play scored well, but turnover should have taken
precedence with the Q still on his rack. LIFTMAN (H8, 15
points) is a better play, despite the 11-point sacrifice.

    My RATTLY must have been a disappointment to Ron, as it
blocked QINTAR (M1), or even better, FAQIR (M2).

Example #46

    Wapnick EEINNR□ TENTERIN⬚, K3 86 245
This move, plus Ron's challenge of it, turned the game
around. I knew that TENTERS was good, and I had memo-

rized TENTERED, so I was fairly sure that my play was
acceptable.

7.	**Tiekert**	ABENOQT	*Challenged*		
			TENTERIN⬚G⬚		
			lost his turn	0	186
	Wapnick	ADEGIOO	ZOOID, D8	30	275

Nice play: it scored the maximum number of available
points and dispensed with three of the five vowels. The -s
hook location at 13D isn't all that dangerous, especially
considering that similar hook locations already exist at B6
and N6.

8.	**Tiekert**	ABENOQT	BATON, B6	33	219

Best. NOB, NEB, or TAB (B4, 29 points) are all safer, but it was
imperative for him to pick more replacement tiles. BEANO
(B6) would be much weaker than BATON, as it would leave a
vowel adjacent to the triple word square at A8.

	Wapnick	AAEGIOU	AGUE, A8	26	301

With no US showing on the board, AGIO (A8, 26 points) to
save the U is not particularly good. AGUE allows the remote
possibility of AGUEWEED, and AGIO permits a possible AGI-
OTAGE, but such things are not serious factors in the determination of what move to play.

At first glance it appears that the AIO leave after AGUE is
less inviting than the AEU leave after AGIO. However, only
four ES were showing on the board before my turn, whereas
seven IS and six OS were already out. The probability of
letter duplication was therefore much higher after AGIO
than AGUE.

9.	**Tiekert**	CENQVW⬚	VIEW, 11C	20	239

Down by 62 points after this play and with three chances to
pick a U, I would have exchanged instead. Ron's leave of
CNQ⬚ could work out if he picked the right vowels, but such a
pick would be a real longshot. WINCE (11C, 20) would allow
him to pick an additional tile, but QV⬚ is not a particularly

desirable leave. Also, WINCE creates a dangerous opening
from H10 or H11 to H15. With the board as open as it was at
this point in the game, I would have kept EN ☐ and prayed.

Wapnick AAEEIIO   Exchange   0   301
                        AAEEIIO

On my last two turns I played away six vowels and two
consonants. I didn't deserve this.

AINEE (10I, 7 points) is a reasonable alternative to passing, as it blocks bingos down column H, across row 10, and
partially blocks column M. The AIO leave would pretty much
ensure continued vowelitis, however. In addition, there were
quite a few good tiles yet to be played. I wanted my share of
them.

10. **Tiekert** ACENQR☐   Q[U]IRE, 2B   39   278
Although this play definitely beats exchanging, it is not as
good as either FACE (1L, 27 points) or RANCE (8K, 24 points).
Q[U]IRE spent the blank for the extra 12 to 15 points plus the
privilege of dispensing with the Q, but with only one U
showing, it's not enough compensation. I would have
played RANCE over FACE, both to increase my chances of
picking a U and to decrease the probability of having no
vowels on my next rack.

Wapnick EEGRTUU   REFUGE, 1J   30   331
I was fortunate to be able to make such a nice play, given the
contents on my rack.

11. **Tiekert** ACEEOON   RACON, 8K   24   302
ROTE (J1, 17 points) balances the rack better, but RACON has
three advantages: it scores 7 more points, opens up the
board for a potential bingo, and doubles the probability of
picking one of the two all-important remaining ss. The last
two factors make RACON the preferred play.

Wapnick DEIJSTU   JUSTED, 13B   48   379
After this play, Ron needed a bingo just to break even.

	A	B	C	D	E	F	G	H	I	J	K	L	M	N	O	
				F	A	W	N	S		R	E	F	U	G	E	1
		Q	U	I	R	E			G			I				2
			V					R	A	T	T	L	Y			3
			E	T					N		E	M				4
			A						O		N					5
		B	L	I	M	Y		L	I	C	T	O	R			6
		A		P	A	X			D		E					7
	A	T		Z	O	R	I	L	S		R	A	C	O	N	8
	G	O		O							I					9
	U	N		O							N					10
	E		V	I	E	W					G					11
				D												12
		J	U	S	T	E	D									13
																14
																15

Example #47

12. **Tiekert** AEEHIOP CHEAPIE, M8   36   338
This play gave up the ghost. It didn't even minimize the loss rather than play for a win, since it opened up great counterplay for me.

There were two tiles left in the bag at this point in the game. Ron thus could have retained his bingo opportunities by playing away only one or two tiles. Three possibilities were HO (14A, 28 points), OH (14E, 28 points), and HE (14F, 28 points).

The disadvantage of all of these plays is that they would empty the bag. After any of them, I would know *exactly* what Ron's remaining tiles would be, and could therefore easily block any potential bingo of his. However, had Ron played only one tile away, I would not know for sure where to block. Imagine, for example, that he had played JO (B13, 18 points), setting up HEAP (15A, 46 points) and preserving CHEAPIE for his next play if necessary. From his point of view, he would have a one in nine chance of picking the s for CHEAPIES, his only possible bingo (since I didn't have the s, the actual probability was 50 percent). Furthermore, JO might have lured me into blocking row 15 rather than defending against the bingo. He would therefore retain a slim practical chance of winning, which is certainly better than no chance at all.

From my point of view after the hypothetical JO play, Ron would have seven of the following eight tiles on his rack: AAEEHIPS. Only if I were playing my very best could I ensure my victory, and to do so I have to block both CHEAPIES and SAPHENAE (O3, 64 points) with a play such as OBI (N8, 7 points). This play also conserves HA+ on my rack, should I need it for 14F. Imagine how I would feel if I play HAIKU (14F, 38 points), and Ron then bingos out with CHEAPIES to win, 420-417! Or if I block CHEAPIES with BRICK (M5, 19 points), but then lose to SAPHENAE. OBI wins the game for sure, but only by a few points.

Wapnick ABDHIKU HIKED, 14J 42 421
Better by the barest of margins is HAIKU (14F). Ron's best play after it would be SOLA (C4, 11 points), and my winning margin would be one point greater than it actually turned out to be.

13. **Tiekert** AOS SODA, G11 16 354
Nice play.

plus ABU X 2 = 10 364

BEST PLAYS
  Tiekert: Turns 1, 2, 3, 4, 5, 8, 11, and 13.
  Wapnick: Turns 1, 2, 3, 4, 6, 7, 8, 9, 10, and 11.

GOOD PLAYS
  Tiekert: Turn 6.
  Wapnick: Turn 12.

BEST PLAY PERCENTAGES
  Tiekert: 8.5 ÷ 13 (8.5 out of 13 moves, one of which was a pass resulting from the icorrect challenge of TENTERIN[G]), 65 percent.
  Wapnick: 10.5 ÷ 12 (10.5 out of 12 moves, no challenges), 88 percent.

Game #5: Joel Wapnick versus Steven Polatnick

1980 North American Championship, Santa Monica: Round 13

This was the sixth and last game of the second day of competition. After attaining a 6-3 record, I had dropped three games in a row preceding this one. I don't know how Steven was feeling, but I was tired, dispirited, and feeling a bit like ground up meat.

Our game was nevertheless an exciting, tightly fought contest. It was also inconsistently played. We both made big mistakes at times and played like champions at other times. The game is interesting not only because it was a nip and tuck affair, but because it presents a considerable number of strategic and tactical considerations worth studying.

Since 1979 or 1980, Steve Polatnick has been the best player in the South, and one of the top players in North America. He finished eleventh in this tournament.

Move		*Rack*	*Play*	*Points*	*Total*
1.	**Wapnick**	GILOUYZ	ZIG, 8G	26	26

A LOUZY and UGLY rack! The additional ten points make this play better than UGLY and LOGY. It is also very good defensively, especially if Steve does not have an s.

	Polatnick	CFINORU	FOCI, 9H	19	19

So much for ZIGGURATS or ZIGZAGGED! FOCI is about as good as FORCING (I2, 15 points). My preference is FORCING, however, for the additional tile turnover. It opens the triple word score at H1, but the 8K–O opening after FOCI is even more dangerous.

2.	**Wapnick**	EILLOUY	LOUIE, 8K	20	46

The only reasonable alternative plays, OILILY (K6 or K8, 18

points) are inferior. Both retain two vowels instead of LY. In addition K8 placement is dangerous (e.g., OXIDE or OZONE, 8K, would be devastating). K6 placement unnecessarily opens the triple letter square at J6.

Polatnick EFNRUUW   Exchange   0   19
EFNRUUW

Overlooking CURFEW (J9, 20 points). This play is well worth the risk: it scores well and retains a nice UN leave. Less good are UNFREE (O3 or O4, 10 points) or FUNGO (I5, 10 points).

At this point you may be wondering why it is acceptable to create an -s hook location at 15J after CURFEW and unacceptable to open up the triple word square at 8O by playing OILILY, K8. The difference is related more to the plays than to the openings. Both openings are dangerous, but OILILY offers no compensation: LOUIE is better and gives the opponent little, whereas competing moves to CURFEW cannot compare with it in terms of scoring and rack leave.

3.   **Wapnick** AADLOVY   DAILY, N6   21   67
Not even close to VALIDLY (K6, 28 points), despite its two-vowel leave.

Polatnick AHIMOOT   HOMO, M3   21   40
MOTH (M10, 25 points) is 4 points more, but the poor leave more than negates the points. Better than HOMO is OHIA (M10, 19 points): its leave is much superior, and it is certainly no more risky than is HOMO. OHIA also prevents a play from O10 to O15. OOLITH (K6, 18 points) opens up the J6 triple letter square for no apparent reason.

4.   **Wapnick** ACEOOUV   Exchange   0   67
ACEOOUV

My mind took a vacation on this one. Better than passing, but too risky when compared with other options are VOUCH (3I, 17 points; the setup here is likely to backfire), AVOUCH (3H, 18 points), and OVUM (5J, 18 points). The two best plays are probably VOE (N2, 19 points) and OVOLI (K5, 16). I like OVOLI, for the better leave and for inhibiting play down column L.

Polatnick AAIITTY   Exchange   0   40

AAIITTY

It's a toss-up between exchanging and TAT (L4, 18 points). The points are hard to pass up, but weighing in favor of exchanging is the terrible leave (especially the two IS with the Y) and the fact that *no* good tiles have yet appeared on the board.

5. **Wapnick** EIIKNSS   KINESIS, 10B   79   146
I got lucky.

Example #48

Polatnick ELQRSU☐   REL⬛QUES, E4   114   154
He got very lucky! Actually, I cannot rate his beautiful find as a best play, as it is not quite as good as the brilliancy SQU⬛LLIER (K3, 118 points)! Still, REL⬛QUES was quite a shock to me.

6. **Wapnick** ADEFIOV   FOVEA, D1   34   180
Good play, reminiscent of my play of FIVE against Ron Tiekert in the previous annotation. FERVID (4C, 30 points) is not as good, as it leaves two vowels. FEOD (L1, 35 points)

doesn't get rid of the unpleasant v, and neither do FADO or FADE (L2, 31 points).

Polatnick EEJNNPR   PINER, C9   20   174
Dreadful play, and dreadful of me not to challenge it. His best play by far is the unpluralizable JINNEE (C9, 42).

7.   **Wapnick** DIIMNUW   WID, N2   22   202
Gruesome! There are only two things wrong with this play: (1) there are better plays, and (2) WID isn't a word. The subconscious train of thought instructing me to think this word was okay went something like: FIZ and WIZ are both acceptable. FID is good, so it only follows that WID is also good.

I should have played FUNDI (1D, 27 points) in any event.

Polatnick EEEEJNT   JETE, O1   52   226
After I played WID, Steven called "hold." He knew that WID was not good, and he was checking to see if it was to his advantage to leave it on the board. He allowed it to stay, and he was wrong to do so.

His net gain for the turn was 30 points. However, it would have been much greater had he challenged and then played JET (L4, 46 points). Instead of holding a 24-point lead after JETE, he would be up by 40. True, he would have played only one of his four ES away versus two after JETE. He might also have thought JET would give me a good play down column N, with my w placed on N4. These factors do not compensate for the lost 16 points of point-spread differential, however. I would have been stuck with the same unpleasant rack, and the successful challenge of a three-letter word would have put me in a very bad state of mind.

8.   **Wapnick** CGIMNUV   FUMING, 1D   33   235
Good, as is FUNGIC (1D). FUMING saves the c for L3 or L4, but the m saved after FUNGIC can also be played at L4.

Polatnick AEEENRR   RELEARN, 6C   21   247
Best was NEARLIER (K4, 32 points); you figure out how to use it in a sentence.

9.   Wapnick ACNNRTV   CANTO, L4   36   271

Nice play, if I do say so myself. Had Steven found NEARLIER on his last turn I would be in deep trouble now.

Polatnick AAEGOPS   PEAGS, J2   26   273

A tough choice. More points and a better leave result from KAPAS (B10, 30), but this play is somewhat dangerous despite the fact that only a vowel (and not a high-point consonant) can be placed on A12. Because of the danger and the one additional chance to pick the blank after PEAGS, I would rate the two plays as about equally good. AGAPE (M10, 21 points) retains the last S, but it permits potentially high-scoring plays down column N if I have the H, X, or Y. It's a decent play, but probably not as good as either PEAGS or KAPAS.

Example #49

(game board, 15×15. Columns A–O left to right, rows 1–15 top to bottom; letters placed on the board:)

```
    A  B  C  D  E  F  G  H  I  J  K  L  M  N  O
 1  .  .  .  F  U  M  I  N  G  .  .  .  .  .  J
 2  .  .  .  O  .  .  .  .  .  P  .  .  W  E  E
 3  .  .  .  V  .  .  .  E  .  E  .  .  H  I  T
 4  .  .  .  E  R  .  .  A  .  A  .  C  O  D  E
 5  .  .  .  A  E  .  .  G  .  G  .  A  M  .  .
 6  .  .  R  E  L  E  A  R  N  S  N  O  D  .  .
 7  .  .  .  .  I  .  .  .  .  .  .  T  A  .  .
 8  .  .  .  .  Q  .  Z  I  G  .  L  O  U  I  E
 9  .  .  .  .  P  U  .  F  O  C  I  .  L  .  .
10  .  K  I  N  E  S  I  S  .  .  .  .  Y  .  .
11  .  .  .  N  .  S  .  .  .  .  .  .  .  .  .
12  .  .  .  E  .  .  .  .  .  .  .  .  .  .  .
13  .  .  .  R  .  .  .  .  .  .  .  .  .  .  .
14  .  .  .  .  .  .  .  .  .  .  .  .  .  .  .
15  .  .  .  .  .  .  .  .  .  .  .  .  .  .  .
```

10.   Wapnick AENRRTV   ERRANT, O10   26   297

With the blank not yet out, this was somewhat risky. Nevertheless, I felt that it was correct: I had to play for the blank, and I needed the points. Neither VEER (12A, 22 points) nor VAV (3B, 18 points) would have opened the board for bingos, but because of the low number of replacement tiles following them they would pretty much cede the blank to Steven.

Polatnick AABDDOY   DAY, 14A   25   298

The losing move. With so many high-point tiles still unseen, this play was simply too dangerous. The best play was BADDY (M10, 32 points). The Y should *not* be saved for 2F, as its use there in conjunction with the double word square at 2B is too speculative.

11.   **Wapnick** AEHTUVX   AX, 15A   45   342

Not very creative, but crushing nevertheless. HADE (A12, 36 points) is markedly inferior, as it sacrifices the points without leaving a really good spot for the X on the board.

     Polatnick ABBDIOO   DOBBIN, 14J   30   328

A beautiful play, made out of nothing tiles. Unfortunately for him, I was able to take advantage of the opening this play produced.

12.   **Wapnick** EHOTTUV   HOVE, 15G   33   375

I knew his tiles, and felt that it was extremely unlikely that his rack contained a playable bingo. I was right.

     Polatnick AILOTW□   WRIT, 13B   20   348

Better would be GOW[K] (I1, 25 points), TAL[L]OW (13F, 19 points), and LOW[S] (F12, 24 points). Best was probably WAB (M12, 16 points), which both blocks my going-out play and enables Steven to play out next turn with either TOIL[S] (11I, 15 points) or TRIOL[S] (13B, 15 points).

13.   **Wapnick**   TTU   TUT, M10   9   384
                   plus ALO□ X   2 = 6   390

BEST PLAYS
   Wapnick: Turns 1, 2, 5, 6, 8, 9, 10, 11, 12, and 13.
   Polatnick: Turns 1, 4, 7, 9, and 11.

GOOD PLAYS
   Wapnick: None.
   Polatnick: Turns 3, and 5.

BEST PLAY PERCENTAGES

Wapnick: 10 ÷ 14 (10 out of 13 moves, 1 failure to challenge), 71 percent.

Polatnick: 6 ÷ 13 (7 out of 12 moves, 1 failure to challenge), 46 percent.

Game # 6: Joe Edley versus Joel Wapnick

1983 North American Scrabble Championship: Round 10

Going into this game, Joe had an 8-1 record and I was at 7-2. Dan Pratt was also 8-1. It was therefore very important for me to win if I wanted a realistic chance of taking first place.

Although I drew eighteen blanks in my seventeen tournament games, I was fortunate to win the NAC in this one very significant respect: I drew all four blanks in my two games against Joe Edley, and I was able to play a bingo immediately after picking each blank. Had Joe won either of the two games between us, he would have won the tournament.

This game was remarkably well played. There was a total of only five mistakes between the two of us, and none of them was particularly serious.

Move	Rack	Play	Points	Total
1. **Edley**	AEGLSXY	AGLEY, 8H	26	26

Perfect: AGLEY scores well, does not place a vowel adjacent to the double letter squares on rows 7 and 9, and conserves the valuable s and x tiles. In addition, AGLEY cannot be pluralized.

Wapnick	DEEILW☐	WEEDLI[K]E, K6	72	72

Placement of this word was good defensively, as no vowels or high-point tiles fell adjacent to double word or triple letter squares (other than the harmless contiguity between the w and the triple letter square at 6J). Equally good for the same reason is WEE[V]ILED (K7).

For the record, other playable bingos are WIEL[D]ED (7B and 9B), WIELDE[R] (9B), WEDELI[N]G (I1), WE[R]EGILD (I4), WEEDIL[Y] (9B), and [B]EWAILED (H5).

2.   **Edley**   BDGISUX   GUILD, 10H   9   35

DEBUG (13J, 18 points) was best. True, it would have created an -s hook in a triple word square column, but since Joe would have retained an s on his rack he might well have been able to take advantage of this opening. If I were not to use or block the -s hook, then he would score at least 40 points on his next turn (SIX, O13).

  Wapnick   AFHIIQW   WAIF, 7E   16   88

Good: it plays away the maximum number of tiles, undoubles the IS, and sets up the H at 6F if Joe doesn't take or block the spot. Exchanging tiles is not quite as good, as retention of the H should guarantee a good score on the next turn even if 6F is taken.

Note that I was not particularly concerned about opening up access to the triple word score at 8A, since this opening was unlikely to give Joe 16 or more additional points versus other plays that he might have.

3.   **Edley**   ABILOSX   BIAXAL, F3   31   66

An alternative was AXIL (L12, 35 points). AXIL opens up row 15, but BIAXAL allows potentially high-scoring counterplay down column E which in most cases would prove to be even more lucrative. More conservative attempts such as AX (L12, 29 points) or BOXY (L5, 30 points) do not play away enough tiles.

  Wapnick   AEHINQV   VAHINE, L1   37   125

HAW and HEW (E5, 37 points) are really bad, even though these plays do not open the row 1 triple word squares. Their drawback is that they play away only two tiles. With the Q on my rack, it was vitally important that I play as many tiles as possible to maximize my chances of picking a U.

I was also aware when I made this play that if I picked a u or a blank, I would have a good chance of making at least a 68+ point play from 2J to 2N or 2O on my next turn.

4.   **Edley**   AGOOSTT   TOT, M2   20   86
Much better was GAVOTS (1J, 30 points), taking rather than blocking row 1. Especially with the other three ss unseen, spending the s for 10 more points would have been well worth it.

   Wapnick   ADEOQTU   QUATE, 2J   68   193
I would have played QUA[K]ED (12H, 50 points), had Joe's GAVOTS blocked both my play and QUOTA (J2). Note that QUATE cannot be pluralized, and that hooking on an E- at I2 has its dangers: it opens play down column O, and probably across row 1 as well.

```
    A  B  C  D  E  F  G  H  I  J  K  L  M  N  O
 1                                          V     TWS
 2                             Q  U  A  T  E
 3              B              H        O
 4              I              I  T
 5              A              N
 6              X              W  E
 7        W  A  I  F           E
 8              L  A  G  L  E  Y
 9                          D
10                 G  U  I  L  D
11                             I
12                            [K]
13                             E
14
15
```

Example #50

5.   **Edley**   AGNOOPS   POGONIAS, 4A   80   166
A beautiful find!

   Wapnick   AADEOOT   ADOPT, A1   24   217
TOGAED (C2, 20 points) has the advantage of leaving only two vowels on the rack rather than the three after ADOPT. I

nevertheless felt that, with a slim lead, it behooved me to play somewhat defensively and block column A.

I was not afraid of Joe's playing ADOPTERS or ADOPTEES, since they aren't really devastating plays. ADOPTING was not possible, as all three GS had been played.

6.   **Edley**   ANORRRT   GARRON, H10   24   190
Another fine play from Joe, scoring well and solving his R problem.

Wapnick   AAEIORS   RAISE, H1   15   232
I considered playing ADOPTERS (A1, 33 points) at the time, but rejected it because of the four-vowel leave. Now I'm not so sure—18 points is an awful lot to sacrifice, even considering the leave and the expenditure of the S. It's probably the best play.

AREAL (J4, 17 points) is an option that I didn't see at the time. Its leave of IOS is worse than the AOS following RAISE, however, since four IS but only two AS remain to be played. I was therefore twice as likely to have two IS on my rack next turn after AREAL as I was to have two AS on my rack next turn after RAISE. Another advantage of RAISE is that it prevents Joe from using the 1H triple word square (which he undoubtedly would have done on his next turn had I not eliminated this possibility).

Other options worth considering are AWE (E6, 17 points), ABA (3E), and BAA (3F) both worth 11 points. All of these plays preserve both consonants, and ABA and BAA retain a very bingo-conducive EIORS. These latter two plays also retain ERS for a possible ADOPTERS next turn. The main problem with these plays is that they do not play off enough tiles, particularly vowels.

Finally, ARIA (L12, 14 points) is a possibility. The EOS leave is slightly better than the leaves following RAISE and AREAL. I do not see making a play that opens a triple word square instead of one that uses an already available triple word square, however, especially as I would receive no scoring compensation in return.

7. Edley   EJORRTU   JUROR, 12D   24   214
Not fancy, just good: it scored well, got rid of the U and doubled R, avoided placing the J in line with a premium square, and retained a nice leave of ERT.

  Wapnick   AINOSV□   INVAS⬛ON, 15A   83   315
This play just about put the game out of Joe's reach.

	A	B	C	D	E	F	G	H	I	J	K	L	M	N	O	
	A							R				V				1
	D							A	Q	U	A	T	E			2
	O					B		I				H	O			3
	P	O	G	O	N	I	A	S				I	T			4
	T					A		E				N				5
						X					W	E				6
					W	A	I	F				E				7
					L		A	G	L	E	Y					8
											D					9
							G	U	I	L	D					10
							A				I					11
			J	U	R	O	R			K					12
							R			E					13
							O								14
	I	N	V	A	S	I	O	N							15

Example #51

8. Edley   CEKRRTZ   RECK, 13J   20   234
With no S on the rack and only three replacement tiles coming, RECK was not wise. Perhaps he believed that any counterplay by me down column N would in turn open column O for him.

  ZERO (D1, 23 points) and DRECK (2A, 24 points) are both slightly better than RECK, though they partially block the column C bingo alley. This is not a big consideration, however, as with a considerable number of high-point tiles to come it is only remotely possible to play a bingo in this spot.

  The play that I think is best is RUCKS (E11, 22). It sets up a T-hook at 10E. Joe might then have been able to play NERTZ (10B, 48 points) on his next turn if he were to pick one of the two remaining NS, or RITZ (10C, 45 points) if he were to pick up one of the two IS still out.

Wapnick DEEHIPS PEISED, N10 41 356

Opening both the O column and the 15 row; but if I had not played here I would have left the -s hook for Joe, and on the basis of his last play I strongly suspected that he was holding onto an s. If he did in fact have an s, it made little sense for me to play PEISE and keep the D for a hook play at 15N.

9. **Edley** EERSTTZ ZEDS, 15L 72 306

He would have played ZEST (15L, 77 points) if I had kept the D.

Wapnick FHLMNNO FON, 13C 23 379

I overlooked a number of superior plays, including HOMO (B1, 33 points), MHO (14F, 28 points), and the best one, FOH (14D, 36 points). Because of the high percentage of high-point tiles still in the bag or on Joe's rack, it was extremely unlikely that he would play a bingo. I could not at any rate block all of his bingo openings (columns B, C, and O) with one move. My best bet was therefore to score well instead of trying to block.

10. **Edley** EMRTTUY MUTTER, O6 30 336

Unlike Ron Tiekert's situation in Game #4, Joe had no realistic chance of winning this game. There were only three tiles left in the bag at this point. Had he tried to dump three or fewer tiles without blocking the two remaining bingo spots, I would have scored sufficiently well down column O to win even if he did manage to bingo out. He was correct to play for minimizing the point-spread differential.

Wapnick EHILMNT MHO, 14F 29 408

Clever, as it both scored well and set up the following going-out plays: LINTEL (8A), TINGLE (C1), and if need be, LINTER (1C). Yes, I did plan it this way at the time.

11. **Edley** BCEY BY, 1N 25 361

  Wapnick EILNT LINTEL, 8A 26 434

  plus EC x 2 = 8 442

BEST PLAYS
  Edley: Turns 1, 3, 5, 6, 7, 9, 10, and 11.
  Wapnick: Turns 1, 2, 3, 4, 5, 7, 8, 10, and 11.

GOOD PLAYS
  Edley: None.
  Wapnick: None.

BEST PLAY PERCENTAGES
  Edley: 8 ÷ 11 (8 out of 11 moves, no challenges), 73 percent.
  Wapnick: 9 ÷ 11 (9 out of 11 moves, no challenges), 82 percent.

Game # 7: Joel Wapnick versus Steven Polatnick

1983 North American Championship, Chicago: Round 13

Of all thirty-two players in the 1983 North American Championship, Steven Polatnick allowed his opponents the fewest number of total points. When playing against other experts, he apparently preferred to avoid taking risks by keeping the board fairly closed. When he obtained a lead, as he did in this game, he was extremely adept at preserving that lead by denying his opponents access to openings for potentially high-scoring plays. In this game, his defensive plays from his eighth move onward made it difficult for me to recover from my deficit.

Move		*Rack*	*Play*	*Points*	*Total*
1.	**Wapnick**	DIMNOWX	MOWN, 8G	18	18

I can tell when I'm not playing well by the degree of paranoia my plays exhibit. I made a good defensive play here, but I should not have been quite so conservative. Better was

INDOW (8H, 26 points), despite its s hooks and the possibility of Steven playing INDOWING. OXID is of course bad, as it forms an -E hook and spends the x for nothing in return.

Polatnick ADEFILY   FLAYED, 9C   26   26
Better than DEAFLY (9B, 29 points), as DEAFLY places a vowel below 8D which might allow me a high-scoring 8A–D play. However, DEAFLY at 9H (29 points) is about equal to FLAYED. This triple letter square at 10J is somewhat risky if I were to have a P, B or Y, but on the other hand only FLAYED allows the possibility of a double-double play. In addition, the triple word square opening at 8A after FLAYED is more dangerous than the triple word square opening at 8O following DEAFLY: it permits plays up to five letters long from 8A, whereas DEAFLY limits plays going to 8O to a maximum of four letters.

IDEAL (9G, 24 points) is interesting, as it sets up the Y at 10J. Its negatives outweigh this positive, however: the FY leave makes it unlikely that a bingo could be played next turn, the 10J spot is not all that wonderful—it may well be blocked or taken by me anyway—and IDEAL sacrifices some points versus FLAYED or DEAFLY.

2.   **Wapnick** AADEIIX   XENIA, J6   30   48
AXE (8A, 35 points) is not as good despite the 5 extra points—it is very important to dispense with at least one I and three vowels, if possible. FAXED (C9, 32 points) is bad for the same reasons. XENIA is also superior to NIXIE (J8, 28 points), as it undoubles both the As and the Is.

AIDE (10C, 24 points) is cute and conserves the x, but at a cost of 6 points plus the formation of a dangerous spot for the z at 11E.

Polatnick EGHIORU   HOURI, K2   25   51
A very good play: it scored well without creating glaring openings, and retained a decent EG on the rack.

3.   **Wapnick** ADIIOTV   AVOID, E9   18   66
A mediocre play from an uninspiring situation. Better is

DAVIT (K9, 23 points), scoring 5 points more and getting rid of one more tile.

Polatnick EGIOQWZ   QUIZ, 4J   44   95
This play did not take much time off his clock! This is his only Q play, but note that had the U not been there he still would have had at least three high-scoring plays with the Z: ZOWIE, at either 7C or 12B (both scoring 34 points), and WIZ (K10, 35 points).

4.   **Wapnick** AAEILMT   MAILE, 11G   27   93
There was no reason why I should not have taken the obvious play, MAIZE (M1, 32 points). It not only yields the most points, but it also prevents Steve from picking up a lot of easy points by making a play through the Z. In addition, MAIZE would have saved the L for a play at 11J next time.

Interesting but inferior plays are MATZA (poorer leave than MAIZE), AMIE (8A, 29 points—leaves the Z spot for Steve), and LAMIA or LAMIAE (11J, 27 and 29 points, respectively—much too risky, especially with the blanks not yet out).

Polatnick AEGHOOW   WHOA, D11   38   133
Nothing else comes close to this play. Nice find.

5.   **Wapnick** AEEIOTT   AZOTE, M3   30   123
With no L available for ETIOLATE, this play is virtually forced.

Polatnick AEEGGOP   AGAPE, H11   30   163
Continuing to pour it on. Alternatives worth considering are OGEE or AGEE (8A, 26 points). I prefer OGEE to AGEE, even though there are three As but only two Os unseen. The AGP leave after OGEE is much better than the GOP leave after AGEE, and in fact may be more than worth the sacrifice of 4 points versus AGAPE and its EGO leave. Steven might even have been able to play AGAPE on his next turn by picking an E as one of his replacement tiles. In favor of AGAPE is that it took the more dangerous opening, and Steven might have been able to play OGEE next turn had he picked one more E.

6.   **Wapnick**   EFINOTU   FOP, 14F   16   139
I do not include this in my personal collection of inspired plays. Actually, I should have simply played FIE (8A, 23 points). FOE in the same spot is not quite as good, since I duplication after it is both more probable than O duplication after FIE, and O duplication is less of a problem anyway.

FOUNT (at either 12K or N7) is a poor idea, despite the opportunity to pick two more tiles. These moves are not only risky, but their leaves portend vowelitis.

Polatnick   BCEGO □□   BAG, 13G   18   181
Getting rid of his two least bingo-conducive tiles. He unfortunately overlooked a bingo: BO[S]C[A]GE (L9, 79).

The second-best play, spotted by Jim Neuberger, was the prettiest: BODEGA (13C, 34 points)!

	A	B	C	D	E	F	G	H	I	J	K	L	M	N	O	
																1
								H								2
								O		A						3
							Q	U	I	Z						4
								R		O						5
								X	I	T						6
								E		E						7
					M	O	W	N								8
			F	L	A	Y	E	D		I						9
				V					A							10
			W	O	M	A	I	L	E							11
			H	I			G									12
			O	D			B	A	G							13
			A		F	O	P									14
							E									15
	A	B	C	D	E	F	G	H	I	J	K	L	M	N	O	

Example #52

7.   **Wapnick**   EINRSTU   ESURIENT, 15H   77   216
More good fortune than I deserved, especially considering my weak turn preceding this one. ESURIENT was the best of my available bingos. The others were TRIUNES, in either of two places (7B, 69 points; N7, 60 points).

Polatnick   CEORS□□   ROC[K][I]EST, O8   74   255
So much for my short-lived lead. It's often difficult to find

the right play with two blanks in the rack, as there are just too many possibilities to calculate. A better play than ROCK-IEST was OVERCAST (O8, 83 points), and the best play was SPROCKET (O8, 83 points). The advantage of SPROCKET over OVERCAST is that it does not place a vowel adjacent to the triple letter square at N10. It does place the E adjacent to the double word square at N14, but with the K positioned at O13, this opening is inconsequential.

8.   **Wapnick** AELLNNU   NAE, C13   16   232
ULNAE (7C, 13 points) would have been an improvement, as it undoubles both the Ls and Ns and plays away five tiles in the hope of picking an S or the J.

  Polatnick ACENRSV   CRAVEN, 7C   25   280
He could not have been too disappointed about being unable to play his bingos (CAVERNS and CRAVENS), since CRAVEN put him in the driver's seat. This fine defensive play took away the most likely bingo spot on the board and scored well to boot.

VENAE (7F, 26 points) is also possible, but CRAVEN is more thorough defensively: it blocks plays from 8A to 8C or 8D, and closes down column D to bingos. CARVE (L9, 28) is decidedly inferior, as it does not block Row 7 at all.

9.   **Wapnick** AKLLNTU   TALUKA, E2   20   252
An attempt to open the board. Another possibility is LAKH (2H, 21 points). With three Es out and none of them on my rack, the probability would have been high that Steven would have hurt me with a big play along row 1 after this play. However, LAKH would also have made it very difficult for Steven to close off all openings for bingos on the upper part of the board. LAKH is nevertheless too much of a desperation attempt. With the J still out, a deficit of only 28 points, and a fairly open board after TALUKA, I did not need to play for a bingo as my only method of salvation.

	A	B	C	D	E	F	G	H	I	J	K	L	M	N	O	
1																1
2				T				H								2
3				A				O		A						3
4				L			Q	U	I	Z						4
5				U				R		O						5
6				K			X	I		T						6
7			C	R	A	V	E	N	E	E		E				7
8						M	O	W	N						R	8
9			F	L	A	Y	E	D		I					O	9
10			V					A							C	10
11			W	O		M	A	I	L	E					K	11
12			H	I		G									I	12
13			N	O	D	B	A	G							E	13
14			A	A		F	O	P							S	14
15			E					E	S	U	R	I	E	N	T	15

Example #53

Polatnick GIOPRST   TROPIC, C2   20   300

A very good blocking play, preventing bingos through all four of the open letters in TALUKA. He might also have tried TOPIC (C3) which saves the R for L7 or L11 (there are no AS left for an ATOPIC hook play), or ORGIC, leaving a nice PST on the rack.

Perhaps slightly safer than TROPIC would have been POSIT (F1, 19 points), which would have made it much more difficult for me to open column A than did his TROPIC. This is a very fine point, however, since it would have been only very remotely possible for me to create an opening that Steven would not be able to block or use.

10.   **Wapnick** DEELNRS   DROLL, 4A   16   268

There were three unplayable bingos on my rack: LENDERS, RELENDS, and SLENDER.

Before my play, there was only one bingo opening on the board: L7-13. I had to open another front, or else Steven would win by simply closing up this opening. Unfortunately, all of my setups were at least partially blockable. If I played ROLL (4B), Steven could make a play down column A with either of three tiles still unaccounted for: a D or one of the two TS. Even if he did not have these tiles, he might have been able to block with a play down column B.

Polatnick BDEGSTY TEDDY, A1 30 330
Good play, both scoring well and blocking.

11. **Wapnick** EEINSTU ENSUE, L9 18 286
With no tiles in the bag, my goose was cooked. This play at least guaranteed an out play on my next turn.

Polatnick BGJINS JIN, N1 22 352
His margin of victory would have been 6 points greater after JINS (F1, 26 points).

12. **Wapnick** IT IT, F2 10 296
My margin of defeat would have been two points less after FIT (C9, 12 points).

plus BGS x 2 = 12 308

BEST PLAYS
  Wapnick: Turns 2, 5, 7, 9, 10, and 11.
  Polatnick: Turns 1, 2, 3, 4, 5, 8, 9, and 10.

GOOD PLAYS
  Wapnick: Turn 12.
  Polatnick: Turn 11.

BEST PLAY PERCENTAGES
  Wapnick: 6.5 ÷ 12 (6.5 out of 12 moves, no challenges), 54 percent.
  Polatnick: 8.5 ÷ 11 (8.5 out of 11 moves, no challenges), 77 percent.

Game # 8: Daniel Pratt versus Edward Halper

1983 North American Championship, Chicago: Round 13

This was one of the most exciting games of the tournament, and it featured just about everything but the kitchen sink: setups, Q strategy, phony words, defensive considerations, conservation of resources, and voluntary rather than forced passing near the end of the game. Considering the complexities involved, it was admirably played by both competitors.

Before we proceed to the annotation, I must mention a word or two about the playing style of Dan Pratt. Dan is a contributor to *Letters for Expert Game Players,* and it is clear from his commentary that he plays the Game a little bit differently from the rest of us. Specifically, he likes to play for bingos and setups, and will often forgo plays of 15 points or more so that he can exchange tiles instead. Several players have commented to me over the years that they do not understand how he can be so successful in tournament play with such a "defective" strategic sense. My answer is usually something like "he doesn't miss much," and I truly believe that this is the reason for his success. On the other hand, it may just be that his emphasis on playing for the big score is not so bad—for him. He has a huge bingo vocabulary and rarely if ever overlooks bingos and other high-scoring plays.

In this game, Dan made what I believe was a very questionable exchange on his second turn. You should be aware, however, that he knew exactly what he was doing when he made this play; if you asked him today, he would probably still claim that it was best. And it's tough to argue with a player who finished second in two NAC's and fourth in the other.

The performance of Ed Halper should not be overlooked. Though his lack of word knowledge hurt him in this game, his plays generally reflected important strategic considerations that might at first not be obvious to the casual player. Ed finished an excellent fifth in the 1983 NAC.

Move		Rack	Play	Points	Total
1.	**Pratt**	CDEGGIQ	Exchange	0	0
			CDEGGIQ		

With no high-scoring alternative available, exchanging was mandatory.

| | **Halper** | EHJOPSS | JOSHES, 8D | 48 | 48 |

The best play here is the very unusual bingo, JOSEPHS (8D, 104 points). I would have missed it, and so would have just about everyone else in North America except perhaps two or three players.

| 2. | **Pratt** | BBDIOUW | Exchange | 0 | 0 |
| | | | BBDIOUW | | |

This exchange cannot be correct. It certainly must be worth 25 points to keep BDIU on the rack and play BOW (9C, 25 points). If he wanted to play away more letters, the s-unpluralizable BUBO (7H, 16 points) was a possibility, as was BUBOED (H4, 14 points). My preference is for BOW (9C) or for BUBO (9A, 20 points); the latter play is a lot less risky than it looks.

| | **Halper** | ACEEIPR | JAPER, D8 | 28 | 76 |

He could have put Pratt in a big hole by playing PEACHIER (G4, 69 points).

| 3. | **Pratt** | IMRRTUX | OMIT, E8 | 24 | 24 |

This move was presumably a setup for a possible SAX or SIX (F8, 59 points) next turn. He had a much better play, however: OXIM (E8, 47 points).

| | **Halper** | CEGINT☐ | E⬛ECTING, H8 | 83 | 159 |

GENT⬛ICE (H1, 83) is a little safer: unlike Ed's play, it does not place a vowel adjacent to double letter squares. Given Dan's setup, however, it would have been best to sacrifice some points and block the triple letter square at F10. This is best done not by making a play like GEN[E]TICS (F1, 64), which scores relatively poorly and opens the board, but by playing [D]EPICTING (10B, 73 points) or PIC[K]ETING (10D, 71 points).

4.   **Pratt**   ARRUWXY   SAX, F8   59   83
Had SAX been blocked, he would have had WAXY (13A, 52 points). Though Ed's lead is greater after the sequence of E[L]ECTING followed by SAX than it would have been after [D]EPICTING followed by WAXY, [D]EPICTING would have forced Dan to play the X and the Y simultaneously. In the actual game, he was able to conserve the Y for the 13D hook next turn.

      Halper   BDEINUR   BUN, 14F   11   170
This is a fishing play; the idea is to play a bingo next turn from 15A ending in -ING. Two superior plays are CURBED (11H, 22 points) and REBID (C11, 21 points). REBID is not really all that defensive. It neutralizes the potency of the -Y or -S hook at 13D, but it also opens another valuable square for the Y: 15D. With the G at 15H open, the IN leave after CURBED is better than the UN leave after REBID, since it maximizes the possibility of playing a word ending in -ING on a subsequent turn.

5.   **Pratt**   MRRTUWY   WRY, 13B   36   119
TRY or MY are a lot safer, as they don't create the A- hook at A13. WRY has much going for it, however: it dispenses with one letter from the unsightly WU combination, scores the highest number of points, and gets rid of one of the two RS. If the scores were reversed WRY would be a mistake, but with Dan behind it was a good gamble.

      Halper   DEHIINR   HERDING, 15B   19   189
Fine play! He could not take advantage of the A- hook, so he blocked its most likely and valuable potential application.

6.   **Pratt**   IIMORTU   CORIUM, 11H   20   139
Good play, as it opened the board but without creating

undue risks. TRITIUM (12H, 16 points) takes unnecessary chances, and OMIT (13F, 23 points) fails to undouble the IS.

Example #54

(Scrabble board diagram showing the following letters:)
Row 8: JOSHES
Row 9: AMA L
Row 10: PIX E
Row 11: ET CORIUM
Row 12: R T
Row 13: WRY I
Row 14: BUN
Row 15: HERDING

Halper   AFIRRTV   FIAR, 13G   22   211
Good play, as it scored as well as possible, created no glaring openings, and undoubled the RS.

7.   **Pratt**   BEITUY□   BUY, L10   16   155
[D]UBIETY was on his rack, but there was no place for it on the board. I do not recommend UBIETY (7I, 15 points), as it does not really open the board very much and may give Ed good counterplay along row 8 (from 8K or 8L to 8O).

Dan played away his two least bingo-prone tiles, but he had to close up the board a little in order to do so. Still, BUY was probably his best play.

Halper   IIORTVW   VROWS, 4I   15   226
No! This play was probably meant to close off row 7 bingos and bingos originating at I1, but it really opened the board much more than it closed it. The presentation of three tiles out in the open for Dan to play through is like dangling raw meat in front of a hungry dog. Also, in the long run a play such as VROWS may have unforeseen consequences by even-

tually opening up the entire upper half of the board. A play through its V, R or O might open hook locations for bingos across rows 3, 4, 5, or 6, as well down columns K, L, M, N, and O. With a 50+ point lead, unforeseen consequences are not desirable at all.

If Ed believed that CORIUM took an -S, and we shall see that he apparently did, he should have played VIM (M9, 15 points). Otherwise, he might have further closed up the board with VROW at B10, 18 points.

8.   **Pratt**   AEIKTU□   KA, A12   21   176

No doubt he would have preferred to dump the K where it would not have interfered with any of his openings, but the best he could do was to take the opening least likely for a bingo. Plays like KAME (M9, 24 points) and MAKE (M11, 25 points) are bad not because they give Ed access to good openings, but because the leave of IU to go along with the blank is not very helpful for bingo formation.

After KA, both players should have been aware of possible TROIKA and TALUKA plays at A8.

Halper   AAIIOTU   ATRIA, 5G   10   236

This play opened up much too much: bingo alleys from 4A and 6A, an -L hook at L5, and possible play through the A at K5. In addition, the IOU leave is awful. Perhaps his best chance for preventing bingos is OATH (G5, 9 points), though it produces both an -L hook at 4G (with no LS yet played) and a spectacularly poor leave. I think that I would have exchanged all of my tiles except perhaps the U in this situation.

9.   **Pratt**   EEISTU□   E[Q]UITES, N5   69   245

His play formed a phony word (CORIUMS) when good bingos were available elsewhere (E[Q]UITES, 6A, and EUTA[X]IES, K2). His play was the "best" bingo if unchallenged. It was risky, however; for, if challenged, Ed would subsequently have been able to block both legitimate bingos easily (e.g., OOT, 6H, could have been played from his next rack).

Halper   AEILOTU   LOUIE, 8K   18   254

When I first examined this position, I thought that TALUKA (A8, 30) was the correct play. Now I'm not so sure. With three DS, two AS, and the Q unaccounted for, QAID (8L) would be a devastating alternative to Louie. Also, the last U must be kept at all costs. ILIA (8L, 15 points) is thus probably better than both LOUIE and TALUKA. To (O8, 14 points) is also worth considering, as it guarantees an excellent score next play if the Q is picked (QUAIL, L1 or QUIET, O1).

10.   **Pratt**   CEFGNOQ   GONEF, O1   35   280

His second phony in a row! It's easy to see how both he and Halper could have gotten confused, considering that GANEF, GANEV, GANOF, GONIF, and GONOF are all *OSPD*-acceptable.

Example #55

Halper   ADGILNT   GLAND, 4C   17   271

A difficult situation for Ed, as he now needed both to score points and pick as few tiles as possible in order to avoid the Q. VANG (4I, 20 points) offers better chances than GLAND, however. It lowers the risk of picking the Q versus GLAND, and it sets up QAID (J3) if Ed should pick the Q. TIDAL and NIDAL (L1, 20 points), like GLAND, play away too many tiles.

11. **Pratt**   CENOQSV   Exchange OQV   0   280

With twelve tiles in the bag, exchanging rather than making a play was a must.

      Halper   ADIILPT   PIT, 4K   14   285

Good. He kept AID for QAID if necessary, did not block spots where QAID might be played, and used only three tiles. He might have reduced even further his chance of picking the Q by simply playing PI (4K).

12. **Pratt**   CEENOSZ   AZO, E4   24   304

This play doesn't look impressive, but it is. Not only did it score well while playing away only two tiles, it also blocked both spots for QAID (E4 and 6D).

  Even better, however, is RE (J13, 4 points), saving AZO for next time if necessary and setting up COZENS (15J, 86 points). Note that if Ed were to make a play from 15J to 15O following RE, he would be extremely likely to lose the game by picking the Q from the bag.

      Halper   ADEILOV   VOLT, M1   14   299

He saved AID for QAID again. With no place to play it if he should pick the Q, however, it would have made more sense to play PIXIE (10D, 14 points), scoring decently and minimizing the likelihood of picking the Q.

13. **Pratt**   CEEENST   Pass   0   304

With four tiles in the bag, Dan wanted to make sure that he would not pick the Q for the third time in the game. This play forced Ed to make a play rather than also to pass, as Dan undoubtedly would have passed again had Ed passed. Since Ed was losing, he could not afford to let the game end through successive passes.

      Halper   AADEILO   ON, F3   2   301

Brilliant! This superb play more than made up for all his previous errors. It lured Dan into thinking that Ed had the Q and was setting up QAID (2C) for his next play. It also forced Dan to play, for if he continued to pass Ed would indeed eventually play QAID.

Example #56

14. **Pratt**   CEEENST   CEE, 2F   22   326
Dan played this not to block Ed's QAID, but to win if Ed were
to play QAID at 1D (30 points) following CEE. Dan could then
respond with SEE (H1, 54 points). What he failed to notice
was that he could have achieved the same goal by simply
playing CON (F2, 11 points). CON gives him only a one in
three chance of picking the Q if it's still in the bag, whereas
CEE guarantees his defeat if Ed does not already have the Q
on his rack.

It is conceivable that Dan could lose after CON to a bingo
along row 1 by Halper. Had Dan therefore played TON (F2)
to prevent the bingo, however, Ed could have responded
with ET or AT (2E), again setting up QAID (1B) and forcing
Dan to make a play with one tile left in the bag. Rather than
eventually having to pick two tiles from the bag instead of
one, I would have taken my chances with CON.

     Halper   AADEILN   DALE, 1H   24   325
He missed the beautiful NAIAD (1D, 38 points).

15. **Pratt**   DEINQST   PIXIES, 10D   17   343
SEND (13L, 18 points) would have been better. Note that
NIDGETS (C1, 20 points) would not have. With only the Q left
on Dan's rack, Ed could have maximized his margin of

victory by playing his tiles away separately: PIXIE (10D, 14 points), MA (M11, 9 points), plus MAN (M11, 10 points). Or PIXIE, plus KA (12A, 11 points), plus BUNN (14F, 8 points).

| **Halper** | AIN | MAIN, M11 | 17 | 342 |
| | | plus DENQT x 2 = 30 | | 372 |

BEST PLAYS
Pratt: Turns 1, 4, 5, 6, 7, 8, 9, 10, 11, and 13.
Halper: Turns 5, 6, 11, 13, and 15.

GOOD PLAYS
Pratt: Turns 12 and 15.
Halper: Turns 3, 10, and 12.

BEST PLAY PERCENTAGES
Pratt: 11 ÷ 15 (11 out of 15 moves, no challenges), 73 percent.

Halper: 6.5 ÷ 17 (6.5 of 15 moves, 2 failures to challenge), 38 percent.

$$\boxed{\text{P} \mid \text{A} \mid \text{R} \mid \text{T} \mid \quad \mid \text{V} \mid}$$

Exceptional Plays

One of the unfortunate aspects of SCRABBLE® brand crossword game is that few experts record their best plays. Every now and then I hear about incredibly imaginative finds, such as Ron Tiekert's ten-letter bingo (RESONATORS) on a board that seemed bereft of bingo opportunities, or Nick Ballard's legendary play of PISTAREEN in a game against Ron. Plays like these are inspiring, creative, and aesthetically beautiful. It is unfortunate that all too often they are not shared with other players who would really appreciate them.

This quiz presents positions in which exceptional plays were found either over the board or from postgame analysis. There are a variety of plays to be found in these positions: unusual bingos, unexpected inside plays, multiple overlaps, strategic gems, setup plays, and endgame maneuvers. In endgame situations, I have included either the tiles unaccounted for or the tiles on the opponent's rack. I have thus provided you with the advantages of tile tracking.

These plays range from fine moves that are somewhat difficult to find to dazzling and unexpected brilliancies of considerably greater depth. See how many of them you can solve. Don't feel too smug if you discover most or all of them, however. Remember that you, unlike the original solvers of these problems, *know* that there is something to be found in each of the examples given. Remember too that many of these problems were solved over the board, under time con-

straints. It's much easier to find the needle if you know the
haystack contains one, and if you are not being rushed to
locate it.

	A	B	C	D	E	F	G	H	I	J	K	L	M	N	O	
1																
2			V				U									
3			I	F			R									
4			T	A	N		J	A	G	G	E	D		C		
5			A		O			E		H	E	R	O			
6		P	L	Y		D	E	I		K			Z			
7			I			O	N			A						
8			S	C	O	O	T	E	R	S						
9			T	I		M	I			N						
10			T			A	A		F	E	R	N				
11			I				W		V							
12			N				H		E					M		
13			G		Q	U	I	L	T	S				E		
14							R				B	O	W	L		
15							L	O	U	D	E	R		D		

Example 57

Position #1

Score	You: 322	Opponent: 216
Opponent's last play		COZ (N4, 34 points)
Rack		AADEEIX

Solution: WEAVE (11H, 18 points). This move eradicates
the rack's vowelitis and creates a nice setup for the x. On my
next turn in this game I played REX (L10, 38 points).

Position #2

Score	You: 22	Opponent: 27
Opponent's last play		FLOTA (9C, 27 points)
Rack		AHILNPR

Solution: ALPHORN (E5, 48 points), a double-double and a lovely word extension play.

___

Example 59

Position #3

Score	You: 25	Opponent: 52
Opponent's Last Play		WAIVE (D8, 22 points)
Rack		EIQTTZ ☐

Solution: Q[U]ARTZITE (H5, 77). This problem, which was not supposed to have one indisputably correct solution, was first presented in *Letters for Expert Game Players*. Fifteen of the twenty-three expert commentators found the solution.

Example 60

Position #4

Score	You: 199	Opponent: 145
Opponent's last play		TAU (C3, 13 points)
Rack		ADEEJNT

Solution: NANA (4B, 4 points). This low-scoring but beautiful setup play was made by Stephen Fisher, in a club game played against me. I'm normally pleased when my opponents make 4-point plays, but in this case I was alarmed. NANA sets up the J at 4A, as JNANA is an *OSPD*-acceptable word. A J play using one of the triple word scores at A1 or A8 would be worth a barrelful of points.

Stephen's play could have been blocked by LATI, SATI (use the last s for only 6 points? If so, pray that he cannot play MASJID, A1!), YETI, SITI, or TITI (all at 3A). It might have been partially blocked by a word using the -s or -T hook at C6. I did not have these resources, and on his second play following NANA, Stephen killed my winning chances with EJECTA (A3, 89 points).

Example 61

Position #5

Score	You: 87	Opponent: 113
Opponent's Last Play		LENGTH (3B, 28 points)
Rack		AEPTXY☐

Solution: APTE[R]YX (O6, 130). The best play in which the blank is not spent is PYXIE (1K, 63 points), but it obviously doesn't compare with APTE[R]YX.

```
    A  B  C  D  E  F  G  H  I  J  K  L  M  N  O
 1  .  .  .  .  .  .  .  .  .  .  .  .  .  .  D
 2  .  .  .  .  .  .  .  P  U  N  N  Y  .  N  Y
 3  .  .  .  .  .  .  .  O  .  .  .  .  .  .  A
 4  .  .  .  G  .  .  .  L  .  .  .  .  .  .  D
 5  .  .  .  O  .  .  .  A  I  .  .  .  .  .  .
 6  .  .  .  U  .  .  .  N  O  .  .  .  .  .  .
 7  .  O  T  T  O  .  .  C  A  Y  .  .  .  .  .
 8  .  .  .  I  .  .  U  N  H  I  P  .  A  X  .
 9  .  .  .  B  E  F  I  T  O  .  E  .  N  U  .
10  .  .  .  E  S  .  .  .  W  .  E  .  S  .  .
11  .  .  .  E  T  .  .  .  .  .  E  .  E  R  .
12  .  .  .  R  .  .  .  .  .  .  I  .  R  .  .
13  .  .  .  .  .  Z  A  G  .  B  E  D  I  M  .
14  .  .  .  .  .  L  I  A  I  S  O  N  .  N  .
15  .  .  V  A  L  V  A  T  E  .  .  W  E  D  .
```

Example 62

Position #6

Score	You: 363	Opponent: 305
Opponent's last play		CAY (7H, 17 points)
Rack		EEEIKOR
Tiles as yet unseen		ACEFGHJLMQRRSTT

Solution: LEK (4K, 14 points). In contrast to the last problem, which was among the easiest of these positions to solve, this one is much more demanding. It first appeared in *Letters for Expert Game Players,* and was solved by only one player, Steven Polatnick of Miami, Florida.

LEK is outstanding because it virtually guarantees the victory. The only way to lose this game is if you draw an unplayable Q after making your play, and your opponent then bingos or makes some other high scoring play. LEK, however, guarantees that you will be able to play the Q away if you draw it. In Polatnick's own words, it "sets up an escape hatch for the Q if I draw it—QUEER at L1. Unless opponent draws the last E and [an] R, it will be a unilateral escape hatch. If he bingos now, I simply block the Q spot [by EN, M1]. LEK also stops JURA for 44 and other high-scoring chances at the upper right."

Example 63

Position #7

Score	You: 104	Opponent: 119

Opponent's last play	GLARE (11C, 15 points)
Rack	AMMORZ☐

Solution: MAHZOR☐M (15F, 73 points). It is not very often that so many high-point letters can be combined to form a bingo. In this sense, MAHZOR☐M is perhaps the most unusual bingo I have ever played.

```
     A    B    C    D    E    F    G    H    I    J    K    L    M    N    O
 1  TWS             DLS            TWS            DLS            TWS
                                    S                                          1
 2        DWS            TLS        T        TLS            C         DWS
                          B                                            2
 3             DWS        R        DLS   O   DLS             DWS   O
                                                                      3
 4  DLS             DWS        DLS                DWS        DLS
                    T    R    O    I    K    A              J    O               4
 5                       DWS                      DWS
                         E    N    D    E    D         P    A                   5
 6        TLS             TLS            TLS
                         Z                   V    A    W    S                   6
 7             DLS             DLS        DLS             DLS
          L    O    O    S    E    S    T         G         C                   7
 8  TWS        DLS                           DLS        TWS
    Q    U    A                   O    B    I    A         H                    8
 9             DLS             DLS        DLS             DLS
          G    R    I    G         W    R    Y    N         L                   9
10  TLS             TLS                      TLS
                         U    V    E    A         I         E    H              10
11                  DWS                      DWS
               F    I    T                        S         P    E              11
12  DLS             DWS                 DWS                 DLS
          F    A    N              T    O    N    I    E    R         N    A     12
13        DWS             DLS        DLS             DWS
    T    A    X                              D    E    Y         M              13
14        DWS             TLS             TLS             DWS
                                                                    I           14
15  TWS        DLS             TWS             DLS             TWS
                                                                    E           15
```

Example 64

Position #8

	You: 336	Opponent: 342
Score		
Opponent's last play		QUA (8A, 43 points)
Rack		DEEILRU
Opponent's Rack		EILMNU☐

Solution: BYLINED (I8, 22 points). In this situation it is necessary both to score well and to block the opponent's [D]EMILUNE or, better yet, [R]ELUMINE at 15H. Opponent may yet win, but BYLINED makes it much more difficult to do so.

Example 65

	A	B	C	D	E	F	G	H	I	J	K	L	M	N	O	
1	C			Q				V			J	E	T	O	N	1
2	A			U				I						L		2
3	R	E	L	A	T	I	O	N	S					O		3
4				D				Y				Z	I	G		4
5						G	A	L	E	A				I		5
6								D	E	B				E		6
7							B	U	M		W	O	T	S		7
8						R		T	E	L	E	X			C	8
9						U		M	I	S					R	9
10						G	I	R	O	N				W	E	10
11								E		E	F			H	A	11
12								D		D	O			A	T	12
13							K	I	F		I	T		P	I	13
14								A			N	O		O		14
15								E				Y	U	A	N	15
	A	B	C	D	E	F	G	H	I	J	K	L	M	N	O	

Position #9

Score	You: 362	Opponent: 387
Opponent's last play		CAR (A1, 24 points)
Rack		DEINORV

Solution: CARNIVORE (A1, 45 points). DRIVER or DROVER (8A) are both okay, but CARNIVORE is a bit better (and a great deal more creative).

	A	B	C	D	E	F	G	H	I	J	K	L	M	N	O	
1																1
2																2
3												S	H		F	3
4					F	E	Y				B	A	I	Z	A	4
5					A	N	E	R	O	I	D				U	5
6															N	6
7					W				I	V	Y				A	7
8			R	O	O	T	E	D			A	M	P	L	E	8
9			O	R												9
10			Q	K												10
11			U	E												11
12		A	E	D												12
13		G														13
14		I														14
15	L	O	O	T												15
	A	B	C	D	E	F	G	H	I	J	K	L	M	N	O	

Example 66

Position #10

Score	You: 149	Opponent: 170
Opponent's last play		FEY (4F, 28 points)
Rack		NRSSTX □

Solution: YESTERN (H4, 20). This play rids the rack of four of its six consonants and scores quite decently. Also to be considered is YESTER (H4). Retention of the N would allow INFAUNAE (O1, 33 points) if the opponent does not play it first and one of your replacement tiles is an I. Also, YESTER does not block a potentially useful spot for the x at 11G. I chose to play away the extra consonant, however, and was rewarded by being able to play EX[S]ERTS (B6) on my following play.

Example 67

Position #11

Score	You: 97	Opponent: 115
Opponent's last play		DUD (2H, 9 points)
Rack		EFILNOP

Solution: PINOLE (N1, 41 points). This five-way overlap is much safer than it might appear at first glance. The second best play, OLEFIN (H10, 33 points), is more dangerous, as it opens the board for potential eight-letter bingos. Opponent's last play was most likely a fishing expedition, so one should especially beware of opening up the board any more than it is already.

Example 68

	A	B	C	D	E	F	G	H	I	J	K	L	M	N	O	
1	TWS			DLS				TWS				DLS			TWS	
2		DWS				TLS				TLS				DWS		
3			DWS				DLS		DLS				DWS U			
4	DLS			DWS V			DLS F	A	Q	I	R	DWS S		DLS		
5				I	DWS			L			DWS		E			
6		TLS		D		TLS		I		TLS			D	TLS		
7			DLS	E		E	DLS	N	DLS				DLS			
8	TWS			DLS O	V	E	R	T				DLS			TWS	
9		DLS	W			L		DLS		DLS			DLS			
10		TLS J	A	N	T	Y		TLS			TLS			TLS		
11			S		DWS						DWS					
12	DLS		P		DWS		DLS		DLS			DWS			DLS	
13			DWS I			DLS		DLS					DWS			
14		DWS		E			TLS			TLS				DWS		
15	TWS Z	E	R	DLS O				TWS				DLS			TWS	

Position #12

Score	You: 121	Opponent: 123
Opponent's last play		USED (M3, 28 points)
Rack		MMNOTY☐

Solution: METONYM[Y] or METONYM[S] (14B, 92 points). In the game, I chose METONYM[Y] simply because it was weider than METONYM[S]. Both are about equally good defensively. Note that M[E]TONYM is playable in two other locations, but neither of the other placements scores nearly as well as do the eight-letter plays at 14B.

Example 69

Position #13

Score	You: 124	Opponent: 130
Opponent's last play		RAISERS (13B, 66 points)
Rack		ABEJMRY

Solution: JAMBED (12A, 71 points). JERRY (B10, 62 points) is a nice-scoring play, but JAMBED is even better (and prettier).

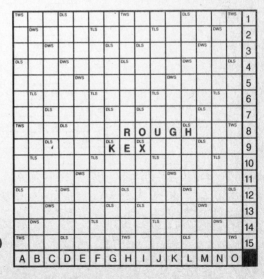

Example 70

Position #14

Score	You: 26	Opponent: 46
Opponent's last play		KEX (9G, 46 points)
Rack		ADFLRSY

Solution: ROUGHDRY (8H, 48 points). This position comes from a game played in the first North American Championship in 1978. The players were Jerold Lowenstein and Charles Goldstein, and it was Lowenstein's turn. The entire annotated game appeared in the September/October 1978 issue of *Games Magazine,* and the annotator was R. Wayne Schmittberger. Both Lowenstein and Schmittberger overlooked ROUGHDRY, which is certainly not the easiest play in the world to come up with.

Example 71

Position #15

Score	You: 377	Opponent: 356
Opponent's last play		TAR[O]T (13B, 34 points)
Rack		CGIJMW
Opponent's rack		EL

Solution: CWM (3J, 21 points). This position is a hypothetical variation of a problem first presented in the December 1980 issue of *Letters for Expert Game Players*. The original problem was submitted by Alan Frank. In it, BOXY and TAR[O]T were not yet on the board. The score was You: 340, Opponent: 322, and your tiles were BCGMOXY.

The original problem turned out to be the most complex one ever to appear in *Letters for Expert Game Players*. Comments from the expert panel included remarks such as: "I'm positively exhausted from working on [this problem] . . . a problem of enormous complexity" (Charles Goldstein); "problem is so complicated I can't begin to dent it" (Ted Rosen); and "calculating to the limits of my endurance, I submit no solution" (Linda Gruber). I will not go into the details of this problem other than to say that the major options selected by panel members were CONY (10C, 30 points), MIX (13G, 23 points), CYMA (D12, 22 points), and BOXY (14A, 37 points).

One of the panel members, Nick Ballard, wrote a monograph on this position titled "Anatomy of an Endgame." This thirty-page unpublished manuscript is a brilliantly conceived and nearly flawless presentation of the various best-play outcomes resulting from each of the four moves mentioned above. It analyzes many variations for each of the four moves, and one of the variations is shown above in Position #15. Ballard thought that the best play here was JOW (N13, 13 points), after which the opponent's LEV (B1, 12 points) wins by four points. He overlooked the very unusual CWM, however, which wins no matter what the opponent does.

Example 72

Position #16

Score	You: 337	Opponent: 374
Opponent's last play		ZIP⑤ (H1, 42 points)
Rack		AEMOOPS

Solution: IPOMOEAS (14A, 109 points)! There is nothing like a six-way overlap bingo play to brighten up the day. One almost needs a calculator to tally up the score.

Example 73

Position #17

Score	You: 92	Opponent: 96
Opponent's last play		MOVER (13B, 20 points)
Rack		EGNORS☐

Solution: HANGO[V]ERS (H7, 86 points). This position arose from a game analyzed by Mike Senkiewicz in *The Official* SCRABBLE® *Players Handbook,* an out-of-print work published in the mid-1970s. Mike apparently did not see HANG-O[V]ERS, since he considered IGNORE[R]S (10E, 64 points), the play actually made in the game, to be best.

Example 74

Position #18

Score	You: 68	Opponent: 157
Opponent's last play		PLOTTING (D8, 76 points)
Rack		AEMORT☐

Solution: [B]ERGAMOT (15A, 140 points). This beautiful triple-triple bingo was played by Dan Pratt in a 1982 tournament game.

The first Scrabble board (Example 75):

							A								1
		F	A			L	I	T	O	T	E	S			2
		J	O	E		I									3
		U	N			E									4
		I	T			N									5
		C				A				G					6
	R	E	F	I	T	G				O				7
		A	D	O	R	E	R	S		G	A	M	E	8
		N					O	H	O						9
V	I	E	W				X	I						10
		G						C						11
		A					Y	O	K	E				12
														13
														14
														15

Example 75

Position #19

Score	You: 155	Opponent: 218
Opponent's last play		YOKE (I12, 35 points)
Rack		ABIIILS

Solution: ALIBIS (1J, 40 points). A nice five-way overlap,
played by Sam Kantimathi in the 1984 Boston Championship.

The second Scrabble board (Example 76):

										D	U	C	K		1
S	N	E	A	P	I	N	G					A			2
			E						H	I	V	E		3
A	U	R	A							I			4
		R							T				5
		I			J	O	W	L	Y				6
		E			E							7
M	A	Z	E	S		C	L	A	G				8
	Q						N					9
U	P	D	R	I	E	S					10
	I										11
	T									12
	A								13
	N	A	M	E	N	I	T	Y				14
F	O	E	T	O	R						15

Example 76

Position #20

Score	You: 316	Opponent: 302
Opponent's last play		A**M**ENITY (14F, 67 points)
Rack		DEHINX ☐

Solution: **P**HENIX (4J, 75 points). Much better than HEX (H13, 39), as it puts the game out of reach. PHENIX is another of those words in the *OSPD* that appears to be misspelled but isn't.

Example 77

Position #21

Score	You: 61	Opponent: 45
Opponent's last play		DRY (10F, 11 points)
Rack		EEEMSSW

Solution: TMESES (11D, 38 points). Played by Alan Frank, an expert player from the Boston area. He used the only word in the *OSPD* beginning with TM- (other than its singular, TMESIS) to create this elegant and surprising overlap play.

Example 78

Position #22

Score	You: 97	Opponent: 93

Opponent's last play   ⓄUTLAIN (7H, 59 points)

Rack   BCOORSU

Solution: MICROBUS (D8, 60 points). A beautiful combination four-way overlap and word extension play.

Example 79

Position #23

Score You: 247   Opponent: 301
Opponent's last play   OX (J9, 52 points)
Rack   CEHILOS

Solution: CUBICLES (1A, 45 points). This extension play was
made by Jeff Reeves in the last game of the 1984 Grand
Canyon tournament. It got him back into the game, which
he won by one point after bingoing out with ORGANON (2H).

Example 80

Position #24

Score You: 22   Opponent: 31
Opponent's last play   ZEIN (9C, 31 points)
Rack   AABOSUU

Solution: ABOULIAS (E4, 40 points). This move, which was
played by Robert Felt of San Francisco in a club game, is
thematically similar to my play of ALPHORN in Position #2.

	A	B	C	D	E	F	G	H	I	J	K	L	M	N	O	
		L														1
		I	F													2
		B	E	N					C	A	M	E	O	E	D	3
			N	A								T				4
				R							P	A				5
				R							E					6
			O	F			J	A	K	E	S					7
			W	A	V	E	R				T	A	C	E	T	8
			I		T					L	E					9
	W	O	R	R	I	E	D				E	N				10
			Y							S		T				11
											R					12
											A					13
		D	E	M	I	R	E	P				L				14
	V	I	A	L			H	A	U	G	H	S				15

Example 81

Position #25

Score	You: 269	Opponent: 360
Opponent's last play		VIAL (15A, 30 points)
Rack		BOQSTUZ

Solution: TOD (O1, 12 points). This absolutely brilliant desperation setup play was made by Stephen Fisher in the 1984 Grand Canyon tournament. He needed a big score to get back in the game, and this play set up BEZIQUE (N2, 102 points) on his next play if he were to draw an I. There were four Is among the nineteen tiles still unaccounted for at this point in the game, so his chance of drawing at least one I in his two draws was a fairly decent 39 percent.

Stephen's opponent played YONI (J10) on her next turn, and Stephen did in fact follow with BEZIQUE. Alas, he still lost the game, but by only 4 points (424-428).

```
    A   B   C   D   E   F   G   H   I   J   K   L   M   N   O
 1 TWS         DLS             TWS             DLS  G   A   M  TWS E
 2      DWS         TLS                 TLS  K   O   I   N DWS E
 3           DWS             DLS     DLS             E DWS
 4 DLS         DWS             DLS  Q   A   I      DWS D         DLS
 5                DWS                     DWS X
 6      TLS             TLS             TLS  T             TLS
 7           DLS  W         DLS  H   DLS     L      DLS
 8 TWS         DLS  O         O   G   E   E DLS         TWS
 9      DLS         V         DLS  R DLS         DLS
10      TLS  V   I   E   W   E   R      TLS             TLS
11 F              N             I             DWS
12 DLS A    DWS             DLS  F             DWS         DLS
13 T   O DWS  U   C   H   I   L   Y DLS             DWS
14 E    DWS             TLS             TLS             DWS
15 TWS D        DLS             TWS             DLS         TWS
```

Example 82

Position #26

Score	You: 132	Opponent: 171
Opponent's last play		WOVEN (E7, 22 points)
Rack		AACEJNU

Solution: ACAJOU (8A, 69 points). I made this play in the
1984 Grand Canyon tournament, and it helped me turn the
game around.

Example 83

Position #27

Score	You: 24	Opponent: 24
Opponent's last play		Exchange 7 tiles
Rack	AEEOPTU	

Solution: OPERATE (K5, 52 points). A great double-double, played by Joe Edley.

Example 84

Position #28

Score	You: 368	Opponent: 351

Opponent's last play   JAB (9C, 44 points)

Rack   DDEEISV

Tiles unaccounted for   DGGIOOQRXZ ☐

Solution: TINE (H7, 4 points). This very sophisticated play was made by Jeremiah Mead in a Massachusetts tournament. Its purpose was to block Q⬛OTING (H4, 26 points), which was the only realistically conceivable play for dispensing with the Q. With seven tiles on the opponent's rack but only four in the bag, chances were excellent that his opponent had the Q. The fact that two Os and two Gs were still unseen meant that opponent's Q⬛OTING was not at all a far-fetched possibility. Another nice aspect of TINE was that it played away only one tile, and this minimized the chance of picking the Q if it was still in the bag.

And the Q was not in the bag: Jeremiah's opponent would have played Q⬛OTING had it not been blocked.

Incidentally, there are two phonies on this board: LEPIDUS and REBUDS.

Example 85

Position #29

Score	You: 143	Opponent: 73
Opponent's last play		RAXED (C3, 35 points)
Rack		CEIOQSV

Solution: COSTIVE (5E, 48 points). Another example of a double-double, played by yours truly in the 1984 Grand Canyon tournament.

Example 86

Position #30

Score	You: 263	Opponent: 281
Opponent's last play		FEOD (2F, 28 points)
Rack		DOPSTT□

Solution: PROETT**E** (E5, 32 points). This magnificent play was made by Ron Tiekert, in the last game of the 1983 North American Championship. A lesser player might have hoarded the blank for a higher scoring play, but Ron correctly realized that such a play was unlikely to be forthcoming, given the rather closed nature of the board.

Concerning his play, Ron writes: "PROETT**E** gave me a lead that, considering my case s and the spot created for it, was likely to stand up unless Steve [Polatnick, his opponent] was able to make a play at 1A. Even then I'd certainly have winning chances. As it happened, PROETT**E** stopped him from playing WINZE (E11) on his turn, and blocking the z was something I'd considered."

A "case" tile refers to the last tile of a particular letter to appear in a SCRABBLE® game. The -s hook that PROETT**E** created therefore belonged exclusively to Ron. Incidentally, REALE was a phony.

Example 87

Position #31

Score	You: 42	Opponent: 51
Opponent's last play		FOH (9F, 25 points)
Rack		AILNNU ☐

Solution: No, it's not **I**NGUINAL (L3), it's **A**NNUALIZING (5B, 90 points)! This remarkable play was made by Chris Cree, in the 1984 Grand Canyon Tournament. It was challenged by his opponent, and Chris actually lost the challenge.

At the time of the tournament, the eighth edition of *Webster's New Collegiate Dictionary* was the official arbiter for deciding whether words that were nine letters or more in length (other than variants of shorter words appearing in the *OSPD*) were acceptable. The ninth edition had been available for well over a year, however, and it turned out that though ANNUALIZE was not in the eighth edition, it was in the ninth!

As a result of Chris's experience, the ninth edition became the official dictionary for the very long words. When Merriam-Webster, Inc. comes out with a tenth edition, it will undoubtedly supercede the ninth, since it makes no sense to have as an official dictionary one that cannot be purchased at a bookstore.

Though Chris was haunted by this play throughout the tournament weekend (he heard announcers on television and radio use ANNUALIZE three different times), justice prevailed. Not only did he win the game, he won the tournament as well.

Example 88

Position #32

Score	You: 214	Opponent: 238
Opponent's last play		PEED (L1, 20 points)
Rack		FGNOTU ☐

Solution: FOUG[H]TEN (5D, 90 points). This position comes from a 1980 game that I played against Stephen Fisher. FOUG[H]TEN was one of seven bingos played, three by me and four by Stephen (the other bingos were SUBANAL, QUAKERS, SAVORING, CASTRATE, REGULINE, and SLATIER). For a discussion of the phonies SUBANAL and BOOGY, see page 108.

Despite the play shown and all the bingos, we really did not play this game all that wonderfully. Nevertheless, we amassed 1,001 points between the two of us. I won, 566-435.

```
     A   B   C   D   E   F   G   H   I   J   K   L   M   N   O
 1                       M   O   H   E   L
 2       L   A   R   D   E   R           U   P
 3   V   O   N       I   N   S       A   X   I   O   M
 4       T   Y   N   E   D           A   E   R   Y
 5                                                   O
 6                                               G       Z
 7                           P   I               E
 8   V   I   T   A       J   I   B   E               E   S
 9       B   R   O   O       A   W           F       E
10       A   H   A       B   I   K   I   N   I   E   D
11       O   R   C   I   N   G               T       E
12                                                       R
13                                           W   E   U
14                           Q   U   A   D           N
15                       G                           T
```

Example 89

Position #33

Score	You: 346	Opponent: 392
Opponent's last play		VITA (8A, 30 points)
Rack		AEFNSSU
Opponent's rack		CLLOT

Solution: US (N2, 19 points). This problem appeared in *Letters for Expert Game Players,* and was submitted by Joe Edley and Nick Ballard. Ballard wrote concerning play following US: "If opponent plays OTIC (B6) for 8 = 400, threatening to go out with ⒷILL (H10), you go out with FANES (12A) [to tie]. . . . You also tie with the same play if opponent plays COL (5G) for 8, threatening to go out with TIL (B7)." Ballard also noted that BLIN (I8) loses by 2 to FANES, VOLT (A8) fails against FANE (1L, 36 points), and COIL (B6, 12 points) leads to a 418-418 tie after FANE (1L), opponent's BLIN (I8), and your SQUAD (14I). All options other than US, including INFUSES (B8, 36 points); FANES, FAUNS, or FUSES (12A, 31 points); FUSE, FUSS, or FESS (N1, 29 points); INFUSE (I10, 25 points); and STAR (12L, 24 points) lose to opponent's best play.

Is it realistic to expect an expert player to find a play such as US over the board? In response to this problem, Steve Williams wrote: "The luxury of analyzing each play by yourself and your opponent is not available to the player who must produce points against time and pressure. The real issue is that the player give a worthy account of himself and his game by making it close. Win, lose, or draw he can hold his head high—the game, thank heaven, is still played by human beings." I agree with these sentiments, but I nonetheless believe that a strong expert should be able to find plays like US—not by calculating out all of the variations following US and other potential plays, but by thinking in terms of strategic principles. Us does two things that no other play accomplishes: it creates a high-scoring setup that the opponent can neither use nor block, and it allows the option of playing out with FANES (12A), if necessary. In a timed game situation one might well be unsure of the ultimate outcome after playing US, but careful consideration from a strategic viewpoint should make one reasonably certain that US is the best chance for winning.

Example 90

Position #34

Score	You: 253	Opponent: 276
Opponent's last play		FELON (O1, 36 points)
Rack		ABEHSSX

Solution: HEXOSANS (6H, 43 points). A charming play through three separate letters, which I unfortunately did not see when the game was played.

Example 91

Position #35

Score You: 142 Opponent: 178
Opponent's last play DATE (12L, 20 points)
Rack DEGORUV

Solution: LOUVERED (O8, 36 points). A nice eight-letter, non-bingo play.

Example 92

Position #36

Score	You: 365	Opponent: 352

Opponent's last play — SOVIET (N9, 22 points)

Rack — KMN

Opponent's rack — IL

Solution: AMI (11B, 9 points)! This great defensive play saves the game by preventing the opponent from playing out with what would have been another great play: WHIRL-IGIG (A7).

Example 93

Position #37

Score	You: 324	Opponent: 317

Opponent's last play — ZOA (6B, 32 points)

Rack — AIMNQST

Opponent's rack — BOOST

Solution: INS (C12, 23 points). This play creates an un-blockable Q setup for the next turn, QUA (11A, 17 points). Note that QAID (12G, 15 points) loses to opponent's BOTS (K4,

25 points), followed by JO on her next turn. If INS is instead played, however, you win by 2 points.

Example 94

Scrabble board (Position #38), rows 1–15, columns A–O:

```
   A  B  C  D  E  F  G  H  I  J  K  L  M  N  O
1  .  .  .  .  .  .  .  .  .  .  .  C  A  V  E
2  .  .  .  .  .  .  .  .  F  .  R  .  .  .  .
3  .  .  .  .  .  .  .  .  I  .  O  .  .  .  .
4  .  .  .  .  .  .  .  .  N  .  W  A  .  .  .
5  .  .  .  .  .  .  .  .  I  .  N  A  .  .  .
6  .  .  .  .  .  K  A  N  A  S  .  C  .  .  .
7  .  .  .  G  L  I  M  .  H  .  .  T  .  .  .
8  .  .  .  .  H  A  T  A  B  L  E  V  I  R  L
9  .  .  .  .  E  .  .  .  R  .  .  N  .  .  .
10 .  .  .  .  R  .  .  .  S  E  P  O  Y  .  .
11 .  .  .  .  A  W  .  .  .  .  .  N  .  .  .
12 .  .  .  B  O  O  .  .  Q  U  I  E  T  S  .
13 .  .  .  O  .  R  .  .  A  .  .  .  .  .  .
14 .  .  .  Z  .  T  .  .  I  .  .  .  .  .  .
15 G  O  O  F  .  .  .  D  E  L  O  U  S  E  S
```

Position #38

Score   You: 342   Opponent: 370

Opponent's last play   DELOUSE[S] (15H, 77 points)

Rack   BEIJNUX

Solution: BIJOUX (3I, 50 points). This is an approximate reconstruction of a club game in which I was a kibitzer rather than a player. It required considerable willpower on my part to refrain from saying something like "What a great play you could make!"

Example 95

Position #39

Score	You: 169	Opponent: 181
Opponent's last play		INVERSES (5D, 70 points)
Rack		ALOORTZ

Solution: ZOOLATER (M1, 84 points). This play comes from one of my 1983 North American Championship games.

Example 96

Position #40

Score   You: 329   Opponent: 346
Opponent's last play   VIA (H11, 12 points)
Your Rack   EMNTT
Opponent's rack   AAOU

Solution: THAIRM (4A, 12 points). This is the only winning play! In the analysis presented below, the opponent sometimes has more than one winning response to plays other than THAIRM. In these cases, only the play that yields the largest winning margin is given. Note also that there is a phony word on the board: YOR (6B).

I. EM, EN, or ET, (12A). These are the three highest-scoring plays available to you, but their rack leaves allow the opponent to win by playing out:

You	Opponent
1. EM (12A, 20 points) = 349 or EN or ET (12A, 18 points) = 347	1. TON (5J, 10 points) = 356
2. Any play; no matter what your move is, you cannot prevent your opponent's next play.	2. AURA (E2, 8 points) wins.

II. NETT or TENT (B10). These plays permit you to play out on your next turn, but opponent still wins:

You	Opponent
1. NETT or TENT (B10, 12 points) = 341	1. OCA (2B, 12 points) = 358
2. SIM (13D) or MEL (11C) or AIM (13H) = 346 plus 4 for playing out = 350. You lose by 8.	

NETT or TENT at B11 serve no particular purpose, and are simply 2 points worse than these plays at B10.

III. NET or TEN (B10). These plays allow you to play out next turn with THAIRM.

You	Opponent
1. NET or TEN (B10, 11 points) = 340	1. OCA (3B, 12 points) = 358
2. THAIRM (4A, 12 points) = 352 plus 4 for playing out = 356. You lose by 2. Playing away one tile at a time is even worse.	

Similar plays such as TERM and TERN (both at either B10 or B11) or DENT (M12) also lose against opponent's OCA.

IV. TERN (E2). Opponent's OCA is no longer possible, and THAIRM is again threatened. However:

You	Opponent
1. TERN (E2, 8 points) = 337	1. TON (5J, 10 points) = 356
2. THAIRM = 349, plus 6 for playing out = 355. A 1-point loss.	

Playing the T and the N separately loses by more: TERM at E2 also loses to TON.

V. THAIRM. This play wins because the rack leave of NET is flexible enough to combat all of the opponent's potential plays:

You	Opponent
1. THAIRM (4A, 12 points) = 341	1. OCA (3B, 12 points) = 358
2. NOH! (B2, 12 points) = 353. NET or TEN (B10, 11) ends the game, but loses by 2. ET right after THAIRM would lose to opponent's TAU (B12). EN (12A) followed by REFT (K10) only ties.	2. TUN or TAN (5L) = 368

2. ARE (12C, 3 points) = 361.
   This play blocks your ET.

3. ET! (B11, 8 points) wins, 363-361. REFT also wins, but by 1 rather than 2.

3. ET! (12A) =371 plus 2 for playing out = 373. A win! But opponent has one more option after playing OCA:

Opponent has other options besides OCA, but they also lose:

You

1. THAIRM = 341
2. TENT or NETT (A1, 12 points) = 353 plus 2 for playing out = 355 after AURA; and plus 6 for playing out after TON = 359.

Opponent

1. AURA = 354, or TON = 356

This last example demonstrates how complicated an endgame can be, even when both players have fewer than seven tiles on their racks. Incidentally, in the actual game I was the opponent, and my last play prior to the position shown above was not VIA but AURA. My opponent subsequently played EM (12A), and I then won the game by playing out with NAOI (14I). AURA loses to best play, however, as do NAOI, OCA, and all other attempts. How? Since this is the book's end, it is only fitting that I let you figure that one out for yourself.

Appendix A: Resources for the Interested Player

SCRABBLE® CROSSWORD GAME PLAYERS® INC. For only five dollars (U.S.), you can become a member of SCRABBLE® PLAYERS® for one year. Membership entitles you to six bimonthly issues of SCRABBLE® PLAYERS® NEWS. Issues are 16 pages long and contain listings of upcoming tournaments, news of past tournaments, quizzes of various sorts, word lists, articles on how to improve your play, news from SCRABBLE® PLAYERS® CLUBS, occasional annotated games, and so forth. You can join by sending your check or money order to SCRABBLE® CROSSWORD GAME PLAYERS® INC., 4320 Veterans Memorial Highway, Holbrook, New York 11741.

Letters for Expert Game Players (*LEGP*). The following description of *LEGP* is excerpted from information provided by Albert and Donna Weissman, for whom *LEGP* is a labor of love:

History and Rationale: Monthly *Letters for Expert Game Players* were initiated in October 1980, as an informal forum for discussing strategic issues in the Game. They were prompted by our belief that SCRABBLE® brand crossword game is deserving of a serious technical literature similar to the literatures of chess, bridge, and backgammon, and that such a literature is not otherwise available.

Format: Each month a set of six problems is sent to a panel of approximately two dozen expert players. In each

273

position, opponent is assumed to be an experienced, expert player. Without cross-consulting, these experts select the single best play according to their judgment and also provide brief notes justifying their choice against alternative plays. The moves are tabulated in the next mailing, along with a compilation of salient rationales for the various choices. (On occasion the format has been altered.) In addition, puzzles, humor, word lists, statistics, opinions, and detailed analyses of positions have often been included. All such materials are intended to appeal to expert players.

If you are serious about this Game, a subscription to *LEGP* is a must. This is the best periodical publication I know of for learning about SCRABBLE® strategy—nothing else comes close to it. A subscription costs $12.00 (U.S.), and back issues are $1.00 each. Write to *Letters for Expert Game Players,* Al and Donna Weissman, 11 White Rock Road, Westerly, Rhode Island 02891.

Matchups. A four-page newsletter, *Matchups* is published eight times a year. It lists results from recent tournaments, provides information on upcoming events (it fulfills these functions more thoroughly and promptly than does the SCRABBLE®*Players News*), and prints lists of players' ratings. The national rating system was developed some years ago by Dan Pratt. It was modeled on Arpad Elo's widely used chess rating system, though there are some significant differences between the two systems. Pratt's system was subjected to further minor modifications by Alan Frank, who both publishes *Matchups* and calculates ratings from tournament data.

To subscribe to *Matchups,* send a $6.00 (U.S.) check or money order to Alan Frank, 16 Oak Road, Medford, Massachusetts 02155. Back issues are $1.00 each.

Tile Rack. This bimonthly publication is produced by Joe Edley, winner of the 1980 North American Championship and many other strong tournaments. It consists of various types of puzzles, all of which are designed to enhance

SCRABBLE®-playing skills. These puzzles focus on anagramming skill, word knowledge, and ability to find high-scoring plays from complex board positions. You can subscribe by sending a check or money order for $15.00 (U.S.) to Joe Edley, Box 4760, San Francisco, California 94101.

The Monthly Duplicate SCRABBLE® Brand Crossword Game. This newsletter presents positions and racks for three different games in each issue. Subscribers send back their responses, and they are tabulated and discussed by Kevin Lawler, the creator of this publication. Subscriptions cost $12.00 for five months, or $24.00 (U.S.) for twelve months. Checks or money orders should be sent to SCRABBLE® Players Club No. 111, East Route 59, Spring Valley, New York 10977.

Appendix B: Basic Rules of SCRABBLE® Brand Crossword Game

Equipment. The equipment that makes up a SCRABBLE® brand crossword game consists of one hundred tiles, a tile bag, two to four tile racks, and the game board. Also needed are scorepads for each player and the *OFFICIAL* SCRABBLE® *PLAYERS*® *DICTIONARY*.

Individual letters of the alphabet are printed on ninety-eight of the tiles. The other two tiles are blanks, and have the same function as do jokers in a deck of cards: the player can choose the letter the blank is to represent. Printed on every lettered tile is a number that appears slightly below and to the right of the letter. This number is the tile value of the letter (a blank has a tile value of zero). Tile values are essential for determining the number of points earned for a play.

A letter's tile value is determined by the frequency of usage of that letter in the language. The common letters A,E, I, O, U, L, N, R, S, and T are worth one point each. On the other hand, less common letters such as F and V are worth four points each. The rarer J and X are valued at eight points, and the still rarer Q and Z are each worth ten. The low-value tiles predominate in the tile distribution. There are twelve ES among the one hundred tiles, but only one each of the K, J, X, Q, and Z.

The board is a 15 by 15 matrix of squares. However, all of the squares are not alike. Some of them are shaded in blue or red. These squares are called premium squares, and there are four varieties of them: double letter, triple letter, double word, and triple word. The double and triple letter squares are colored light blue and blue, respectively. The double and triple word squares are pink and red, respectively. The square at the center of the board is starred, and like the other squares shaded in pink, is a double word square.

Beginning the game. In order to start a game, each player draws one tile from the tile bag. The person who draws closer to the beginning of the alphabet goes first, with blanks taking precedence over As. In the case of three or four players, play proceeds clockwise from the person who goes first. Most serious players refuse to play a game involving more than two players. There is simply too much luck involved, and the player who goes third or fourth is at a great disadvantage. The rules presented here will deal solely with the Game as played by two people.

The player who goes first picks seven tiles and places them on the rack. The second player then does the same. Players are not permitted to look at each other's tiles.

The first player begins the game by making a two- to seven-letter word from the tiles picked, and placing that word on the board. One letter must cover the star on the board, and the play may be made either vertically (down column H) or horizontally (across row 8). The first player may also begin by exchanging any or all of his tiles, or by simply passing (no tiles exchanged). Procedural details related to exchanging and passing are described on pages 37-38.

Allowable Plays. Three criteria must be met for a play to be allowable. First, the tiles added to the board must all be located on the same column or row. Second, they must either be placed adjacent to each other to form a word, or must be placed so that they combine with previously played tiles already on the column or row to create a word. Finally, the tiles played must connect to tiles that have already been played. It is also permissible to play only one tile from the rack, even if the sole purpose of the tile is to tack an -s onto a pre-existing word.

Players often create more than one new word on a given play. Such plays are called hook plays or overlaps, and are described on pages 59-60.

How to score a play. Plays are scored basically by adding up the tile values of the word formed. HOME is worth 9 points, for example, since the tile values of its constituent letters are 4, 1, 3, and 1, respectively, and these values add up to 9.

More often than not, however, the value of a play is modified by the premium squares. These squares function exactly as they are labeled: double and triple letter squares double or triple the value of tiles falling on them; double and triple word squares double or triple the *total value* of an entire word, if any tile from that word covers the square. Words whose tiles cover *two* double word squares are called double-doubles. In this case, the total value of the word is quadrupled. Similarly, words whose tiles cover two triple word squares are called triple-triples, and the total value of such a word is multiplied by nine.

In order to calculate the value of plays whose tiles cover both premium letter and premium word squares, it is necessary first to adjust the value of the letter(s) falling on the premium letter square(s), and then to double or triple the value of the entire word. Imagine, for example, that you begin a game with QUICK, 8D. The Q is normally worth 10 points, but since it covers a double letter square it is worth 20. In addition, the entire word is doubled, as the K covers a double word square (the star). The play is thus worth 60 points: 20 for the Q plus 1 each for the U and I, plus 3 for the C, plus 5 for the K = 30, and this sum is doubled.

Once a tile has been placed over a premium square, that square is of no particular value later in the game. If your opponent were to add -ENED onto QUICK, for example, only the D on the double letter square at 8L would be doubled. The

Q would not now be doubled, nor would the total value of the entire word. QUICKENED (8D) would be worth only 27 points.

The value of a play that forms more than one new word is calculated by adding up the values of the individual new words formed. In Example #3 (page 23), for example, the play of NI⬚US (N9) totals 27 points: 6 for NI⬚US itself (remember that the blank has no point value), plus 8 for KANA, plus 4 for IT, plus 1 for ⬚E, plus 8 for DIGITS.

Plays which use all seven tiles on the rack are called bingos, and are worth the value of the play plus a bonus of 50 points.

Details related to scoring at the end of a game are presented on pages 28-29.

One last obvious but essential point: the winner of the game is the player who outscores his opponent!